W9-AZZ-101

# INDIA

## Southern India

**Second Edition
completely revised
1994**

# *TABLE OF CONTENTS*

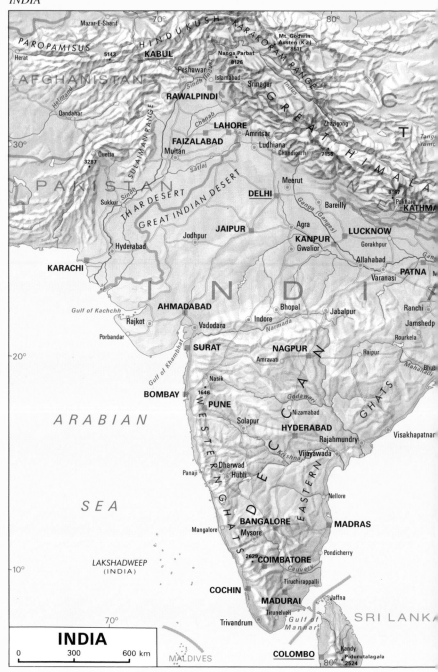

INDIA

0     300     600 km

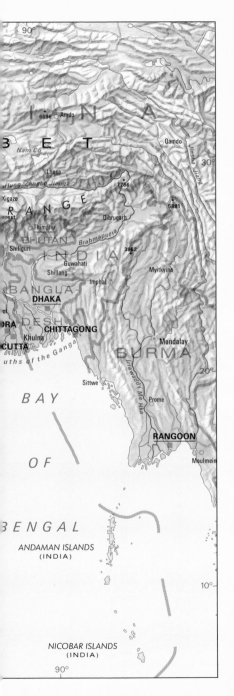

## LIST OF MAPS

Please note: in some cases the spelling of the place names on the maps is not the same as in the text, because the spelling on the maps is according to UN guidelines, whereas the usual English spelling is used in the text.

# Nelles Guides        ... get you going.

## AVAIABLE TITLES

Australia
Bali - Lombok
Berlin
*and Potsdam*
Brittany
California
*Las Vegas, Reno, Baja California*
Caribbean
*The Greater Antilles, Bermuda,*
*Bahamas*
Caribbean
*The Lesser Antilles*
Crete
Cyprus
Egypt
Florida
Hawaii
Hungary
India
*Northern, Northeastern*
*and Central India*
India
*Southern India*
Indonesia *West*
Kenya
Mexico
Morocco

Munich
*and Surroundings*
Nepal
New York
*City and State*
New Zealand
Paris
Philippines
Provence
Spain
*North*
Spain
*South*
Thailand
Turkey

## IN PREPARATION

Cambodia - Laos
Canada
*East*
China
Malaysia
Moscow - St. Petersburg
Rome

---

**INDIA**
**Southern India**
©Nelles Verlag GmbH, D-80935 München
All rights reserved

2. Edition completely revised 1994
ISBN 3-88618-405-6
Printed in Slovenia

---

| | | | |
|---|---|---|---|
| **Publisher:** | Günter Nelles | **Cartography:** | Nelles Verlag GmbH, |
| | | **Color** | |
| **Chief Editor:** | Dr. Heinz Vestner | **Separation:** | Priegnitz, München |
| **Project Editor:** | Shalini Saran | **Printed by:** | Gorenjski Tisk |

---

No part of this book, not even excerpts, may be reproduced without prior permission of Nelles Verlag
- 05 -

# AN INVITATION TO INDIA

*"India is like an ancient palimpsest on which layer upon layer of thought and reverie have been inscribed. This is the complex and mysterious personality of India. ... About her is the elusive quality of a legend long ago; some enchantment seems to have held her mind. She is a myth and an idea, a dream and a vision, and yet very real and present and pervasive."*

Jawaharlal Nehru

Indophiles are unable to define the true essence of India, but all agree that there are certain characteristics which yield a glimpse of it. India's infinite variety, clichéd as it has begun to sound, is one of these features that frequently overwhelm even the experienced Indian traveler.

This variety has arisen, to a large extent, from the assimilation of alien influences into the Indian mainstream throughout the course of history. While some of these influences underwent further changes, geographical factors and the sheer size of the country prevented their simultaneous and even impact.

Before the advent of British rule in the nineteenth century, political unity had been experienced only in the third century B.C. While, in the span of 2000 years and more, highly evolved and very sophisticated achievements were made at the many centers of religion and power, there were – and still are – vast areas where folk and tribal cultures remained virtually untouched.

This diversity is increased by the coexistence of ancient and contemporary beliefs and ideas, occupations and lifestyles and differing modes of creative expression. It accounts for contradictions, and for quaint, and sometimes startling, juxtapositions; but it also lends an extraordinary vitality and texture to life. It makes for a lively range of possibilities, and reveals the astonishing ability of the Indians to take the most incongruous situations in their stride.

As unique and deep-seated as this diversity is the unmistakable presence of a deeply unifying factor, an "Indianness" that is pervasive, vital and enduring. Even today, in the face of rapid industrialization and change, and in the midst of poverty and hardship, there is a certain poetry to life in India.

It is not merely the poetry of the picturesque, and less still of the legendary erotica often associated with India, but a far more profound poetry, integral to a world-view that is not entirely materialistic. It manifests itself through inspiration rather than design, and at many levels – in the brilliant marigolds that the wayside vendor scatters upon his heap of purple berries; in the reverence with which hill folk regard the majestic Himalaya; in the full-throated song of the desert dweller; in the sublime ecstasy of classical art; in the beauty of symbolic expression.

You will experience this poetry if you can look beyond the crowds and the confusion; if your vision is not clouded by preconceived – and often, misconceived – ideas; and if you do not try to resist the Indian pace of life. It can move you to question much that you have always taken for granted. And it can touch you so deeply that it remains more than just a memory when you return to your own country.

Today, India is the world's largest democracy and the phase of transition into a modern society, though not without its traumas, is a dynamic one. It is as necessary to respond to this, as to the splendors of the past, if you wish to un-

*Preceding pages: A Lakshadweep fisherman. A modern Bombay beauty. Bharat-anatyam dancers. Fishing from a coracle at Karnataka. Woman at the flea market at Anjuna.*

derstand India. We hope that this Nelles Guide will be a helpful and inspiring companion on your journey through India.

India has been covered in two books – **Northern India** and **Southern India**. They are complementary; although to attempt to cover the exuberance, complexity and diversity of a country such as India within even two books is a task both challenging and frustrating.

The challenge has been admirably met by a team of knowledgeable and experienced writers, each of whom is Indian. What you read, therefore, is valuable information combined with the insights of Indians into their own country; insights which have evolved and matured through years of work related to a specific region or interest, and also through having lived or traveled extensively in a particular area. The text is supplemented by wonderfully evocative photographs. There are also over 30 historical and city maps throughout the text.

**Southern India** begins with "A Brief History of South India" by a well-known archaeologist and Sanskrit scholar. The history of this region, which has differed from that of the north, is briefly outlined to reveal the forceful religious and cultural patterns that emerged through the centuries and remain intrinsic to the fabric of contemporary life. However, it would be instructive to read the corresponding essay in **Northern India**, as many basic and vital factors of the south Indian ethos originated in the north.

The main travel section follows this introduction. **Southern India** covers Bombay, Maharashtra and Goa; Orissa; Karnataka and Andhra Pradesh; Madras and Tamil Nadu; Kerala; and the Andaman, Nicobar and Lakshadweep islands, states and cities that offer a varied range of experiences. Each state is supplemented by a *Guidepost* which lists details of accommodation, restaurants, tourist offices, museums and festivals.

The next part of this book focuses on specific interests. These are arranged as six itineraries, each of which concentrates on a single interest: Indian cuisine; beach resorts; Indian painting; the dance forms of South India; the important *ashrams* in the south; and the major groups of temples.

In the features section that follows, some perspectives on Southern India are offered through concise essays on nine aspects of India that are likely to draw your attention. The subjects of these essays range from temple rituals and the worship of the *linga*, to the population explosion, the caste system, women, the media, the colonial experience and the phenomenon of untouchability.

The next part, *Guidelines*, deals with traveling in India, and is a comprehensive list which contains, among other details, information on arrival and departure formalities, currency and exchange, health regulations and precautions, telecommunication, tours, and special schemes offered by airlines and the railways in India. The addresses of airline offices in Bombay and Madras, of embassies, high commissions and consulates in India, and of tourist offices abroad have also been included.

*Guidelines* also gives some useful words and phrases in Malayalam and Tamil, the latter being understood practically everywhere throughout the southern states.

The credits acknowledge the work of the writers and photographers. They are among several people who made a valuable contribution to the creation of this book, and who, together, invite you to share the beauty of India.

- Shalini Saran

# A BRIEF HISTORY
# OF SOUTHERN INDIA

The peaceful and responsive nature of the people of south India has, to a considerable extent, been determined by geographical factors. The peninsula is bound by the Arabian Sea, the Bay of Bengal and the Indian Ocean in the west, east and south, and barricaded from the north by the high Vindhya mountains which cut across the middle of India in an east-west direction. Compared with the north, there were few violent invasions by foreign powers until technological developments in the 16th and 17th centuries brought maritime powers to the coasts, especially from Europe, enabling them to get a foothold and acquire territorial overlordship. Maritime contacts with other countries had existed for almost 2000 years before the 16th century; but these contacts were mainly commercial in nature, and the changes they initiated in the lives of the people were insignificant. Of far greater significance to the lifestyle of the people of peninsular India were the influences that came from the north across the Vindhya ranges, through the great southern route, the Dakshinapatha.

### The Geographical Factor

Southern India almost forms a triangle. To the south of the Vindhya ranges are two great rivers - the Narmada, flowing westwards into the Arabian Sea, and the Mahanadi, flowing towards the east and entering the Bay of Bengal in Orissa. These two rivers and the Vindhya ranges are looked upon as the natural and traditional northern boundary of south India. Two mountain ranges complete the

*Preceding pages: Chowpatty Beach. Left: Temple donor, Pattadakal, 8th century A.D.*

triangle: the Western Ghats begin north of Bombay and run parallel to the west coast almost to the tip of the peninsula; the Eastern Ghats begin in Orissa and run parallel to the east coast almost up to Madras, from where the ranges take a south-western course and join the Western Ghats in the Nilgiri mountains. The steep Western Ghats rise from a height of 700 m (2297 ft) in the north to almost 3000 m 89843 ft) in the cool moist Nilgiris, and run continuously, with very few passes, to link the narrow coastal strip with the hinterland.

The Eastern Ghats, on the other hand, are neither high nor continuous. Contained within the span of these two coastal ranges is the rocky Deccan plateau (Deccan is derived from the Sanskrit *dakshin*, meaning south).

Most of the great rivers of south India, such as the Godavari, Krishna and Kaveri, rise in the western ranges and flow through the eastern passes into the Bay of Bengal. The Europeans who arrived three centuries ago, christened the coastal belts along the east and the west the Coromandel Coast and the Malabar Coast, respectively.

The southwest monsoon clouds that meet the Western Ghats bring very heavy rain to Kerala and the Konkan region, whereas the area immediately to the east of the Ghats gets very little rain.

The east coast receives its major rainfall from the northeast monsoon, between the months of October and December. This monsoon is sometimes accompanied by cyclonic storms which strike the Coromandel Coast. However, compared to the west coast, the rainfall is lighter. By and large, south India has a uniform and temperate climate, ranging mostly from 20°C to 30°C, and shooting up to 40°C at some places in the interior in the month of May.

Climatic conditions and geographical factors contribute to the varied vegetation of the peninsula. The southwest coast was famous even in the ancient world for its wealth of spices, in particular, pepper. In fact, there was a time when pepper was dearer than gold, and many fortunes were made in the spice trade. Thick forests grow on the slopes of the Western Ghats; the Malabar Coast is known for its teak and rosewood, while the Mysore plateau is rich in sandalwood.

The Nilgiris proved to be ideally suited for the extensive cultivation of tea and coffee. Paddy rice is the main crop in the fertile plains south of the Deccan plateau in Tamil Nadu, and also in coastal Kerala. Other crops grown in south India include sugarcane, cotton and tobacco. However, large areas of the plateau are too rocky for cultivation of any crops.

### The Age of Iron

South India was inhabited by people from Paleolithic times. Stone Age tools have been found all over the south, although they are considered to belong to a later point of time than the ones found in the north.

A sudden change is apparent to archaeologists in south India dating from around 1000 B.C. and evident from the large-scale use of iron weapons and swift horses, both of which contributed to a dramatic change in the life of the people. This period coincided with the last phase of the Indus Valley civilization that flourished in the north from about 3000 to 1500 B.C. In fact, there is a general consensus among scholars that the Indus Valley civilization was Dravidian in content; seals that have been found especially suggest this possibility. However, as the Indus script still awaits decipherment, this remains pure speculation.

The Iron Age is widely represented in the entire south. Tridents, spears, long-

bladed swords, and horses provided tremendous striking power that aided swift colonization. The origin of the people who swarmed over the southern region in such large numbers is still a matter of debate. Apart from their weapons and horses, two characteristics distinguish them from their predecessors in the south and their contemporaries in the north.

These Iron Age people have left a large number of megaliths, funerary monuments built of stone and varying in form. Some of these contain skeletal remains of the dead, while others are memorials, containing pottery and other deposits. The custom of erecting such megaliths was so widespread that literally thousands of them can be seen throughout the southern region.

These Iron Age people are identified with the Dravidians by most archaeologists. The view that they came in a great wave of migration from the Caucasus region via Baluchistan, the Punjab and Sind and penetrated southwards through the western route, seems possible because of the occurrence of megalithic monuments - and also of an isolated language called Brahmi, akin to the Dravidian languages - that is found in Baluchistan.

The other significant trait of these people is the use of a distinct type of pottery called black and red pottery, the exterior of which is red and the interior, together with the rim, black in color. Such pottery is found in predynastic Egypt in the third millennium B.C., with the result that some scholars have suggested an overseas migration.

The examination of skeletal remains from these burials has revealed a variety of different racial groups. Some were Proto-Australoids with long heads and broad noses; a few of the surviving tribes of the south, such as the Chencus, Kurumbas and the Malayans are considered their linear descendants. The other races that have been identified so far are the

*Right: Temple priest with Vaishnav symbol on his forehead.*

Negroid, Proto-Mediterranean and Armenoid types, indicating different waves of migration.

### The "Aryanization" of the South

The other factor that greatly influenced the life of the people of the south, and almost simultaneously, was the Aryan migration from the north. A wealth of legends and material remains tells of the gradual Aryanization of the south before 700 B.C. Aryan chieftains of the ruling class moved southwards with their Brahmin priests, burning forests en route to clear the way. At the same time they brought land under cultivation.

The sage Agastya, who lived in the early Vedic age, is said to have been the first to initiate the southern colonization. According to a legend, he destroyed the demon Vatapi and his brother in the Dandaka forest and reached as far south as the Podiyil hills in the Tinnelveli district of Tamil Nadu. He is considered the father of the Tamil language. Another

Vedic sage, Parasurama, is associated with the colonization of the west coast, especially Kerala. Ancient Tamil texts speak vividly of the migration of Aryan chieftains over more than 47 generations.

These waves of Aryan migration had a profound and formative impact on the social and cultural evolution of south India. The Aryans brought with them their literature, incorporated in the four Vedas; and Sanskrit, their language. For the people of the south, this also meant exposure to the world-view embodied in the Vedas, and to the Vedic gods - Agni, Varuna, Rudra or Siva, and Prajapati or Vishnu. The rituals and rites of passage which had been devised by the Brahmin priests, and which were so deeply entrenched in the lifestyle of the Aryans, became integral to the south Indian ethos. They have survived here to this day in their most original forms.

The division of society into castes was also an important part of the Aryanization of the south. The Brahmins were the learned, priestly class; the Kshatriyas

comprised the chieftains and warriors; the Vaishya, the next in order of hierarchy, comprised farmers and peasants; the Sudra, on the lowest rung of the ladder, were the inferior class.

The two great epics, the *Mahabharata* and the *Ramayana*, which have permeated the Indian psyche, came with the Aryans too. It is now believed that the *Ramayana*, which narrates the story of the exiled hero Prince Rama of Ayodhya and his victory over the demon king of Lanka, is a poetic retelling of the southward expansion of Aryan tribes. These aspects of Aryan culture were adopted over the course of centuries, and their impact was lasting. In the north, pervading foreign influences formed a continual part of the historical and cultural reality. This was not the case in the south, and, as a result, traditions brought by the Aryans

*Above: Ancient Pampatira, Hampi, closely associated with the Ramayana. Right: Buddhist chaitya (prayer hall) at the Kanheri Caves, Bombay.*

became firmly rooted, and are still adhered to in the daily life of the people.

**Buddhist Deccan**

Two events which took place in the north proved to have a powerful impact on south India as well. In the sixth century B.C. the voice was heard of the Sakyan Prince Siddhartha (born 566 B.C.), known to the world as the Buddha, or the Enlightened One. He preached a way of life that considered the source of human suffering. His teachings were not based on caste or ritual, which had already begun to plague the Brahminical religion. The story of his life, and the profound wisdom of his words attracted a large following. The Buddha also established the Sangha, a monastic order, thus providing institutional support for his ideas.

Mahavira (b. 540 B.C.) was a contemporary of the Buddha, who founded the Jain faith. It was a far more puritanical religion, the main tenet of which was non-violence. Its followers believe that

only non-violence, accompanied by austerity, can purify the soul that exists in every living being; and that all knowledge should be directed towards this purification of the soul, which can then attain eternal bliss. The practice of non-violence in Jain faith was carried to an extreme, leaving few professions other than trade open to the Jains.

### Buddhist and Jain Monks

Besides the Aryan chieftains and the Brahmins, the southern route brought traders and religious mendicants as well. Jain and Buddhist monks, with large numbers of followers, also moved in a southward direction.

One such journey of great significance to the Jain faith was that of Bhadrabahu, a Jain monk, who traveled accompanied by the Mauryan Emperor Chandra Gupta in the third century B.C. They reached Sravanabaler, in Karnataka, and both died there. It has been a dominant center of Jainism ever since. The Jain faith

greatly influenced the trading communities, who carried it to the extreme south, including Tamil Nadu. As a result, large numbers of merchants made donations to Jain settlements near the capitals of ancient Tamil kingdoms.

The Enlightenment of the Buddha, and the subsequent religious aspirations personified by the monks and the lay disciples, which were represented mainly by the merchant community, underwent a great change with the accession of the Mauryan Emperor Asoka in the third century B.C. By the early years of his reign, Asoka already ruled a large part of southern India. He was the first Indian ruler to unite the major part of India (except for south of Kanchipuram, in Tamil Nadu) under one authority, a feat repeated only briefly by the Mughal Emperor Aurangzeb nearly 2000 years later in the late 17th century, before the advent of British rule. Asoka's conquest of Kalinga, a part of Orissa, proved to be a turning point not only in his own life but also in the religious ethos of India.

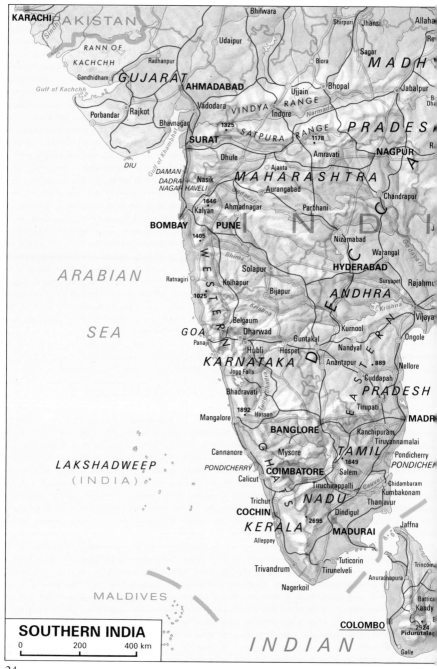

SOUTHERN INDIA

0      200      400 km

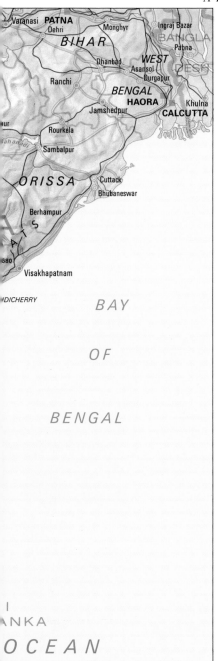

## Asoka's Metamorphosis

The terrible destruction and suffering caused by the Kalinga war made Asoka question his ambition. He embraced the tenets of Buddhism, and instead of conquests of territories through wars, he embarked on the conquest of the mind through love and righteous conduct. He explicitly stated in official edicts that he had renounced the path of war and sent his emissaries to propagate Buddhist *dharma*. Asoka was an efficient ruler and he made his officers preach the teachings of Buddha wherever they were. As a result, a large number of Buddhist stupas were erected in Maharashtra, Karnataka and Andhra Pradesh.

Asoka's edicts have been found in Andhra Pradesh and Karnataka, where stupas enshrining relics of the Buddha were erected. According to Buddhist sources, Asoka built a tall stupa at Kanchipuram, near Madras. Asokan edicts testify that southern peninsular India was ruled by the Cholas, Pandyas, Kerala *putras* and Satya *putras*, who were on friendly terms with the Emperor.

Asoka sent his missionaries to propagate Buddhism, but although they were well received, Buddhism did not have as deep an impact south of Kanchipuram as in the territories directly under Asoka's control. There is very little early Buddhist art in the extreme south, as compared with Andhra, Karnataka or Orissa. By the time of Asoka's death the impact of Buddhism on the life of the people in these three areas was enormous. In Dhauli, near Bhubaneswar in Orissa, as many as eleven edicts of Asoka were found. In one of them we read the famous declaration of Asoka: "Devanamapriya (Asoka), the conqueror of Kalinga has remorse now because of the thought that the conquest is no conquest, for there was killing, death, and banishment of the people in such a conquest. That is felt with profound sorrow and regret by Devanamapriya. Now even the loss of a hundredth or even a thousandth part of all the lives that were killed, or died, or carried away captive at the time when Kalinga was conquered is considered deplorable by Devanamapriya. He considers that even those who wrong him are fit to be forgiven of wrongs that can be forgiven, because he desires that all beings should be left unhurt, should have self-control, have equal treatment, and should lead happy lives. To Devanamapriya, the conquest through righteousness is the most important conquest."

Karnataka, till recent times known as Mysore State, was called Mahishamandala in Asokan times. Two Buddhist missions were sent to Mahishamandala and Vanavasi in north Karnataka from the court of Asoka. Asokan edicts are found in over seven places in Karnataka, such as Maski, Govimath, Brahmagiri, Sid-dhapur and Sannathi.

Besides propagating Buddhism, Asoka is remembered for introducing a script known as Brahmi, used for writing documents. The origin of the script is much debated. After the pictographic script of the Indus Valley era which lasted to about 1500 B.C., the next decipherable script of India dates only from the time of Asoka, whose contact with regions as far away as Persia, suggest Aramaic as its source. Whatever its origin, once it was used by the Emperor it became the script of India, used from Kashmir in the north to Kanniyakumari in the south. It forms the foundation for all modern scripts of India, including Tamil, Malayalam, etc.

## The Satavahana Kings

Closely following the reign of the Mauryan Emperor Asoka, a great dynasty called the Satavahana asserted its independence. The Satavahana kings

*Right: The tranquillity of the sleeping Buddha, Ajanta Caves.*

brought under their rule the whole of Maharashtra, Madhya Pradesh, Karnataka, Andhra and the borders of Kalinga. From the second century B.C. to the second century A.D., their patronage nurtured the flowering of art, literature and philosophy, and implemented a fruitful social cohesion. The Satavahanas were followers of the Vedic religion, observing a number of Vedic sacrifices such as the Asvamedha or horse sacrifice. However, their outlook was catholic and they were also patrons of the newly emerging Buddhist faith. Some of their queens were even followers of Buddhism. Their first capital was established at Paithan (Prathishta-napura) in Maharashtra, but it was soon moved to Dhanyakataka (Amaravati) in Andhra Pradesh.

The language of their court was Prakrit - a form of spoken Sanskrit. It later flowered into a fine form of literary expression called Maharashtri. The newly introduced Brahmi script gave the Satavahanas, and the traders under them, the scope for recording their works on royal edicts. What had earlier been confined to royal usage only, was now available to all, and the large number of epigraphs that were produced are also a record of the world-view of these men.

The Satavahanas encouraged active trade with the west, especially with the Roman world. They emulated the Romans by issuing coins portraying images of their rulers on the observe and their royal emblems, such as the horse and elephant, on the reverse. In north India, a Greek influence had begun to manifest itself in Buddhist art. This trend soon filtered southwards, where the direct contact established with the Roman empire through trade drew Roman influences into the expression of Buddhist sculptural art. If one were to go by the costumes and jewelry depicted in some sculptures it might appear that the Romans influenced contemporary modes of dress among the nobility in south India, too.

It was during the Satavahana reign that Buddhism reached its zenith in Maharashtra. A large number of Buddhist establishments were founded in the hills of Maharashtra, where several monasteries (*viharas*) and prayer halls (*chaityas*) were excavated. Maharashtra thus has the greatest number of Buddhist caves in India; these include Ajanta, Kanheri, Baja and Kondane.

### The Heyday of Buddhism

An impressive range of caves is located in the Poona district, while others are found around Bombay and Nasik. Caves excavated before the Christian era followed the Hinayana Buddhist practice of portraying the Buddha through symbols. In the later caves, the Buddha's images were sculpted. It is known that religious activities continued in these *chaityas* and *viharas* for over 800 years, and they provide us with fine examples of Buddhist architecture, sculpture and paintings. The 30 caves at Ajanta were gradually excavated from around the second century B.C. A number of them were excavated under later rulers, who also embellished the caves with sculptures. But it is for exquisite paintings that Ajanta is internationally renowned. The Ajanta paintings belong to two distinct phases. The earlier ones, belonging to the two centuries B.C., were created under the patronage of the Satavahanas, while the later ones were executed under the patronage of the Vakatakas, in the 5th and 6th centuries A.D.

The great stupa built at Dhanyakataka (modern Andhra Pradesh) was known as the Mahachaitya. While Buddhist stupas all over India had a basic similarity, the Andhra stupas developed certain distinct features, such as the five pillars erected at each of the main entrances. These five pillars, called the *ayaka* pillars, represented the five main stages of the Buddha's life - his birth, renunciation, enlightenment, his first sermon and his passing away. The dome-shaped superstructure was built over a drum, on a plan resem-

bling a wheel. The wheel represented the wheel of righteousness, set in motion by Lord Buddha.

In the central part of the wheel was interred either a relic of the Buddha, any object used by him, or a memorial. Along with the relic, gold leaves, precious gems, and emblems of the Buddhist faith were placed inside a crystal casket, which in turn was de-posited in a stone casket. Often, the cas-ket bore inscriptions recording its contents and the name of the nobleman or guild who offered the enclosed gifts. The core of the stupa was built of brick and encased within carved slabs. It had a path with a railing outside. The inner side of the railing had sculptures depicting scenes from the life of the Buddha, or Buddhist legends. Most of the carved slabs bear inscriptions from devotees, giving a deep insight into contemporary society. The stupa, and there were many in Andhra Pradesh, especially in the Krishna basin, reached its finest form under the Satavahanas, Amaravati furnishing the best example.

A great number of Buddhist stupas and sculptures emerged in the Andhra region in the first three centuries of this millennium, when a considerable section of the people living there were Buddhists. The Buddhist monasteries served as great centers of learning and drew eminent men from all parts of India, from China, the Far East and Sri Lanka. The intellectual activities at these monasteries helped the people to develop a universal outlook, combined with the philosophy of compassion taught by the Buddha. Though Buddhism declined and then disappeared altogether in later years, this great inheritance continued to influence the people of Andhra Pradesh.

The considerable body of literary and philosophical works that have survived mark the Satavahana age of the Deccan

*Left: Detail of an 18th-century sculpture at Mallikarjuna Temple, Pattadakal.*

as an era of great creative activity. At least four of them may be mentioned as of immense importance. The 700 verses, called *Sattasai*, by Hala (second century A.D.) is a poem on love and other secular themes. Written in Maharashtri Prakrit, the poem expresses the gentle feelings of the people who work on the land - the cowherds, and the women who tend the garden or grind corn at the mill, the hunter or the worker. Much of the poetry draws upon the charm and simplicity of life in the village, but the attractions of the city are not forgotten. Unlike anything in Sanskrit poetry, Hala's *Sattasai* remains an outstanding and distinctive example of the ancient literature of India.

A second work of great merit is the *Pancatantra*, a collection of tales in Sanskrit. These tales virtually served as a manual of instructions for princes in their day to day political life. The gripping narration of the tales, which have left a lasting impression on the Indian mind for over 2000 years, is ascribed to the genius of poets who lived in the Satavahana court. The work was translated into Pahlavi before A.D. 570, followed by old Syrian and Arabic versions. Several Indian versions have appeared in abridged form through the centuries.

The third work of great repute is the *Brhad Katha*, written in Paisaci Prakrit, by Gunadhya. The author was born in Paithan, the capital of the Satavahanas, and is said to have been greatly favored by the ruler. Gunadhya is known to have composed his masterpiece in the Vindhya hills, deriving his inspiration from the epic *Ramayana*, Buddhist legends, and also from stories of sea voyages and strange adventures in faraway lands. The original text is lost, but later versions have survived. The fourth work is the philosophical treatise of the great Buddhist teacher Nagarjuna. All these works bear witness to the intellectual fervor of the times and remain the distinct contribution of the Deccan.

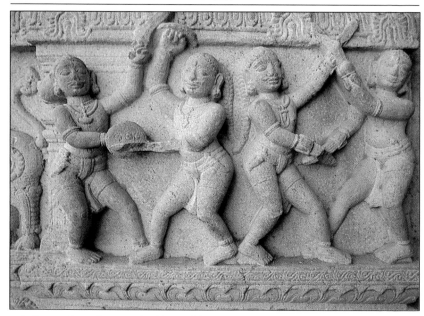

Indian sculptural art reached its zenith under the Satavahanas, and especially at Amaravati, where the great stupa was enlarged and embellished by the rulers, their queens, and noblemen. In the portrayal of the human form the art of Amaravati remains unrivaled. The linear treatment of the body, the flowing contours, the grouping of figures and the dramatic use of space create a remarkably realistic effect. The sculptors were able to imbue their art with emotion, and this is seen in all the images, from the minute figures of joyous dwarfs to the overwhelming figures of the Buddha. The stone sculptures almost resemble delicately carved pieces of ivory.

The great gateways at Sanchi, near Bhopal, known for their profuse sculptures, were, in fact, created by ivory carvers from Vidisa for the Satavahanas. The early paintings of Ajanta also belong to this outstandingly creative era.

*Above: Lively frieze of warriors, Hoysala temple detail.*

**The Sangam Age**

In contrast to what happened in the Deccan, the whole of Tamil Nadu presents a slightly different picture in the period between the 2nd century B.C. and the 2nd century A.D. Even before the 3rd century B.C., Tamil had developed into a classical literary language. The land south of Thirupati Hill (north of Madras), was traditionally known as Tamil country, and this included the west coast. The Cheras, the Cholas, and the Pandyas were the famous "three crowned Tamil monarchs," who ruled this region. The Cholas controlled the east, the Cheras the west and the Pandyas the southern parts of the Tamil land. The Cheras had their capital at Karur in Trichy district, while their rule extended to the west coast through the Palghat Gap in the Western Ghats. Their main port was Muziris. The exploits of ten great rulers of this dynasty (first century B.C. to first century A.D.) are preserved in a body of literature. They performed Vedic sacrifices and were patrons of the arts, and they are referred to in Asokan inscriptions as Kerala *putras*. They were originally rulers of parts of the Tamil country and are thus spoken of as Tamil kings. At a later period, after the 7th century A.D., they confined their rule mainly to the west coast, and came to assume a distinct Kerala culture. The Cheras of the Sangam Age seem to have had a close alliance with the Satavahanas of the Deccan. The capital of the Cholas was Uraiyur, a suburb of modern Trichy.

Karikala, the most illustrious among the Cholas, extended his kingdom up to Kanchipuram. Many rulers of bordering lands established matrimonial alliances with him, and their descendants proudly declared their Karikala lineage. Karikala was also a follower of the Vedic religion and performed several sacrifices. Among his achievements, the erection of an embankment along the River Kaveri, to divert its waters for irrigation, receives special mention. He was already the ruler of the fertile Chola country, and this interest in agriculture further enriched his coffers. One of the rulers of this dynasty performed the famous Vedic sacrifice known as the *Rajasuya*, which was also performed by Aryan kings. Kaveripumpattinam (also known as Poompuhar) at the mouth of the River Kaveri, was the main Chola port.

**The Pandya Dynasty**

Madurai was the ancient capital of the Pandya dynasty. This dynasty has the unique distinction in the history of India of being the only one to rule for over 2000 years, from a few centuries before Christ almost to the 18th century A.D. Korkai, at the mouth of the river Tamraparni, was their main port, known also for its exquisite pearls, and even mentioned in the great epic *Maha-bharata*. The Pandyas were also followers of the Vedic religion, and one of their rulers

performed enough sacrifices to assume the title *Palyagasala*, i.e. one who did many Vedic sacrifices.

As we have seen earlier, Buddhism did not have as great an impact far south as it did in the Deccan. But we know that Jains were received with great favor in the royal courts. Many Jain monks are mentioned in the records of the age, and they were also provided with rock shelters in the hills, mainly near the capitals of Tamil rulers. The merchants dealing in gold, metal, grains and cotton are known to have taken great interest in Jainism. Though the rulers themselves followed Vedic Hinduism, they patronized the Jain monks by making donations.

A monarchical system, with hereditary succession, was the prevalent mode of rule in Tamil Nadu, but the king's role seems to have been confined to the protection of territory, and to establishing a harmonious life, rather than the autocratic enforcement of his will on society. Ministers and poets counseled the king against partiality and hasty or harsh decisions. By and large, poets and wise men were respected for their views and held in higher esteem than the rulers.

The cities, villages, temples and palaces were laid out according to architectural treatises and each occupied an allotted place and function. There were many expert artisans who could execute the plans detailed in the treatises. Each village had a special area where people could meet for leisure and for the discussion of problems relating to the village. Society was divided into castes, and each caste lived in separate quarters. Brahmins who recited Vedic hymns had their own colonies. There were also colonies of different craftsmen, such as jewelers, leather workers, toy makers, blacksmiths, gold- smiths, masons and artists. The trading class led a prosperous life, and were known for their honesty in business and the exchange of goods, barter being the main form of trade. It was

acknowledged that the prosperity of the country and victory in war depended mainly on agricultural wealth and the labor of the peasantry. Agriculture was therefore recognized as being the most important occupation. There were agencies to levy taxes and customs duties on commodities, both inland and at the ports. There were regular guards who kept a watch on reservoirs to prevent the overflow of water or the bursting of banks. The army was well organized and had elephants, horses, chariots and soldiers, the king himself leading in battle.

Temples were built, dedicated to Hindu gods like Siva, Vishnu, Muruga and Durga. Daily offerings were made at the temples and the images were taken out in procession in the evenings. It was customary to build temples first when setting up new villages. Though temple worship was prevalent, the secular aspects of life were of greater importance.

*Above: A floral offering to Siva at Mahakuta Temple, Karnataka.*

**The Sangam Literature**

These details of contemporary life are vividly preserved in a body of Tamil literature collectively known as Sangam literature. This consists of 2239 long and short poems, composed by many poets, including some of the ruling kings. Most of the poems are secular in nature and deal with the exploits, conquests and benefactions of the kings and nobles. These fascinating groups of poems, dating from the 2nd century B.C. to the 2nd century A.D., give a lively picture of contemporary society, and are considered a landmark in the literary and cultural history of India.

Many kings, queens, nobles and poets have become famous through these poems, and recent epigraphical finds have confirmed the authenticity of many of them. A great assembly of Tamil poets existed in the court of the Pandya kings at Madurai. This assembly of poets, known as the Tamil Sangam, had the right to approve or disapprove of the quality and excellence of the poems, a precondition for any poet who wished to be recognized. Three such Sangams are said to have existed. The present collection of poems is said to belong to the third Sangam, the works of the earlier two being irretrievably lost. It is customary to refer to this era as the Sangam Age of the Tamil country. Thus, from the dawn of history, Tamil Nadu showed its love of literature, music and dance, which have been called "the three Tamils".

Among the Indian languages, except for Sanskrit, it is Tamil that has best preserved a classical literature that is 2000 years old. Yet the surviving works are only a part of a vast body of literature created in that era. A large number of Sangam poems deal with human love, set in the natural surroundings of different regions. The authorities classify these poems under two categories - the ones dealing with the external exploits of heroes are called *puram*, while those expressing the love of heroes or heroines are called *aham*.

Further, another classification has been made in which the entire land was divided into five basic regions - namely, the hilly tract, the forest region, the cultivable plains, the coastal region and desert lands. Each *aham* poem of love is said to take place in one of these five regions, and the geographical factors, the flora and fauna, and the customs and manners peculiar to the respective region appear as a distinctive background.

The Tamil language was enriched by the sage Agastya, who migrated to the south in legendary times. However, a very early grammatical work called *Tolkappiam* (i.e. ancient work) with clear-cut rules, ascribed even on a modest estimate to the beginning of the Christian era, has survived. It deals with the language under three headings - syllables, words and meanings.

A remarkable work named *Thirukkural*, by the saint Thiruvalluvar, and also

assigned to the beginning of the first century A.D., is a didactic work par excellence. It consists of 3300 verses, grouped into three books and dealing with righteous conduct, polity and love. In precise and sublime poetic form, the verses impart profound wisdom and a code of conduct. This amazing work has influenced the life of the people for the past 2000 years and has been translated into most of the major languages of the world.

### Contact with the Romans

An important aspect of south Indian society in the first two centuries of the Christian era was the contact established with imperial Rome. The Romans were called the Yavanas, a word also used to refer to the Ionians, who settled in Egypt under the Romans.

Until the beginning of the Christian era, western ships used to reach Barygaza (Broach) in Gujarat, and then sail down the west coast to the ports of the Chera kingdom in the south. The ships then sailed around Cape Comorin (Kanniyakumari) and, passing through Colchi (Korkai), the port of the Pandyas, reached the Chola coast – Poompuhar being their main destination. Roman coins and other artifacts have been found in the south, including the Deccan.

At least three classical works of the western world (first and 2nd centuries A.D.), ascribed to Ptolemy and Pliny and including *The Periplus of the Erythream Sea*, speak of Roman ships bringing commodities to the south Indian port towns and returning with pepper, semi-precious stones and other commodities of interest to the western world.

The Sangam classics refer to Yavana ships, settlements and trade. Various Roman metal objects, glass, pottery and terracotta objects have been found in Tigara (Ter) in Maharashtra, in the environs of the ancient capital of the Satavahanas. In Tamil Nadu, especially around Karur,

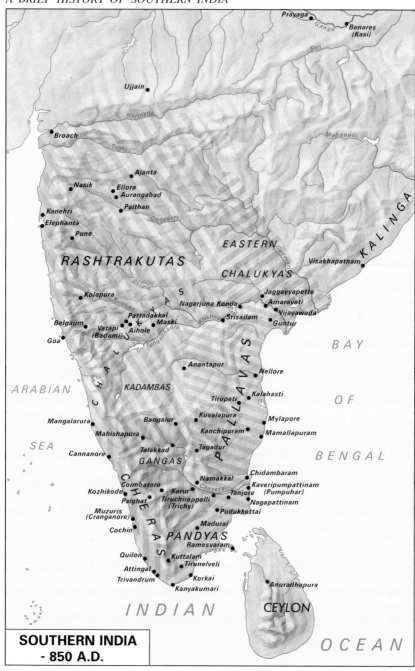

Prayaga • • Benares (Kasi)
Ganga
Son

Ujjain •

Narmada

• Broach
Tapti
Mahanadi

• Ajanta
Nasik • Ellora
Aurangabad
Kanehri • Paithan
Elephanta •
Pune • Godavari

RASHTRAKUTAS
EASTERN

CHALUKYAS
KALINGA
Visakhapatnam •

Bhima
Kolapura • Jaggayyapetta
Nagarjuna Konda Amaravati
Belgaum • Pattadakkal Maski Srisailam Vijayawada
Vatapi Aihole Krishna Guntur
(Badami)
Goa • Tungabhadra

BAY

Anantapur •
Nellore •
OF
Kalahasti •
KADAMBAS Tirupati •
Mangalarura • Kuvalapura
Bangalur • Mylapore •
Mahishapura • Kanchipuram • Mamallapuram
Cannanore • Talakkad Tagadur BENGAL
GANGAS
Namakkal Chidambaram
Coimbatore Kaveripumpattinam
Kozhikode • Karur Cauvery (Pumpuhar)
Palghat Tiruchirappalli Tanjore • Nagapattinam
Muzuris (Trichy)
(Cranganore) • Pudukkottai
Cochin • Madurai
PANDYAS
Quilon • Ramesvaram
Kuttalam
Attingal • Tirunelveli
Trivandrum • Korkai Anuradhapura •
Kanyakumari

ARABIAN

SEA

CHALUKYAS

CHERAS

PALLAVAS

INDIAN CEYLON

**SOUTHERN INDIA
- 850 A.D.**

OCEAN

the ancient capital of the Cheras, thousands of silver and gold Roman coins have been found. Excavations by the famous archaeologist Sir Mortimer Wheeler at Arikkamedu, near Pondicherry, revealed a Roman settlement, and yielded stamped Mediterranean pottery manufactured at a site called Aresso near Rome, as well as Mediterranean wine jars and other artifacts.

Another site, near Rameswaram in the south, produced a special type of pottery manufactured in Tunisia when it was under Roman rule.

Sangam literature attests that many Roman soldiers were employed as the bodyguards of the Tamil kings, and that the gates of capital cities like Madurai were guarded by fierce Roman soldiers, wielding long spears and shields. However, it is also known that most of the Romans stayed only for the brief period of their trading transactions.

The Roman contact deserves to be noted for two other aspects. Indian luxury goods were in great demand in imperial Rome, especially among ladies, and such quantities of gold were bartered in exchange for these items that the Roman economy seems to have been adversely affected, and the Roman emperor is known to have issued a decree prohibiting the export of gold to India.

The second aspect was the establishment of a direct sea route to South India. It was found that the monsoon could be used advantageously to sail ships directly from the Red Sea to Muziris, the port of the Cheras, in 40 days. This revolutionized the maritime trade of the age. Saint Thomas, the Christian missionary, came to the Kerala coast during this period.

Though there are copious references to different art styles in Tamil works, little of the artistic work of the age has survived. Compared to the profusion of Buddhist sculptures and terracotta figurines found in the Deccan, practically nothing has survived in Tamil Nadu. The absence of Buddhism as a guiding force might perhaps explain this.

## The Ascendance of Monarchies

The three centuries following the Satavahana and Sangam eras are marked by varying degrees of advancement in the political, cultural and artistic life of different regions in the south. In Maharashtra, the Vakatakas, who had maintained matrimonial alliances with the imperial Guptas of the north, established their rule. The Vakatakas continued to patronize Buddhism and excavated many caves, the best examples being the later cave temples of Ajanta.

The magnificent cave temples of Elephanta, off the coast of Bombay, also developed under their patronage. The awesome groups of sculpture seen here, representing Trimurti, Kalyanasundara, Andhakasuravadha and Nrittamurti, are among the supreme artistic creations of the age. From moderately sized carvings, sculptural art now came to emphasize overwhelming grandeur; from the delicate depiction of line and movement, it shifted to vigorous display.

In Karnataka, two dynasties emerged during this age – the Kadambas in the northeastern part, and the Gangas in the Mysore-Bangalore region. The former were Brahmins devoted to Vedic learning. The founder of this dynasty, Mayurasarman, went to Kanchipuram, the capital of the Pallavas, to learn the Vedas, but at the borders he was involved in a quarrel with the guards and decided to establish his own kingdom. The Gangas of the south hailed from the banks of the River Ganga, and were related by marriage to the Cholas of the Kaveri region. While the Kadambas lost their identity after the rise of the Chalukyas in the 6th century A.D., the Gangas survived for nearly 800 years by tacitly aligning themselves with the superior powers.

In the Andhra area the Ikshuvakus of Vijayapuri continued the traditions of their predecessors; they also gave great encouragement to the building of temples dedicated to Hindu gods. Vedic sacrifices, Hindu temples and Buddhist stupas embellished with sculptures were the norm of the age. Buddhist art in those days was an extension of the Satavahana tradition, although it was beginning to lose its delicacy and assumed a somewhat heavy form at Nagarjunkonda.

## Tamil Epics

The political history of the Tamil country is not very clear after the Sangam Age, although two great Tamil epics, the *Silappadhikaram*, and the *Manimekhalai*, are ascribed to this period. The *Silappadhikaram* is an epic poem par excellence

*Above: Devotees and musicians at the Srirangam Temple, Tamil Nadu. Right: Dating trom the 7th century: the Chalukya Papanatha Temple, Pattadakal.*

written by a Chera Prince, Ilangaodigal. It has a novel theme, dealing with the life of a chaste woman named Kannagi who was the wife of a merchant, Kovalan. This merchant was in love with a dancing girl. The story is set among the three kingdoms - the Chola, Pandya and Chera. After his romance with the dancing girl, the hero returned to his wife and set out to find wealth in the Pandyan territory. There he was wrongly accused of stealing one of the anklets of the queen and was beheaded by the king. In revenge, the heroine burned the city of Madurai, went to the Chera kingdom and surrendered to death in order to join her husband in heaven. The Chera ruler, Sunguttuvan, who came to hear of the episode, erected a temple to the chaste wife.

The story is narrated in poetry, and vividly portrays extremes of human emotions in different contexts. This long epic poem is also a treasure house of information about various sections of society as visualized by the poet, who tells of merchants, farmers, cowherds, hunters, the

king and his administrators, religious faith and wise men. A remarkable quality of the poem is that it steers clear of partiality and religious bigotry. In this, it anticipates the devotional movement that emerged in the succeeding centuries; the epic is interspersed with devotional hymns in praise of the goddess Durga, Lord Vishnu and Subrahmanya. It also gives details about the mode of constructing temples and the information it furnishes on various arts, especially dance and music, reveals a highly sophisticated society with a remarkably precise understanding of music and dance.

The other epic, *Manimekhalai*, is essentially Buddhist in nature and centers around the life of a Buddhist nun, Manimekhalai, who was the daughter of the dancing girl in *Silappadhi-karam*. This work is thus a sequel to the other epic and chiefly aims at extolling Buddhist ideologies against other faiths. The different philosophical beliefs that were influential in Tamil Nadu are briefly outlined, but the increasing influence of Buddhism is clearly seen in this work. Besides these twin epics, a number of Buddhist texts, written in Prakrit and dealing with the life of the Buddha and the Jataka tales, were composed in Tamil Nadu, especially at the port town of Kaveripumpattinam, a great center of Buddhist learning. A Buddhist *chaitya* and a *vihara*, both from this period, have been excavated here, the former bearing Far Eastern influences.

One great political event of the age which merits attention is the establishment of the Pallava kingdom, with Kanchi as its capital, towards the close of the 3rd century A.D. Pallava rule was confined to the northern boundaries of Tamil Nadu, but extended to the lower regions of Andhra and Karnataka. This dynasty was to play a vital role in molding the cultural ethos of the south.

### The Age of Change

The history of the next three centuries, from A.D. 600 to A.D. 900, is virtually centered around devotional, intellectual and artistic changes, the first two originating in Tamil country, and the third appearing simultaneously all over the south. It is worth mentioning that both the devotional and intellectual movements were spearheaded by common people, the rulers then following suit; the artistic movement, on the other hand, owed its success to the direct influence and patronage of the rulers.

By A.D. 600 several hundred temples, principally to Siva and Vishnu, had already come into existence in Tamil Nadu. Over 300 temple settlements of Saivites and 108 Vaishnavite settlements were under active worship by the beginning of the 7th century. There arose a great movement of Bhakti (devotion) to a personalized God, who was conceived as the universal father, bestowing grace on the devotee, who surrendered all his actions to the service of God.

Among both the Saivite and Vaishnavite devotees, there were many men and women belonging to all castes, who were adored and deified. Nandan, an outcaste devotee of Siva, and Thiruppanalvar of the Vaishnav school, also an outcaste, were deified and worshiped by the Brahmins, kings and others. Similarly, Karaikkal Ammai, a woman devotee of Siva, and Andal, the Vaishnav Bhakta, were venerated by all for their devotion. The Bhakti movement underlined the freedom of the soul and its capacity to rise to the highest realm of consciousness, and dispensed with the shackles of mundane codes of existence. While extolling the path of devotion to a chosen God, both schools mounted an attack on the Jains and Buddhists, especially the former. Buddhism, as mentioned earlier, had only a marginal effect on Tamil society; with this religious upsurge it was destined to be wiped out. But the Jain faith was on a different footing. It had

*Right: Mendicants at the entrance of the Kanheri Caves, Bombay.*

gained influence among the business and ruling classes, and it even had kings in its grip, as demonstrated by the fact that a Pallava king, Mahendra (A.D. 590 - A.D. 630) and a Pandyan ruler, Arikesari, were followers of Jainism before they were converted to the Hindu faith. The Saiva and Vaishnav Bhakti upsurge was a mass movement of the common people against the oppressive influence of followers of other faiths. It resulted in the rulers themselves becoming converts to the Saiva or Vaishnav faiths. However, it did not drive Jainism from Tamil Nadu; it only weakened its hold over the population.

### Paths of Devotion and Knowledge

The essential differences between the Saiva and Vaishnav movements, however, lies in recognition of the supreme God, Saivas holding Siva as the ultimate God, while the Vaishnavs hold Vishnu as the supreme God. In the devotional path two distinct approaches are discernible, one the path of eternal service to God, and the other the path of human love, likened to that of a woman towards her lover. Both were known and accepted by the Saivites and Vaishnavites. The latter liken the individual soul, irrespective of the sex of the individual, to a woman longing for union with God, personified as her lover. It is a metaphysical concept given human dimensions. The Vaishnavite Alwars, by and large, preferred the path of love while the Saivites' preference was towards eternal service to God.

The path of human love attains its fullest expression in the hymns of the Vaishnavite Alwars. Altogether 4000 verses by the 12 Vaishnav saints are recorded and are known as the "four thousand hymns." All these hymns are committed to memory by the followers of the Vaishnavite Alwars and recited at home and in the temple. The different perceptions of the path of love are revealed in

these compositions of the Alwars. In a number of verses, Periyalvar makes God the child of the devotee, and sings His praises with motherly affection. The incarnations of Vishnu as Rama and Krishna are especially conducive to such a portrayal. Nammalvar, who composed the maximum number of verses, emphasized the feminine emotion of love as the aspiration of the human soul. Andal, the woman devotee, dreamed of her marriage with the lord - a union of the human with the divine. Her moving compositions are sung as Vedic hymns in Vaishnav marriage ceremonies to this day, for she has left a poignant impression on the minds of the south Indian people.

Among the Saivites the songs of four great saints are especially revered. Over 7000 verses of three saints - Appar, Sambandar, and Sundarar - have survived and are grouped as the *Tevaram* hymns. The collection of the fourth saint, Manikkavacakar, a minister to the Pandya ruler of Madurai, is called *Thiruvacakam*. The hymns of these saints are sung to this day, set to traditional music known as *pans*. Of the four saints, Appar was born in a farming family, and demonstrated that a true devotee of God can lead a fearless life, so that even the coercive commands of the ruler of the land will leave him unaffected. Appar held that true devotion would lead to knowledge, identical with godhood.

The Bhakti movement inspired by these saints is unique in the history of India. It had a profound impact on temple culture and transformed the entire south into a land of temples. The Bhakti movement also later inspired the devotional ethos of the north in the medieval age.

The intellectual upheaval of the time was symbolized by Sankara, the Advaita philosopher. Steeped in Vedic tradition, Sankara interpreted the Upanishads as embodying the supreme wisdom of the land and held that knowledge alone could bestow redemption. Behind the plurality of the world and the innumerable souls, is the indivisible Supreme Being, beyond time, and beyond space, called Brahman.

All pluralities are only the projections of the same Supreme Brahman. The individual soul (*atman*) and the Supreme Brahman are identical in the light of ultimate truth. The relative existence of this world is illusion (*maya*), which can best be understood only as a lower level of perception. Sankara did not question the existing stratification of society, but he held that these were simple diversities and had no meaning in the ultimate perception. All souls, he said, are essentially one with the Supreme and can realize their true nature. Nor did he reject rituals, which he held to be capable of disciplining the mind; however, he emphasized that true realization could only be attained through knowledge. Sankara has commented on three groups of work - the Upanishads, the *Bhagavad Gita* and the *Brahmasutras*, all from the Advaita point of view. Besides these commentaries, many devotional hymns and minor phil-

*Above: A towering and profusely carved gopuram is typical of South Indian temples.*

osophical works have been ascribed to him, showing that he was not unwilling to guide those souls endowed with lesser intellectual faculties. The date of Sankara is much debated, but it is certain that he traveled throughout India propounding this refined philosophy. It can be said that every school of philosophy or religious faith which developed thereafter in India could not escape the overwhelming force of his exposition. There were attempts, later, to question his theories, but Sankara is still held to personify the height of Indian intellectual clarity.

### Religious Architecture

The third important event that took place during this age is the gradual consolidation and expansion of the regal power. The rule of the king came to be felt by the people with greater force. Traders were losing their preeminent position to soldiers and generals. However, royal involvement in monumental architecture stands out clearly. In the south, the Pallavas ascended to great heights by conquering vast territories and enforcing their rule. In the extreme south, the Pandyas at Madurai also remained powerful. Towards the close of the 6th century, the Chalukyas established their rule with Vatapi (Badami) as their capital. The Chalukya rule extended to Maha-rashtra, Karnataka, Andhra Pradesh and part of Kalinga as well.

The greatest conqueror of all was Pulakesin II (A.D. 609-642) who captured Vengi in Andhra, and appointed his brother as ruler, thus laying the foundation for the Eastern Chalukya kingdom. The two great powers, the Pallavas and the Chalukyas were perpetually at war, and frequently invaded each other's territory. The Chalukyas were exhausted by the middle of the 8th century, and replaced by the Rashtrakutas. A century later, the Pallavas were a weakened power. It was during the early period of this age that the famous Chinese traveler Hsuan Tsang visited almost all of these kingdoms and left an account which has served as a veritable source book of history until now.

Inspired by their mutual competitive contribution to art, the Chalukyas of Badami, the Pallavas of Kanchi, and the Pandyas of Madurai, embarked upon the excavation of caves and monolithic temples of great magnitude.

The finest Chalukyan cave temples are at Badami and Aihole. The Rashtrakutas, who followed them, are responsible for a series of caves at Ellora, dedicated to the Hindu, Buddhist and Jain faiths. The Pallavas have left a number of cave temples of moderate size in different parts of their kingdom, the most famous temples being at Mamallapuram, where monolithic creations and open air sculptures have earned a place in the art history of the world. The Pandyas have left more cave temples numerically, but with less attention to sculptural art. However, their attempt, though unfinished, to carve a

monolith at Kalugumalai, in the Tinnelveli district, stands out as a remarkable creation.

It is interesting to note that after this period cave art totally disappeared. Structural temples, the new expression of religious architecture, were raised by the great rulers of each dynasty, either as dedicatory temples, or in memory of conquests in war. By this time each region had developed its own style of architecture and sculpture. The temples and the sculptures embellishing them now exhibit a boldness of conception, freedom of articulation, and an urge towards new forms with each new creation.

The groups of Brahminical, Buddhist and Jain cave temples at Ellora are well known. Ellora (ancient Elapura) was the capital of the Rashtrakuta rulers before they moved it to Malkhed. Though a few of the caves here date to an earlier period, most of them are assigned to the Rashtrakuta era (8th and 9th centuries A.D.). The amazing group of monuments belonging to three religious sects, all found at the same place and almost adjacent to each other, reveal the catholicity of their builders and the people. The Vishvakarma cave of the Buddhists, the Kailash of the Brahminical faith and the Indrasabha of the Jains are real gems. The Kailash Temple was excavated by Rashtrakuta Krishna, and it exhibits a Dravidian influence. In the sculptural art of Ellora, art historians see a resemblance to Chalukyan art, especially that of Pattadakkal. Some of the Rashtrakutas were followers of Jainism, which received great impetus through them.

The age also witnessed the strict adherence to codified texts, called *Agamas*, in temple architecture and rituals. The *Agamas* are generally divided into four parts, dealing with personal conduct, rituals and festivals in temples, yoga and Jnana, i.e. the metaphysical concepts behind such rituals. Several such Agamic texts have survived and there are specific

references in contemporary records which reveal the extent to which these Agamic texts were followed in temple construction and rituals. Many of the kings were initiated into the codes of worship, especially those of Saivism, which they note in their records. It is worth mentioning that the *Agamas*, which prescribe rigid formulas, allowed some freedom of expression.

### The Flowering of the Arts

The Agamic worship in temples also necessitated the employment of musicians and dancers, who formed an integral part of temple ritual. A family of dedicated dancing girls performed during daily rites and festivals, but also attended to other duties such as making flower garlands. This art enriched the different forms of dance, and was based essentially

*Above: An enchanting detail of the Ajanta frescoes. Right: Carvings of animal forms were widely used in Hoysala temples.*

on the treatises of Bharata. This tradition of dance, in turn, greatly influenced and inspired new forms of poetry which emerged with the temple as a focal center. Dramas, which flowered as another extension of the dance tradition, were also enacted in temples. Some of the rulers themselves were also great composers of music and dance. The Pallava ruler Mahendravarman stands out as one example. He was clearly a genius in the fields of architecture, painting, music, dance, literature and philosophy. Among his creations are two dance-dramas, farces ridiculing the failings of the religious mendicants of contemporary society. For example, he mocks a Kapalika monk, a drunkard and debauchee, roaming the streets of Kanchipuram with a woman, who is also a drunkard, and a Buddhist *bikshu* casting his lustful eyes on the woman. Coming from the pen of an emperor, these farces stand out as unique works in the field of Indian literature. What is more striking is the fact that they have been performed over a

span of 1300 years, to this day, in the temples of Kerala, which is perhaps one of the unique achievements in the history of world drama. This period also witnessed the rise of many eminent poets, some composing biographical sketches of the ruling monarchs in a highly embellished poetic form. It was an age when regional languages flowered into distinct groups, being employed as administrative languages in records, along with Sanskrit.

### The Ebb of Buddhism

This was the time when Buddhism reached its lowest ebb throughout the south, even though, in the 8th century, the Chinese emperor obtained permission from the Pallava ruler, Narasimhavarman, to build a Buddhist *chaitya* at Nagapattinam in Tamil Nadu for the benefit of Chinese travelers. In Orissa, however, Buddhism continued to flourish for nearly 2000 years from the time of Asoka until the end of the 16th century A.D.

Large numbers of Buddhist sculptures, found scattered all over Orissa, attest to the continuity of this faith. A center of Mahayana Buddhism, with Arya Ava-lo-kitesvara as the deity, was established in the 6th century near Jayarampur. In the middle of the 7th century, more than 100 monasteries were active, housing several thousand Buddhist monks. The Chinese pilgrim Hsuan Tsang, who mentions the great activities that went on in the Buddhist monasteries refers to the hill monastery of Pushpagiri, identified with Lalitgiri or Udayagiri in Cuttack district. He also refers to ten Asokan stupas. One of the rulers of the Bhaumakara dynasty sent a Mahayana Buddhist manuscript, bearing his autograph, to the Chinese emperor Te-Tsong in A.D. 795. The Bhaumakara rulers are known to have built many monasteries and other structures for the worship of Buddhist images. Orissa also harbored Buddhist centers; foremost among these was Ratnagiri.

Ratnagiri, in Cuttack district, was a great center of Buddhism from the 6th to the 10th centuries. On top of the hillock, a *vihara* called the Ratnagiri Mahavihara flourished. A large number of excavated structures, sculptures and inscriptions reveal that many Buddhist scholars of great repute resided here. To seek their guidance, monks from far off places arrived in considerable numbers. This is one of the sites where Buddhists kept alight the torch of their faith almost to the 16th century. Besides the main stupa and a number of monasteries, eight brick temples in the Orissa style, dedicated to Manjusri and other Buddhist deities, have been found. Beautiful bronze images of the Buddha, Lokesvara and Maitreya have also been discovered.

According to tradition, Orissa is the home of Mahayana Buddhism. A great number of sites in the state bear witness to this faith. Mention may be made of Achyutrajpur in Puri district, where a great bronze casting center flourished. Among nearly 100 bronze images of exquisite workmanship (9th to 11th centuries A.D.) there are more than 75 Buddhist bronzes of the Vajrayana school, including images of the Goddess Tara, Vajrasattva and others. Buddhism declined and disappeared after the 17th century in Orissa.

In the social and economic spheres during these centuries the king's role assumed greater significance. In both personal and public matters, the king and the people were guided by the *Dharmasastras*, the law books of the ancient Indian sages. The king was only the enforcer of these codes of law, not their creator. Agricultural and commercial taxation, together with several professional taxes, enriched the king's treasury, a part of which was made over to rural maintenance and development. Though different dynasties ruled different regions, and

though there were various regional languages, the lifestyle of the people, guided by these *Dharmasastras*, was the same throughout south India.

## The Golden Era of the Cholas

The 400 years from the 9th to the 13th centuries A.D. have appropriately been termed as the age of grandeur in the history of south India. Within this span of time a remarkable sophistication was achieved in the fields of administration, the arts and literature. Magnificent temples, numbering several thousands, came into existence during this age, especially in the 11th century, when the great temples of Tanjore and Gangaikondacholapuram in Tamil Nadu, the Lingaraj Temple in Bhubaneswar and the Jagannath Temple of Puri were built. Creative activity of such stupendous dimensions became possible mainly because of the thorough and inspiring efficiency of the Chola monarchs, who brought the major part of south India under their rule and also influenced the course of events in other regions.

The Cholas of Tanjore emerged as an imperial power in the middle of the 9th century A.D., and soon expanded their kingdom to include the southern part of Karnataka. The region as far as the Tungabhadra river was annexed by them, and remained under their rule for nearly 200 years. At the same time the Rashtrakutas were uprooted, and later the Chalukyas took control over northern Karnataka, siting their capital at Kalyani. The Tungabhadra river formed the main dividing line between their kingdom and that of the Cholas, with whom they were continually at war until almost A.D. 1200. The Cholas maintained a very well-organized army which earned laurels on all fronts. They were also great navigators, and had a powerful naval fleet. The greatest Chola ruler, Rajaraja I (A.D. 985-1014.), was mainly responsible for the naval and

*Right: Carved dvarpalas, or door guardians, at the entrance to the temple sanctum.*

military prowess of the dynasty. He was succeeded by his son Rajendra Chola (A.D. 1012-1044). The Chola navy conquered Sri Lanka and, sailing across the Bay of Bengal, won decisive battles in what was then known as the Srivijaya Kingdom, which included Malaysia, Singapore, Sumatra and Java.

It is perhaps the only overseas conquest ever achieved by any Indian monarch. The Chola army marched towards the north, and after a succession of victories, reached as far as modern Calcutta. The aim to extend their conquests to the Gangetic plain was thus fulfilled. The victorious Chola army poured the sacred waters of the River Ganga on the heads of the vanquished rulers and, to mark the victory, Rajendra Chola built a capital, Gangaikondacholapuram, which, from then on, became the seat of power for two and a half centuries.

The Cholas reigned supreme until A.D. 1280. The vast territories they conquered were organized into well-knit territorial units that were assigned to the care of efficient administrative officers. The strength of the Cholas lay in their carefully elected village democracy.

The qualifications of the members were strictly assessed, their tenure of service limited, and their accountability to the assembly closely watched. After serving one term, a person was debarred from standing for three succeeding elections, thus giving opportunity to fresh candidates. A defaulter was removed immediately from membership. These structures made village democracies both active and powerful.

The vital participation of the people in this administration marked the success of the Chola empire. Well-organized guilds of farmers, traders and artisans functioned effectively, contributing to the economic prosperity of the people. The Cholas also paid great attention to education and the establishment of hospitals. They founded several Vedic colonies, called *caturvedi mangalams*, and gifted land to the Brahmins, thus enabling them to pursue their learning peacefully. These

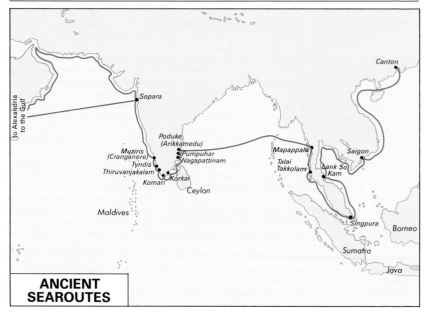

**ANCIENT SEAROUTES**

colonies were divided into several wards, and a representative from each ward was elected to the village assembly, which not only looked after the administration through committees called *variyams*, but was also responsible for the collection of revenue and the administration of the temples. By the side of these centers of learning, the Cholas also established trading nuclei, called *nagaram*, which were administered by merchant communities.

These settlements had their own system of self-government, and concentrated on trade and commercial growth. Great attention was paid to irrigation, and several hundred irrigation canals were laid to bring thousands of hectares of land under cultivation. Periodical assessments of the land, based on fertility and yield, were undertaken and taxation suitably adjusted. Incentives were offered by way of tax exemption for bringing fallow and uncultivable lands under the plow. Regular desilting of village tanks and lakes to augment water sources was an

important function assigned to the village assemblies. A regular watch was maintained on the proper utilization and accounting of village finances and temple endowments by the king's officers, who periodically inspected the accounts. The drafting of records related to sale, endowments or judicial judgements catered to the growing legal requirements. Tens of thousands of records, engraved on temple walls, speak of the thorough administrative organization and the dependence on written documents to enforce the rule of the law.

The condition of trade under the Cholas is brought to life in the account of a Jewish traveler, Benjamin (A.D. 1170): "This nation is very trustworthy in matters of trade, and whenever foreign merchants enter their port, three secretaries of the king immediately repair on board their vessels, write down their names and report them to him. The king thereupon grants them security for their property, which they may even leave in the open fields without any guard. One of the king's officers sits in the market and receives goods that may have been found anywhere and which he returns to those applicants who can minutely describe them."

Great institutions of learning, with well-equipped libraries of manuscripts, and hospitals were established as adjuncts of temples and given liberal land grants. However, it was in building great temples and instituting the arts, including music and dance, that the Cholas excelled. Literally thousands of temples were built or renovated with granite, and every temple was provided with musicians and dancers. It became a regular custom to recite, in the presence of the deity, songs of the great saints as part of daily worship, which enabled the age-old Tamil and Karnatic schools of music to survive to this day.

The number of temples built by the Cholas is amazing. They will also be remembered for their contribution to the art of bronzes. Several thousand bronzes were made and consecrated in the temples for festivals. The Chola bronzes, especially those made in the early phase of their rule, are now known throughout the world for their exquisite beauty and grace. It was also during the time of the Cholas that the form of the dancing Siva, Nataraja, was perfected.

The Cholas also left several thousand inscriptions which give details of benefactors to various temples and institutions, and include the names of many artists and architects.

Maritime contact with the Far East was frequent. Chola traders and emissaries reached as far as China and established colonies there. The king of Srivijaya sought the approval of the Chola Emperor Rajaraja and built a Buddhist *vihara* at Nagappattinam in the name of his father. Buddhist monks from far off places visited the Chola kingdom, while Tamil inscriptions from this time have been found in China and the Far East.

In the coastal regions of Andhra, up to Visakhapatnam, the Chalukyas were allowed to rule as feudal vassals of the imperial Cholas. Their artistic, intellectual and administrative traditions were mainly inspired by the Cholas. Even further north, in Kalinga, the Gangas accepted nominal suzerainty of the Cholas and, inspired by the artistic endeavors of the Cholas, built lofty temples. The great temples at Konark and other sites owe their origin to the Chola influence.

The northwestern Deccan was ruled by the Chalukyas of Kalyani who carried on a relentless war against the Cholas. In the field of the arts, they followed the traditions of the early Chalukyas of Badami.

Chola administration and their zeal for magnificent temple architecture spread to Karnataka. Towards the end of the 12th century, another great power rose in Karnataka: This was the Hoysalas, the builders of the Belur and Halebid temples. Originally, they began as feudatories of the Chalukyas of Kalyani, and, on their behalf, fought against the Cholas. However, they quickly assumed great power, challenged the Chalukyas, and, in the 13th century, turned their attention to the Tamil region. Their power extended to Trichy in the south and this brought the Kannada language and culture right into the Tamil heartland. The Hoysalas of the 13th century established a secondary, new capital near Trichy. Ramanuja, the great Vaishnav saint, had to flee from the Chola country for safety and took asylum with the Hoysalas. Thus, politically and culturally, these two regions became very close. The Hoysalas ruled for about 200 years from A.D. 1100 to 1300.

When the Pallavas rose to eminence in Tamil Nadu, they exerted pressure on the Cheras, who retreated to the west coast, using the high hill ranges as protective barriers. Now they began to move southwards along the entire west coast. By about the 9th century, the Kerala region, from south of Mangalore to Travancore in the extreme south, was divided into three main regions, each ruled by a different dynasty. The middle kingdom was ruled by the Kulasekharas, who gradually asserted great power and tried to unify all three regions. However, several historical factors encouraged the existence of different principalities. The Travancore country later came to be called the Thiruvadi Rajya.

A new factor emerged in trading relations during this reign. Arab and Chinese traders reached the Malabar coast, bringing rich Jewish and Christian merchants to Kerala. In the 10th and 11th centuries the imperial Cholas conquered the Kerala country and put an end to the Kulasekhara dynasty. The Kerala region was again divided into three main principalities - the Venadu rulers of the south, the Zamorin of Calicut in central Kerala and the Kolatri Raja in the north.

### Islam in the Deccan

In the next 400 years (A.D. 1300-1700) the Deccan and the Tamil country, further south, were to be subjected to a greater variety of alien influences than had ever been experienced before. The 13th century witnessed the establishment of the Turkish Sultanate in Delhi, and the supremacy of Muslim rule in north India. A new phase had begun in the history of India, and it was to last for six and a half centuries.

Initially, the Sultanate was confined to north India, but when Alauddin Khilji ascended the throne he sought to fulfil a long-cherished dream of the Sultans - the conquest of peninsular India. Placing his army in the hands of his competent general Malik Kafur, he sent two expeditions to the Deccan in 1307 and 1311. Mysore, Warangal and Devagiri felt the

*Right: Seeking shelter beneath the shadow of royal remains (Mecca Masjid).*

true strength of the Sultanate for the first time, and though their territories were not annexed they had to pay large tributes and acknowledge the supremacy of the Khilji ruler. The army then went even further south, to Madurai. The city was sacked and the booty that was sent back to Delhi is said to have consisted of more than 600 elephants, 20,000 horses and an enormous quantity of gold, jewels and pearls that had been donated to temples.

Alauddin Khilji became the first Muslim ruler to extend his empire beyond the Narmada river, and a new face of Islam was seen in the Deccan. The Arabs had come to the Kerala coast as early as the 8th century A.D., but they were essentially traders and their concern was not with political power.

As a consequence, their interaction with local communities was harmonious. Alauddin's invasion, however, created ripples of insecurity and provoked the kingdoms of the Deccan to unite against the Sultanate in a move that was more anti-Turkish than anti-Islam.

This resistance manifested itself in the founding of two kingdoms - the Muslim Bahmani kingdom and the Hindu Vijayanagar kingdom. The former had been founded in 1347 by an Afghan official of the Sultanate, Hasan Gangu. He claimed to be a descendant of the Persian king Bahman Shah, after whom he named the kingdom, proclaiming himself Sultan under the title of Alauddin Bahman Shah. Gulbarga, in present-day Karnataka, became his capital.

This kingdom lasted for 200 years and its story is fraught with violence and strife. Of the 18 Sultans, two were blinded and deposed, two drank themselves to early death and five were murdered. Added to this was the instability created by the constant bickering of the noblemen. Comparative peace was known only in the reign of Mahmud Gawan, who had two military achievements to his credit. He captured Goa,

which was of strategic importance for trade, and a bone of contention with the rulers of Vijayanagar. He also led a campaign to Kanchipuram, where, though the local people defended the temple of Siva, the Muslim army proved too powerful.

The chaos and intrigue that followed the death of Mahmud Gawan in 1481 eventually led to the break-up of the Bahmani kingdom in 1538 into the five small kingdoms of Bidar, Berar, Bijapur, Gol-conda and Ahmadnagar. This was something of a repetition of the fate of the Sultanate in the north.

Nikitin, a Russian merchant who lived in the Bahmani kingdom between 1470 and 1474, records: "The land is over-stocked with people; but those in the country are very miserable while the nobles are extremely opulent and delight in luxury. They are wont to be carried on their silver beds, preceded by some 20 chargers caparisoned in gold and followed by 300 men on horseback and 500 on foot, and by horsemen and torch-bearers and musicians."

However, the Bahmani Sultans seem to have had a good side to them, too. They are known to have built hospitals, dams and canals, and above all were great patrons of architecture. Some of the magnificent buildings which they raised are still to be seen, and they make a startling contrast, though not any less beautiful for being so, to the exuberance of classical art in south India.

Much of the inspiration for the Islamic architecture of the Deccan came from overseas. The Muslim cities of Bijapur, Golconda and Bidar were not raised near thriving centers of Hindu culture, which eliminated the possibility of using ready-made material from Hindu buildings, as was the case in the north.

The regularity of voyages across the Arabian Sea encouraged craftsmen from Persia and Turkey to enter the service of the Deccan sultans, who therefore did not have to rely on Hindu craftsmen from the south. The significant contribution of the Bahmani Sultans to the Islamic architecture of the Deccan includes the Jami

Masjid at Gulbarga, which is the only mosque in India with a covered court-yard, topped by 63 domes; the Chand Minar of Daulatabad; the school of Mahmud Gawan at Bidar, where there is also the tomb of Ahmad Shah; and the tomb of Mohammad Adil Shah in Bijapur. Minarets, arches, domes and tiled ornamentation were new architectural features which appeared in the Deccan.

The other powerful kingdom in the Deccan, which was contemporary to the Bahmani kingdom, was established in 1336, on the banks of the Tungabhadra river.

Two princes, Harihar and Bukka, had been taken as hostages during the Deccan campaign of one Tughlaq Sultan, and in Delhi they were converted to Islam. They were later sent as peacemakers to quell a rebellion in the south; but, once there, were faced with the temptation of founding their own kingdom.

*Above: The picturesque and tranquil Tunga-bhara River at Hampi.*

They did so with the help of the sage Vidyaranya, who took them back into the fold of Hinduism. Harihar crowned himself king of Hastinavati (later known as Hampi) in 1336. This kingdom of Vijayanagar, also known as Karnataka Samrajya, gradually unified the southern parts of Karnataka, Andhra, Tamil Nadu and a part of Kerala, made effective war on the Muslims and preserved the Hindu faith. It lasted until the 17th century. If, in the south of India, magnificent temples are found in large numbers and are still in use and if the Hindu faith has preserved its vitality and continuity, it is mainly because of this kingdom.

During this period, Telegu literature and art reached great heights, the emperors themselves being eminent poets. Harihar built Vijayanagar, the city of victory, which also gave the empire its name. The city was completed in 1343 and the ruins at Hampi still evoke its splendors.For several years after the founding of this kingdom wars were fought with the Bahmani Sultans, mainly over a fertile tract of land known as the Raichur doab, which was situated between the Krishna and Tungabhadra rivers. Vijayanagar's age of glory began in 1509 when Krishnadevaraya became king. This was a time when the Bahmani kingdom was being torn asunder by ambitious nobles; Krishnadevaraya, however, handled them with a combination of military prowess and shrewdness.

**A Legendary Kingdom**

The prosperity of the Vijayanagar kingdom is legendary. Krishnadevaraya, himself a poet, writes in his Telegu poem *Amuktamalyada*: "A king should improve the harbors of his country and so encourage its commerce that horses, elephants, precious gems, sandalwood, pearls and other articles are freely imported into his country. He should arrange that the foreign traders who land in his country on account of storm, illness, and exhaustion are looked after in a manner suitable to their nationality. Make the merchants of distant foreign countries who import elephants and good horses be attached to yourself by providing them with daily audience and presents and by allowing decent profits. Then those articles will never go to your enemies...". And in fact this is how he treated the Portuguese who had come in 1498 and settled in Malabar.

Ships from Vijayanagar went to Persia, Africa, China and Ceylon laden with rice, sugar, coconut, sandalwood, cinnamon, pepper, cloves, ginger, teak and dyes. Men from different nations were seen in the busy streets of Hampi, while in the countryside too prosperity was assured by adequate public services and an efficient taxation system.

The Vijayanagar kingdom ruled Tamil Nadu for nearly 400 years and from the beginning of the 16th century A.D., the territory was administered through governors called Nayaks, who had their capitals at Gingee, Tanjore and Madurai. Towards the end of the 16th century, however, the Nayaks developed mutual rivalry and failed to support the imperial government properly.

The Vijayanagar rulers and their governors brought into Tamil land Telegu traditions from the fields of art and literature. Many Telegu literary works and musical lyrics were composed in the Nayak courts at Tanjore and Madurai. Telegu dance dramas were also enacted in the courts and temples. Some families of Telegu Bhagavatas settled near the Tanjore region, where they performed dance dramas annually, a tradition that has survived to this day under the name of Bhagavata Melas.

The Telegu rule was not a one-way influence. Many Tamil poets and artists were received at Hampi, the imperial capital. Temples dedicated to Tamil saints and sages were built in Hampi and other Telegu regions; these included temples dedicated to the Vaishnavite woman devotee Andal, and the Vaishnavite teacher Ramanuja. The great emperor Krishnadevaraya wrote about Andal and also translated many of her poems.

In the latter decades of the 16th century the five kingdoms that had emerged from the Bahmani kingdom were constantly at war with one another. This was encouraged by the Vijayanagar ruler in an effort to keep them away from his kingdom. But this strategy did not survive for long. In 1565, the five rulers joined forces and attacked Vijayanagar. For five months after the battle of Talikota enemies ravaged Hampi "with fire and sword, with crowbar and axes... day after day...." A contemporary writer records that "never perhaps in the history of the world has so much havoc been wrought, and wrought so suddenly, on so splendid a city." The Vijayanagar kingdom continued to exist till the 17th century but it lost most of its territory to Bijapur and Golconda long before then.

### European Traders in the South

In the meanwhile the great Mughal Empire had been established in 1526 by Babur. His grandson, Akbar, who brought great energy to the creative expression of Islamic and Hindu cultural traditions, was also the first of the Mughals to bring his army to the peninsula. However, before that happened, other events of some consequence had taken place in south India, linked to trade with Europe and the east.

Those goods from the Orient that were in demand in Europe reached the western continent via a complicated route. The Arabs were in control of trade in the eastern hemisphere, and they brought goods from China and southeast Asia to the Malabar coast of India, where their supplies were augmented by Indian traders. These

*Above: The Bom Jesus Basilica in Old Goa, constructed 1594 - 1605. Right: Vasco da Gama's original contract, written on palm leaf, Church of St. Francis, Cochin.*

treasures of the east were then taken by the Arabs across the Indian Ocean and up the Persian Gulf, from where they were transported to the shores of the eastern Mediterranean. The Turkish conquest of the latter region in 1453 forced the Europeans to sever trade links with the Arabs and search for an alternative route.

The great age of sea explorations began, with the Portuguese at the forefront. In 1487 Bartholomew Diaz reached as far as the southern tip of Africa. In 1497 Vasco da Gama set sail from Lisbon and followed the route taken by Diaz. But he went further, rounded the Cape of Good Hope and sailed up the east coast of Africa, much to the consternation of the Arabs. He managed to find an Arab to guide him across the Indian Ocean and, in 1498, he landed in Calicut on the coast of Kerala.

The Zamorin of Calicut, who was an ally of the Arabs, did not extend any facilities to the Portuguese adventurer, so, instead, Vasco da Gama befriended the Raja of Cochin. The Portuguese conflict

with the Zamorin lasted for almost a century. The Kinjali Marrakan, who served in a hereditary capacity as the admirals of the Zamorin, gave battle to the Portuguese, but nevertheless they managed to establish themselves in the coastal areas. In 1500, Almeida, the first Portuguese viceroy in India, wrote to the powers in Lisbon: "... let all your forces be on sea, because if we should not be powerful at sea, everything will at once be against us. Let it be known for certain that as long as you may be powerful at sea, you will hold India as yours...."

### Alfonso de Albuquerque

In 1509, Alfonso de Albuquerque became viceroy, and within a few years had established Portuguese strongholds at Goa, Diu, Daman, Salsette, Bassein, San Thome, and at Hooghly in Bengal. In the 16th century the Portuguese were an unrivaled power at sea, and their empire extended from Ormuz in the Indian Ocean to Macao in Chinese waters. However,

towards the end of the century their power began to decline, not only because of events at home, but also because of their excessive missionary zeal in India. Christianity had already come to Malabar in the first century A.D. and won converts who, however, retained many old traditions. The vigorous Latinizing enforced by the Portuguese, however, provoked resentment and enhanced their unpopularity. Eventually, they could retain only Goa, Diu and Daman; the Portuguese influence is still evident, at many levels, in the lifestyle of Goa.

It was not long before the word spread that it was enormously beneficial to trade directly with the east. Rival trading companies were rapidly formed in Europe. In 1602 the Dutch East India Company was established. They managed to enter into a treaty with the Zamorin of Calicut and obtained trading facilities. By 1660 they had captured the Portuguese forts at Cochin and Cranganore, and had also established centers at Nagapattinam and Pulicat. However, the Dutch later suffered a terrible defeat at the hands of Martand-varma, the ruler of Travancore, in 1740.

The English East India Company had also appeared on the shores of India, their first ship dropping anchor at Surat, Gujarat, on 24 August 1608. By 1623 there were already a few English factories; 16 years later Mr. Day, a company servant, leased land from the Raja of Vijayanagar and founded Fort St. George, which became the nucleus of Madras. Bombay, with its fine natural harbor, replaced Surat as the main port of the British.

The Danish East India Company entered into an agreement with the Nayak ruler of Tanjore in 1620, and established a trading center at Tranquebar in Tanjore district. A letter in gold leaf, written by the Tanjore Nayak Ragunatha to Christian IV of Denmark is still preserved in Copenhagen. The French were the last to come, in 1664, gaining a foothold in Pondicherry, and in Chandernagar in Bengal. Each of these European powers sought to establish their supremacy and to gain favor with the Mughal emperor. Eventually the French and the English emerged as the major rivals.

While these European influences were filtering into south India, the Mughals had already begun their incursions into the Deccan. Having proved himself supreme in the north, Akbar (1556-1605) turned his eyes to the important states of the Deccan – Bijapur, Golconda and Ahmadnagar. When diplomatic missions failed, he resorted to the use of his army and within a few years was able to take Berar and the city of Ahmadnagar. The kingdom of Ahmadnagar was completely subdued only in 1633, in the reign of Akbar's grandson, Shah Jahan, the builder of the Taj Mahal. In 1636 this emperor set out to include Golconda and Bijapur whithin the boundaries of the Mughal Empire; the former was more easily con-

*Right: Maratha infantry soldier, Forbes, Oriental Memoirs, 1781.*

quered, but the emperor was eventually successful. He left his son Aurangzeb behind as viceroy of the Deccan and returned northwards.

## The Marathas

Aurangzeb's efforts to eliminate his brothers and secure the throne at Delhi, temporarily diverted his attention from the Deccan. He became emperor in 1658, but in the intervening period of his absence, Shivaji, a Maratha chieftain, had risen to power in the Deccan.

The Marathas were a hardy race, mainly of farmers; well-placed families were either commanders or *jagirdars* in the service of the Sultans of the Deccan. As a people, they were united by a certain economic and social uniformity of status. They spoke Marathi and Hindi, and were Hindus, who were brought still closer by the teachings of the Bhakti saints of Maharashtra – Eknath, Tukaram and Dnyaneshwar. Geographically, too, their region was contained within the Satpura, Vindhya and Sahyadri ranges. They were in an ideal position to form a state; all they lacked was political leadership. This is what Shivaji brought to the Marathas. He became a legend in his lifetime, and the Marathas emerged as the most formidable force in the Deccan.

To understand the spirit of modern Maharashtra, one must understand about the great Shivaji. He was born of a distinguished Maratha family in 1630. His father Shahji was a commander under the Sultan of Bijapur and his mother Jijabai a daughter of a powerful aristocrat. During his youth Shivaji roamed the rugged hills and learned the hard facts of life, while his father was fighting for the Sultan. Shivaji grew up with a fierce longing for independence and a determination to master administrative and political concepts which would later stand him in good stead when he cast off the shackles of Mughal domination.

After the death of his father, Shivaji resorted to guerrilla tactics, making use of his well-trained soldiers to capture hill forts and attack the enemy. For a long time he managed to evade the Mughals, and even keep them on constant alert. This, naturally, incurred the wrath of Aurangzeb. A mighty army was sent under none other than the great Rajput Raja Jai Singh, and Shivaji was forced to surrender most of his forts. He was even forced to attend the court of the emperor and was eventually taken prisoner. But he had the last word. He managed to escape by ingenious means and made his way back to the Deccan in disguise. In 1670 he started recapturing the forts he had surrendered and four years later was crowned king of the Marathas.

Aurangzeb returned to the Deccan soon after the death of Shivaji and stayed there until the end of his reign in 1707. It was his determination to conquer Bijapur, Golconda and even the Marathas, which kept him in the Deccan. He was successful with the first two; he even managed to have Shivaji's son executed, and to imprison his grandson. But he was not destined to celebrate his triumphs, for the Marathas were far from subdued. They rose again under Shivaji's other son, Rajaram, who moved his capital to Ginjee, near Madras.

When Rajaram died in 1700, his widow took command, followed by the executive ministers, called Peshwas, who kept up the Maratha supremacy for about a century. While the Marathas never actually fought a battle with the Mughals, they managed constantly to plague the cumbersome army with their guerrilla tactics, which the Mughals were incapable of countering. Eventually, the exhausted Mughal army had to retreat to Ahmadnagar in 1707.

*Right: Elaborately decorated cannon at the Daulatabad Fort, Maharashtra.*

## The Beginnings of Colonial Rule

Aurangzeb had extended the boundaries of the Mughal empire further south than any others of his dynasty, but this vast empire disintegrated very soon after his death in 1707. The Deccan was practically independent; it was the Marathas under the Peshwas who were the superior power. Then a new set of protagonists appeared on the scene: The Marathas, the British, the French, and Hyder Ali, the ruler of Mysore.

The British and the French had maintained a long-standing rivalry in Europe; in India, their trading interests also clashed. This eventually led to three wars in the Carnatic, on the southeast coast of India. The Carnatic was supposed to be a subsidiary of the Deccan which in turn was supposed to be a subsidiary of the Mughal empire. In fact, both were independent. The Carnatic also encompassed the two important trading coasts of Pondicherry and Madras. While the first Anglo-French war on Indian soil was politically inconsequential, it revealed the superiority of both their troops and the fact that the Indian rulers remained spectators. Later, when wars of succession broke out in Hyderabad and the Carnatic, the French saw an opportunity to gain a foothold in Indian politics. Their support of Hyderabad earned them some territory, and for one of them the meaningless title "Suzerain of South India." The British, in turn, supported the rival of the French candidate in the Carnatic. A clever maneuver led to the victory of the British candidate, and it was now the British who became politically ambitious. They eventually defeated their French rivals, allowing them to retain only Pondicherry but not to fortify it. Meanwhile, in 1761, Maratha power was extinguished at Panipat, in north India, by the invader Ahmad Shah Abdali. As a result the Mughal emperor became practically a homeless wanderer; the Maratha

confederacy broke into five states, and the eyes of the British were opened to the prospect of gaining power.

The British began to inch their way inland from their trading posts. The British Governor of Bombay was unsuccessfully embroiled in a war of succession among the Marathas. His counterpart in Madras faced a more formidable enemy - Hyder Ali, the ruler of Mysore. Hyder Ali had been prime minister of the Hindu Raja of Mysore State before he overthrew him and took command. He was an illiterate man who spoke many languages, and whose military genius was spurred by ambition. Under his rule, Mysore grew into a very prosperous state.

In 1776 Hyder Ali invaded the independent state of Malabar, where the British also had a trading outlet. A few years later the Marathas attacked Mysore, but the British did not help Hyder Ali, as they were supposed to in accordance with an earlier treaty. Hyder Ali then combined forces with the Marathas and the Nizam of Hyderabad, swept through the Car-

natic and captured Arcot. Several wars ensued, and when he died, his son Tipu Sultan took over. Peace was established in 1874 but Tipu still remained the deadliest enemy of the British. Two years later he stopped the export of spices from Malabar, which affected British trade with China.

Another complicated war was fought; this time the British formed an alliance with the Nizam and the Marathas against Tipu. Neither the Marathas nor the Nizam foresaw the dangers of siding with foreigners against another Indian ruler. Tipu suffered defeat, but Cornwallis, the Bri-tish Governor-General was wrong when he said: "We have effectively crippled our enemy without making our friends too powerful." In fact, Tipu was already preparing for another war, and sent missions to Afghanistan, Arabia and Turkey in an effort to build up an anti-British alliance. He thought it better "to die like a soldier than to live as a miserable dependent on the infidels, in the list of their pensioned rajas and nawabs."

The British again formed an alliance with the Marathas and the Nizam, and challenged Tipu in 1799. Tipu met a hero's end, his troops staying with him until the last. Most of his territory was annexed by the British; the remainder was given to the reinstated Hindu Raja, who was entirely dependent on the British.

Tipu Sultan emerges as one of the most extraordinary rulers in Indian history. Apart from his remarkable qualities and achievements, was the fact that he alone recognized the true threat of the British to India.

The British had now established their supremacy from the Malabar to the Coromandel Coast in south India. The Peshwas had been dethroned and replaced by a descendant of Shivaji who functioned merely as a puppet in the hands of the British, who continued to ac-

*Above: Europeans enjoying the luxury class on a 19th-century train. Right: Mahatma Gandhi who is still revered as the Father of the Nation.*

quire territories through a variety of means. By 1818 the British were the real rulers of most of India, and had come a long way from the little strip of land Mr. Day had purchased almost 200 years earlier in the year 1639.

**The Era of Transformation**

By 1818 the Company's dominion in India had been transformed into the Company's domination of India. Britain's Indian empire had become a reality. The Bombay and Madras Presidencies, ruled directly by the British, spanned the coasts of peninsular India; the states of Cochin, Travancore, Hyderabad and Mysore were overtly "independent." The token representation of Indians in the administration and in political decision-making could not disguise the realities of a rule that was racist and despotic. Yet the British were able to find the necessary local support for the smooth functioning of their administration, while in the post-1857 era, they

earned the unstinting support of the native rulers, who stood by them until the end of the British rule.

It is not the intention here to go into details of British rule or the freedom movement, but rather to highlight certain events which represented an era of transformation. For even as the British enjoyed their heyday, the mind of India was in ferment, and western ideas were being seriously examined. Western education, foreign officials and methods of administration strengthened the impact of this "ideological invasion." From this arose the phenomenon of Indian nationalism. The Indian National Congress was established in 1885, although three years later the Viceroy described it as a "microscopic minority" which, in reality, was confined to the elite English-educated professionals. The incorporation of the peasant millions into the national movement was to take place a few decades later, under the leadership of Mahatma Gandhi. By 1936, the Congress was "the largest organization of the common people drawn very largely from the village population and counting among its members lakhs of peasants and cultivators and a sprinkling of industrial and field workers."

Meanwhile, alongside the political movement against foreign rule, considerable social changes were taking place, and many of these were linked to caste. While the broad hierarchy of the caste system recognized four basic divisions, there were innumerable sub-divisions of local *jatis* united by occupation, rites and customs. At the turn of the century these *jatis* began the process of establishing a higher status for themselves by adopting the distinctive characteristics of a superior group (see The Caste System and Untouchables in this book).

The traditionally outcaste Ezhavas of Kerala were inspired by Sri Narayana Guru (1854-1928) to attack Brahmin domination, which had been an influential aspect of south Indian society for centuries. He encouraged them to strive for entry into temples and also to upgrade

59

their own castes. The Dharma Paripalana Yogam was established through the combined efforts of Narayana Guru, Dr. Palpu, the first Ezhava graduate, and N. Kumaran Asan, the great Malayali poet.

In the 1920s this organization was closely linked to Gandhian nationalism. Later, the Ezhavas were the foremost supporters of communism in Kerala.

Somewhat similar movements appeared in Tamil Nadu and Maharashtra. In the former, the untouchable toddy tappers and the agricultural laborors developed a mercantile upper stratum, claimed Kshatriya status, and called themselves Nadars (they were originally called Shanans).

Their attempt to gain temple entry rights led to riots in Tirunelveli in 1899. The Pallis of northern Tamil Nadu acted along similar lines and called themselves Vanniya Kula Kshatriya, imitating Brahmin customs. In Maharashtra (which perhaps more than any other state had developed a community spirit that transcended the barriers of caste) the Mahars raised their voice against caste discrimination and asserted their rights for wider job opportunities.

They were later to form the backbone of a movement against untouchability spearheaded by Dr. Ambedkar, who converted to Buddhism, as did many of his followers, and who also played a key role in the formulation of India's constitution. In 1870 Jyotiba Phule established the Sat-yashodhak Samaj which questioned the caste system itself.

This movement adopted a populist and radical stance. The literature it generated was in Marathi and its influence permeated to tiny rural settlements. The propagation of its message was achieved through a form of traditional folk theater known as *tamasha*, which is still active in Maharashtra today.

*Right: Bridal finery at a south Indian wedding ceremony.*

## The Tamil Brahmin

The Brahmin predominance in education and administration in the Madras Presidency was a source of deep resentment among lower castes who now articulated a desire to save themselves from "hypocritical Brahmins and their opportunistic scriptures."

First a word about Tamil Brahmins, who are in some ways unique. Through the centuries they have memorized the scriptures, which has given them extraordinarily retentive brains. They also have a capacity for intellectual development, while at the same time they are staunch preservers of tradition. It is therefore not uncommon to meet an orthodox Tamil Brahmin who performs religious rites at "auspicious" moments, and who may at the same time be a leading scientist.

The Brahmin community has produced some outstanding intellectuals in recent times. Srinivasa Ramanujam whose centenary was celebrated in 1988 is an acknowledged mathematical genius. C.V. Raman (1888-1970) was awarded the Nobel Prize for Physics in 1930 for the discovery of what is known as the Raman Effect. In 1983 Prof. S. Chandrasekhar shared the Nobel Prize for Physics with an American. The late Dr. S. Radhakrishnan, an honored philosopher who became the President of India, also belonged to this community. However, despite these illustrious figures, the privileged position of the Brahmins at the expense of lower castes through the centuries remains a fact.

The British, following their policy of divide and rule, encouraged anti-Brahmin sentiments which were growing into a kind of Dravidian or Tamil separation. At a meeting held in 1886, the Gov-ernor of Madras said: "You are a pure Dravidian race. I should like to see the pre-Sanskrit element amongst you asserting itself rather more. You have less to do with Sanskrit than we English

have...." The wider implications of "Sanskrit", of course, involved the Aryanization of the south all those centuries before. However, the four regional languages of south India also played a part in the process of change.

### The Languages of the South

Tamil, Malayalam, Kannada and Telegu (on which foundations were created the post-independent states of Tamil Nadu, Kerala, Karnataka and Andhra Pradesh, respectively) are called the Dravidian group of languages, and are somewhat different in structure and mode of expression from the north Indian languages, which form a part of the Indo-European group of languages. Though these two major groups are distinguished by experts, they were never exclusive, and have borrowed liberally from each other from time immemorial.

Among all the Dravidian languages, Tamil has the most ancient classical literature, and over 2000 years of continuous literary history. Kannada and Telegu, which emerged as classical languages around the 3rd and 4th centuries A.D., were earlier known as Prakrit (a form of spoken Sanskrit). Malayalam, which was essentially Tamil with a regional variation in the early period, appeared as a distinctive language around the ninth and tenth centuries. Except in the extreme south, Prakrit was used as the official language for royal charters, documents and inscriptions.

In the Tamil south, Tamil, together with a mixture of Prakrit, was employed. But from the 4th century A.D. until almost the 16th century, Sanskrit was employed as the only proper court and administrative language throughout the length and breadth of the south including Tamil land. However, from about the 9th

*Right: Queuing for water beside political posters promising progress.*

century, regional languages were employed by the people simultaneously with Prakrit; thus the recording of documents in bilingual languages became customary. This not only helped the regional languages to flower into great classical languages but also retained the essential cultural unity of the entire south.

In relation to Tamil Nadu, the establishment of the "Justice Movement" launched in Madras in 1915 by C. N. Mudaliar, T. M. Nair and P. Tyagaraja Chetty against Brahmin domination, was of political significance too. A more radical anti-caste movement also emerged here under E.V. Ramaswamy Naicker. Mysore State saw the rise of the Vokkaligas and Lingayats (see Karnataka in the main travel section) while its first political organization, founded in 1917, had an anti-Brahmin base.

In Travancore State missionary influences, especially among the Ezhavas, had brought about a 36 percent literacy rate, then the highest in India (Kerala continues to maintain its leading position in literacy). A considerable section of the population of Kerala was comprised of Christians and Muslims. Among the Hindus the prominent communities were those of the Ezhavas, the Nairs and the Namboodris. The Namboodris were orthodox and high caste Brahmins (who considered even the sight of an untouchable polluting) wholly involved in religious activities. Interestingly, this community produced E.M.S. Namboodripad, a leading member of the Communist Party of India.

Historically, the Nairs had been at the forefront in defending the honor of Kerala and proved themselves able soldiers. At the turn of the century the Nairs found themselves threatened from three directions - by the non-Malayali Brahmins who held positions of power in Travancore State; by the prosperous Syrian Christians who owned, and still own, vast plantations; and by the rising Ezhavas.

The Nair matrilinear system and its complicated practices were out of keeping with the times. This resulted in social reforms, in the voicing of anti-British sentiments, patriotism and even radicalism. The first Malayalam modern novel, *Indulekha* (1889), by Chander Menon raises crucial social issues related to Nairs, while C.V. Raman Pillai's *Martanda Varma* (1891) recalls the military glories of the Nairs. The Nair Service Society, established in 1914, combined social reform with caste aspirations. In the same year the first Malayalam biography of Karl Marx was written by Ramakrishnan Pillai. The first decades of this century witnessed the emergence of powerful literary and cultural trends in various regional languages. In Kerala, Gandhian ideas were propagated through the powerful verses of Vallathol.

In Andhra, there were complaints about lack of Telegu representation in services, which eventually led to the demand for a separate "linguistic" state. In Tamil Nadu, Tamil Sangams were formed in Madura, Madras and elsewhere. These Sangams sought to vitalize the Dravidian heritage. They encouraged interest in ancient Tamil classics and even went so far as to sing the praises of the villains of the epic *Ramayana*. In Maharashtra, Shivaji was now looked upon as a rebel against caste tyranny.

During the years 1917 to 1927 the Non-cooperation Movement penetrated southwards, where it found expression in various forms - in labor unrest; in the picketing of liquor stores; in the rise, in Madras, of Singaravelu Chettiar as the first Communist in south India; and in the rise of C. Rajagopalachari, who later became the Governor-General of India.

Meanwhile, as the ability of Congress to organize an all-India agitation came under trial, a significant movement took place at Vaikom, in Travancore State in 1924-25. The temple at Vaikom is one of the most beautiful in Kerala. Here the Ezhavas, in the first of the temple entry movements, tried to assert their rights to use a road near the temple. This peaceful agitation carried on for a while, but eventually the state government built separate roads to avoid any further confrontation. A more radical trend of protest was also emerging at this time. In Tamil Nadu E.V. Ramaswamy Naicker severed his ties with the Congress Party to establish the rationalist Self-Respect Movement which first advocated temple entry rights and then outright atheism.

## Resurgence of Gandhian Politics

The years 1926 to 1937 witnessed a resurgence of Gandhian politics in the south. C. Rajagopalachari organized a march, like Gandhi, to break the salt law. The agitation, which also included the picketing of foreign cloth shops and anti-liquor campaigns, was not always nonviolent. Salt marches were also organized in Kerala. This was the time when R. Krishna Pillai, who later founded the Kerala Communist Party, rose to fame.

By 1946 the Communists were entrenched in Shertallai, Alleppey and Ambalapuzha, which together formed the "coir" belt of Travancore State. Their task was made easier by the proximity of factory workers to fishermen, toddy tappers and agricultural labor. They faced the full onslaught of state government repression, but they emerged as martyrs. Ever since 1957, when Kerala became the first state in the world freely to elect a Communist government, Punnapra and Vayalar, the two places associated with the martyrdom of the Communists have been visited by new ministers before assuming their office.

Another significant event took place in Andhra. Between 1946 and 1951 there was a massive peasant guerrilla war, particularly in the Telengana region. A Communist-led agrarian revolt also incorporated a struggle against the Nizam

*Right: Giant-sized cardboard cutouts of political Indian leaders.*

and his Razakars. It remained active until a year after independence and in those areas held by the guerrillas, reforms were instituted. Then, with the changed political circumstances of the country, the guerrillas were faced with the larger Indian army; with the new government the anti-Nizam appeal was no longer applicable. The guerrillas were driven into the hilly, interior tribal districts and the movement died down. Yet it was not futile because it brought an end to the Nizam's autocratic rule and it also paved the way for the creation of Andhra Pradesh on a linguistic basis.

Post-independence legislation has made temples accessible to all castes and this is no longer an issue in south India. But the caste factor continues to be integral to Indian politics. Although the beneficiaries of the social reform movements are mostly the better off among the lower classes, there are still those below them who continue to try fighting for their rights. The aim in the latter part of this introduction has been to give some indication of the social changes that have occurred in a deeply traditional society still in the throes of transformation.

In the last 40 years there has been significant progress. India has emerged as a powerful democracy and overcome political crises. But the phase of transition into a modern society continues. Deep-rooted traditions – social, religious and cultural – continue to face the onslaught of modern ideas and the impact of industrialization. The results of this process are not invisible, but they have been frequently expressed in film, theater and literature.

This introduction has been confined to the history of south India for practical reasons, but south India cannot be seen in isolation from the rest of India, despite regional variations. It is undergoing the same phase of transformation as the rest of the country, one that is more dynamic than any witnessed before.

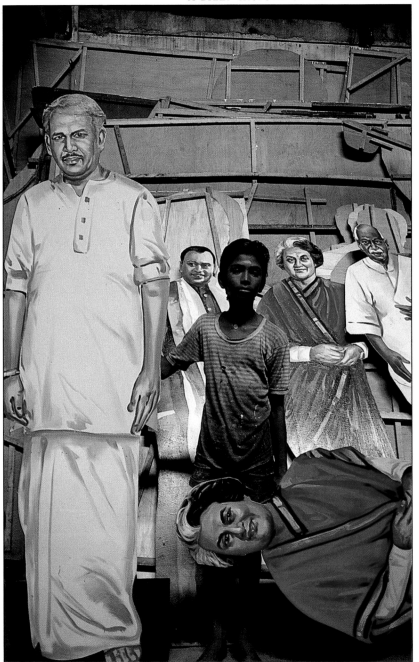

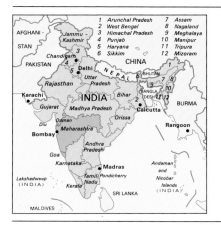

| | | | |
|---|---|---|---|
| 1 | Arunchal Pradesh | 7 | Assam |
| 2 | West Bengal | 8 | Nagaland |
| 3 | Himachal Pradesh | 9 | Meghalaya |
| 4 | Punjab | 10 | Manipur |
| 5 | Haryana | 11 | Tripura |
| 6 | Sikkim | 12 | Mizoram |

# SKYSCRAPERS
# SEASHORES
# SACRED SPLENDOR

## BOMBAY
## MAHARASHTRA
## GOA

## BOMBAY

**Bombay**, one of the world's great cities, has earned several epithets, all of them richly deserved. This Jewel on the Arabian Sea is India's answer to New York, an Asian Hollywood, a truly contemporary City of Gold, the Gateway to India. It has a character and ambience that defies description, yet lends itself to the most vivid imagery. Everything is larger than life here, and paradoxes abound. But beneath all its urban chaos is a tangible vitality, a warmth that is welcoming, and above all, a deep sense of live and let live.

India's commercial, economic and financial hub is the world's seventh-largest city, and also its most densely populated. Thousands flock here from the rural areas every day, in search of the proverbial pot of gold. While some do unearth it, and rags-to-riches stories abound, others hover above the poverty line, subsisting on the overflowing garbage bins of affluence. Nowhere is the division more sharply noticeable, where giant slums stand cheek by jowl with flashy skyscrapers, as tattered beggars stretch their

*Preceding pages: A view of Bombay harbor.*
*The Cathedral of St. Catharine, Velha Goa.*
*Left: The Taj Mahal Hotel, Bombay.*

palms into chauffeur-driven Mer-cedes Benzs. There's no getting away from the fact that this land of opportunity suffers all the chronic ills of burgeoning urbanization: air and water pollution, an abysmal shortage of housing, poverty, and the perpetual feeling that the city is bursting at its seams. Bombay's notorious underworld is tightly controlled by Mafia-type thugs, yet there isn't another place in the country where women feel as safe. The sweltering crush of humanity here is benevolent, if hectic. It can best be appreciated when the local transport system of electric trains belches out thousands in a veritable tidal wave into the city's center for a hard day of toil. Here, the day seems to last forever: Bombay never sleeps. Certain localities come alive only after dark. The city is as vivacious by night as by day. For in all that scramble to amass wealth, Bombayites somehow find the time to spend it. They work hard, but they play hard as well. Entertainment is big business in this city, like everything else.

The Bombay film industry is the world's most prolific, producing over a film a day, 365 days a year. Much of the city's razzle-dazzle is contributed by its celluloid stars, their lifestyles as flashy as the hoardings they adorn. Bombay's escapist potboiler movies and the values they promote become yardsticks of suc-

71

cess for the ordinary man whose mind is utterly seduced by the films he sees: on Bombay's streets, only a thin line divides fantasy from reality.

Bombay is big on statistics. India's richest and fastest moving city is the most important seaport on the Arabian Sea, and accounts for two-fifths of India's sea and airborne trade. The natural beauty of Bombay is unsurpassed in the region; some believe that the name Bombay is derived from the delighted exclamation, *Bom Bahia* (the beautiful bay), of seafarers sailing into its lovely natural harbor, where ships are secure from the wildest storms. The wide harbor is dotted with little green islands and framed by the Western Ghats on the mainland, making it a panoramic view. Bombay pays the largest amount of tax in the country: about a third of the country's revenue originates here. The city's fortunes were made in cotton textile mills in the 1800s; even today, textiles account for much of its trade. But there have been other diversifications, and now Bombay manufactures almost every imaginable industrial and consumer commodity. Bombay also serves as the headquarters of the Western Naval Command and the Indian flagship's base, besides housing the Atomic Energy Commission's nuclear reactor at Tarapur across the bay. The nation's leading banking institutions and most prosperous stock exchange are situated here. And last, but not least, Bombay is the capital of Maharashtra.

### A Brief History

It is difficult to imagine that this fabulous city was once a troublesome no-man's land, notorious mainly as a malarial swamp, if 17th century travelers are to be heeded. In many ways the story of Bombay is as incredible as that of some

*Right: The typical, exciting chaos of a Bombay wholesale market.*

of its inhabitants who have made their fortunes here. Located on the site of an ancient settlement that spanned seven islands, the place derived its Indian name, **Mumbai**, from the goddess Mumba Devi, an incarnation of Parvati, Lord Shiva's consort. The original inhabitants were Koli fisherfolk, who still continue to live off the fruits of the sea. Despite her reputation for being inhospitable, Bombay attracted Persian, Roman and Assyrian travelers from the earliest times. Ptolemy, the Greek astronomer and geographer, came here in A.D. 150 and christened the trapezoid-shaped Bombay island Heptanasia, seven islands. The islands were part of Emperor Asoka's kingdom in the 3rd century B.C., and were ruled by the Chalukyas from the 6th to the 8th centuries A.D., as the Elephanta temples testify.

In 1348, Bombay was conquered by invading Muslim forces and became part of the state of Gujarat. The British may have built Bombay, but it was the Portuguese who founded it. In 1508, a Portuguese attempt to conquer the Mahikavati (Mahim) settlement failed. Twenty-seven years later, Sultan Bahadur Shah, the ruler of Gujarat, ceded the islands to the foreigners, who divided them into fiefs and manors and gifted them to individuals or religious orders as rewards. In 1661, Bombay formed part of the dowry that Princess Catherine of Braganza brought with her when she married King Charles II of England. Not knowing what to do with the islands, he in turn, leased them to the fledgling East India Company for the princely sum of 10 pounds in gold per annum.

It was only after 1783 that the area became the Company's main base for its activities on the subcontinent. With the opening of the Suez Canal in 1869, the foundations of Bombay as we know it today were laid. A massive land reclamation scheme and an ambitious building program changed the face of the city. As

it acquired a reputation as an important port and shipbuilding center, its burgeoning population was plagued by a chronic lack of space, and the city fathers turned their attention to the political and technical feasibility of reclaiming land from the sea, a process that had been begun in 1662, with the gradual fusion of the seven islands. In the 1940s reclamation created the spectacular sweep of Marine Drive along part of Backbay. Most recently, Nariman Point and the Cuffe Parade area have encroached upon the sea, their hundreds of skyscrapers boasting property values on a par with those of New York, but having a minimal effect on Bombay's urban crush.

### The People

Bombay's growth since the 1940s has been phenomenal, almost alarming. At the turn of the century its population was 85,000; today it is an estimated 10 million. The influx of people in search of employment is never-ending; poverty in rural areas has driven thousands to this El Dorado. The city's people are cosmopolitan in the truest sense of the word; they came from all over the country and even from abroad, and brought with them their customs, their rituals, their culture, their language, and also their food. Bombay is, to use a worn but effective cliché, India's melting pot, a potpourri of peoples and nationalities, each adding to the richness of the city's fabric. Bombay has become home to them all, welcoming and assimilating everyone, even at the cost of brimming over. That is the hallmark of a great city. Bombay's many-faceted urban society is a complex blend of communities. Prominent among these are the Gujaratis, the Parsis and the Goans; these and other smaller communities like the Sikhs, the Armenians and the Chinese, have contributed vastly to the city's growth. In 1947, after Partition, there was a major influx of Hindus from Sind (called Sindhis); the huge city also has a significant Muslim population. Gujaratis, who are mainly traders and businessmen

73

(they still dominate the stock exchange) constitute a substantial proportion of the city's population. This is not surprising, considering that Gujarat, the state just north of Bombay was carved out of the Bombay presidency. The Parsis, also from Gujarat, were originally Persians who fled their homeland in A.D. 630 to avoid persecution by the Muslims and conversion from Zorastrianism, the religion they still follow. The history of the Parsis in India is inextricably woven into the fabric of Bombay: it is said that Parsi shipbuilders did more for the city's growth than the English merchants. This tiny community (about 100,000 the world over) has been phenomenally successful; most notably the Wadia family, Bombay's original shipbuilders, and the Tatas, whose industrial empire includes textile mills, hydroelectric works, the country's largest steel manufacturing plant, and iron-ore mines, and extends far beyond the boundaries of Bombay. It was Tata Airlines, founded in 1932, that went public as Air India; and that Bombay landmark, the **Taj Mahal Hotel**, is also owned by the House of Tata.

The Goan Christians of Bombay are either direct descendants of the Portuguese who came to the island in the 16th century, or converts from Hinduism by zealous Roman Catholic missionaries, who still have a presence in the city and run some of its best educational institutions. The Muslims of Bombay have merged with the rest of the communities, though a flavor of Islam and its rich culture may still be experienced at the city's **Mohammedali Road**, with its eateries and Muslim shops. The Jews also made Bombay their home, though, like the Parsis, their numbers are dwindling. The family of David Sassoon left its imprint here: he came to Bombay from Baghdad and built a formidable trading empire. The family no longer lives here, but the **Sassoon Docks** and the **David Sassoon Library** maintain their memory. Bom-

bay's Hindu population is largely Maharashtrian, though there are non-Maharashtrian Hindus too. Each of these diverse peoples make Bombay what it is today.

### Culture

Bombay's cultural life mirrors its polyglot population. Perhaps no other city in India boasts such a high degree of both cultural and entertainment facilities; throughout the year, the cultural calendar is filled with dance, music and theater events to cater to the diverse tastes of its population. Hundreds of cinema halls are strewn all over Bombay, the stronghold of the Indian film industry. Other bastions of culture include the **National Center for the Performing Arts**, a beautifully designed complex housing the Tata Theatre, and located on Nariman Point, the **Birla Matushri Sabhagarh** and the **Patkar Hall**, both on Marine Lines, the **Tejpal Theatre** in the Malabar Hill area, and the **Bhulabhai Desai Auditorium** on Backbay Reclamation. In the suburbs, the **Shanmukhananda Hall** and the very ritzy **Prithvi Theatre,** owned by the Kapoor family who have dominated the Hindi film industry for three generations, are popular. The English language theater is as alive and well as the Marathi *tamasha* and the Parsi *nataks*, which are often bawdy comedies. The city's diplomatic cultural centers include the **American Center**, the **British Council**, the **Alliance Français de Bombay**, and the **Max Mueller Bhavan**.

### Eating Out in Bombay

There is a great tradition of eating out in Bombay. Nobody has the time to make packed lunches, and in the afternoons the commercial **Fort** area becomes one giant fast-food feast. Bombayites value time, and fast foods were popular here long before American food joints swamped the

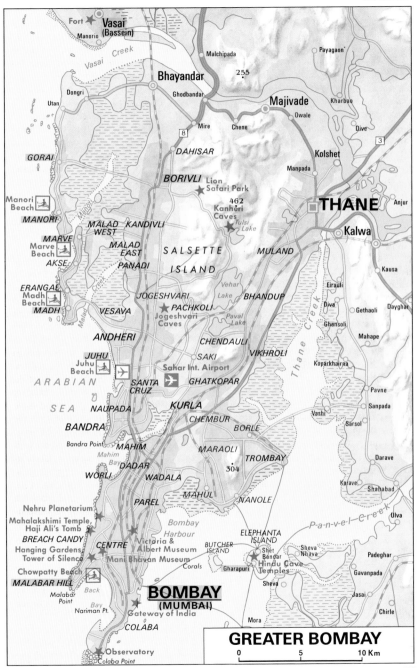

Fort
Vasai
(Bassein)
Manorio
Vasai Creek
Payagoan
Malchipada
Bhayandar
255
Ghodbandar
Dongri
Majivade
Kharbau
Utan
Owale
Mire
Chene
Dive
8
Kolshet
DAHISAR
Manpada
GORAI
BORIVLI
Lion
Safari Park
THANE
Anjur
Manori
Beach
462
Kanheri
Caves
Kalwa
MANORI
MALAD KANDIVLI
WEST
Tulsi
Lake
Kausa
MARVE
S A L S E T T E
MULAND
Marve
Beach
MALAD
EAST
AKSE
PANADI
I S L A N D
Eirauli
ERANGAL
Madh
Beach
Vehar
Lake
BHANDUP
Diva
Gethaoli
Dayghar
JOGESHVARI
PACHKOLI
MADH
VESAVA
Jogeshvari
Caves
Paval
Lake
Ghansoli
Mahape
ANDHERI
CHENDAULI
Koparkhairna
JUHU
Juhu
Beach
SAKI
VIKHROLI
Sahar Int. Airport
A R A B I A N
SANTA
CRUZ
GHATKOPAR
Pavne
S E A
NAUPADA
KURLA
Vashi
Sanpada
CHEMBUR
Sarsol
BANDRA
BORLE
Bandra Point
MAHIM
Mahim
Bay
MARAOLI
TROMBAY
Darave
DADAR
304
WORLI
WADALA
Karave
Shahabad
MAHUL
NANOLE
PAREL
Ulva
Nehru Planetarium
Bombay
Harbour
ELEPHANTA
ISLAND
Panvel Creek
Mahalakshimi Temple,
Haji Ali's Tomb
BREACH CANDY
Hanging Gardens,
Tower of Silence
CENTRE
Victoria &
Albert Museum
BUTCHER
ISLAND
Sheva
Nhava
Padeghar
Mani Bhavan Museum
Corals
Shet
Bandar
Hindu Cave
Temples
Chowpatty Beach
MALABAR HILL
Gharapuri
Gavanpada
Malabar
Point
Back
Bay
Sheva
Jasai
Nariman Pt.
BOMBAY
(MUMBAI)
Gateway of India
Mora
Chirle
COLABA
Observatory
Colaba Point

## GREATER BOMBAY

0          5          10 Km

city. The traditional Irani Parsi restaurants with their ornate marble tables and spicy Mughlai delicacies, the ubi-quitous roadside vendors hawking everything from *samosas* (a popular savory) to Chinese noodles, the south Indian Udipi eating houses and the hundreds of regional cuisine restaurants make eating out a gourmet experience. Try a Bombay *bhelpuri* snack on **Chowpatty Beach**, a creamy *kulfi* (Indian icecream) at **Parsi Dairy**, or if you're looking for the exotic and expensive, a meal at any of the specialty restaurants.

## Sightseeing in Bombay

Forty years after independence, the imprint of the Empire still remains. All of Bombay's concrete mass and matchbox style apartment blocks cannot completely shadow the architectural heirlooms liberally built by the British, especially in the city center. A tour of Bombay could start appropriately from the **Gateway of India** where in earlier times shiploads of visitors from overseas alighted. This triumphal arch was built on **Apollo Bunder** (pier) to commemorate the arrival of King George V and Queen Mary on a state visit in 1911. Today this handsome yellow basalt gate is the city's symbol, with a panoramic view of the harbor and its crowded sea. Opposite is the imposing **Taj Mahal Hotel**, and the extension of it in a modern skyscraper luxury hotel. Built in 1903, the hotel is one of the world's finest, with a superb view of the harbor. A short walk away is **Colaba Causeway**, a shopper's paradise and bargain-hunter's delight. Bombay street chic is formulated here: from summer casuals to trendy shoes, leather bags and exotic jewelry stores. Minutes away is the **Prince of Wales Museum**, built in the Indo-Saracenic style to commemorate King George V's first visit to India in 1905. It houses a fine collection of Mughal and Rajasthani miniature paintings,

archaeological and natural history finds, and a fabulous porcelain and jade collection. The basalt and sandstone building has an imposing dome; its architect, George Wittet, was responsible for the Gateway of India and the grand **General Post Office** at **Victoria Terminus**. The **Jehangir Art Gallery** stands within the museum compound, and is the city's first permanent art center. Its café, **Samovar**, attracts a motley crowd of "creative" people, artists and students. The **Bombay University** building, built in the Gothic style, is dominated by the 80-m-high (262 ft) **Rajabai Clock Tower** with all four of its faces telling the time. The **Bombay High Court** next door, with its ornate statues of Justice and Mercy, was completed in 1878, and designed in the early English style. This is the city's heart as it were, the hub of all business activity, the **Fort** area. This bustling business district derives its name from the British fortifications erected here from the late 17th century to the middle of the 19th century. The old buildings jostle with new high-rise horrors like the Bombay Stock Exchange. There is a proliferation of many different architectural styles, often an interesting blend of Victorian Gothic and Indo-Saracenic, derived from Arab influences. The city's parks or "lungs" are three large adjoining green belts, called *maidans*: the **Oval Maidan**, fringed by the Cooperage area, the **Cross Maidan** at **Churchgate** and the **Azad Maidan**, where many historic meetings were held during the struggle for independence.

One sight that Bombayites never tire of, and miss when they leave the city, is the grand sweep of **Marine Drive**, with the **Malabar Hill** in the distance, dotted with neon signs that flash on the dark sea. Down this promenade, which is called the Queen's Necklace because the lights viewed from afar in the night remind one of jewels, is the **Chowpatty Beach**, which has an interesting atmosphere even

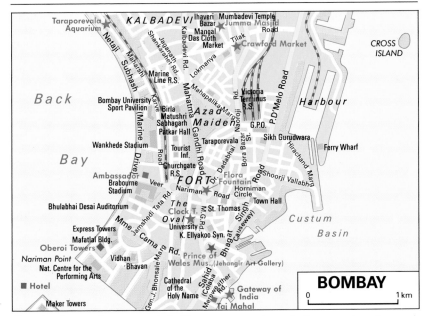

if it is dirty and overcrowded. Here, children have pony rides on the sand, fly kites or eat at one of the numerous *bhelpuri* and *kulfi* stalls. Up Walkeshwar Road are the **Hanging Gardens**, built on a water reservoir, and the **Kamala Nehru Park**, both excellent vantage points because of their sheer height over the city. This is Malabar Hill, Bombay's most exclusive residential area, and with good reason.

Carved into the hillside and surrounded by acres of wooded land is the Parsi **Tower of Silence**, where, in keeping with an ancient custom, the dead are left for vultures and other birds of prey. A deep pit, well out of human sight, is used for the purpose because earth and fire are not to be defiled according to Zorastrian scriptures. **Breach Candy** and **Scandal Point** are popular seaside promenades, especially with Bombay's jet-setting teenagers. Descending from Malabar Hill and following the coastline leads one to the **Mahalakshmi Temple**, where thousands of devout Hindus pray and ring sonorous brass bells every day. Appropriately enough the racecourse nearby is named after this goddess of wealth. Races are held on these tracks, running parallel to the sea, every Sunday from November to March; fortunes are made and lost with equal panache. Off the coast is the **Haji Ali Tomb** and mosque, commemorating the Muslim saint who is believed to have drowned here. A rocky causeway leads to the mosque, and can be traversed at low tide; those who do not worship here may spend a quiet evening by the sea, so close to the city's buzz, yet so far. The **Nehru Planetarium** at Worli has an instructive *son et lumière* show, and fascinating exhibits. Other places of tourist interest include the **Mani Bhavan Museum**, where Mahatma Gandhi stayed when he visited Bombay, and the **Zoo** with its quaint **Victoria and Albert Museum** containing documents pertaining to Bombay's colorful past.

Returning to the city, head towards the splendid **Victoria Terminus**, headquarters of Central Railways and one of the

three main rail terminals in Bombay. This grand edifice, florid and Victorian-Gothic in style, is replete with ornamentation and gargoyles, and rivals even London's elaborate St Pancras station. The **Crawford Market** which supplies the city's fresh fruit, meat and vegetables was built in the same style in 1871, albeit with a lot less fuss. This remarkable bazaar's spacious halls and flagstone paving see much action during the day; the author Rudyard Kipling's father was responsible for the lovely bas reliefs that adorn the entrance. He was the principal of the **JJ College of Art** nearby and this is where young Kipling grew up. Another monument from the Victorian era that is now a landmark is **Flora Fountain**, an ornate structure built to honor Sir Bartle Frere, Bombay's British governor in 1869. The statue of Flora, the Greek god-

dess of flowers, stands at the junction of five broad thoroughfares, and must have been a pretty sight when the fountain played. However, the area was rechristened Hutatma Chowk after the formation of Maharashtra state when the city fathers sought to wipe out memories of the Raj by banishing regal statues and non-Indian foreign-sounding names.

Surrounded on three sides by the sea, it is only natural that Bombay's jagged coastline boasts some pretty beaches. **Juhu**, near Santa Cruz, is dirty and over-crowded with food-stalls and hawkers, a sort of suburban Chowpatty. You should try some beaches further out: **Madh**, **Marve**, and **Manori**. By far the nicest is **Gorai** beyond **Borivili** which also has a sanctuary. Unfortunately modern tourism is changing the face of this once secluded beach with its little Catholic town.

*Above: The Gateway of India in Bombay, built for the visit of George V and Queen Mary in 1911. Right: Peace and tranquillity in the cave temple of Elephanta.*

### Elephanta, Kanheri and Bassein

While Bombay's comparatively recent history means that there are no ancient or

even medieval monuments here, three excursions out of the city are steeped in history. About an hour's ride away by motorboat from the basalt façade of the Gateway lies **Elephanta**, a cave-temple shrine hewn out of solid rock some time in the 8th century A.D. by the Rashtra-kuta dynasty who ruled the Deccan from A.D. 757 to 973.

Probably intended as a private place of worship for the ruling family, the exact date of its construction will never be known. The island was later plundered by the Portuguese in the 16th century; they destroyed the plaque that bore details of its history.

It was the Portuguese who named the island after the large stone elephant that guarded it; the original name is **Ghara-puri**, the fortress city. The elephant has since been moved and reassembled in the compound of the Bombay Zoo, as guides are quick to point out. The caves represent what is probably the last example of the golden age of art that flourished in the Gupta period, even though it dates from

after that time. Though not as impressive in scale as Ellora, the Elephanta caves are unsurpassed in terms of beauty and eloquence. The **Siva Temple** originally had three entrances, giving it a cruciform shape; the play of light is constant. The inner sanctuary, beyond the realm of images, has a plain and unadorned *yoni-lingam*, the symbol of strength and creativity. Amidst irregular pillars in the Dravidian style, a celestial drama unfolds, the most dramatic of which are Ravana shaking Mount Kailasa and the marriage of Siva and Parvati. The **Trimurti** of Siva is the focal point.

At **Kanheri**, 42 km (26 miles) from Bombay, are 109 Buddhist caves dating from around the 2nd to the 9th centuries A.D. **Cave 3** is worth a visit, to see its grand *chaitya* (prayer hall) and long colonnade of pillars. **Bassein**, on the coast north of Bombay, was once a splendid Portuguese stronghold. Its magnificent fort, where only the Hidalgos (aristocracy) lived, is now in ruins, though vestiges of Portuguese glory still remain.

## BOMBAY
### Accommodation

*LUXURY:* **Centaur**, Santa Cruz, Tel: 6116660. **Holiday Inn**, Balraj Sahani Marg, Juhu Beach, Tel: 6204444. **Taj Mahal Intercontinental**, Apollo Bunder, Tel: 2023366. **Oberoi Towers**, Nariman Point, Tel: 2024343. **President**, 90 Cuffe Parade, Colaba, Tel: 2150808. **Ramada Inn Palm Grove**, Juhu Beach, Tel: 6112323. **Ritz**, 5 Jamshedji Tata Road, Churchgate, Tel: 220141. **Welcomgroup Searock Sheraton**, Lands End, Bandra, Tel: 6425454.

*MODERATE:* **Apollo**, 22, Lansdowne Rd., Apollo Bunder, Tel: 2020223. **Citizen**, 960 Juhu Beach, Tel: 6117766. **Shalimar**, August Kranti Marg, Tel: 3631311. **West End**, 45 New Marine Lines, Tel: 299121.

*BUDGET:* **Delamar**, 141 Sunder Mahal, Marine Drive, Tel: 2042848. **Sea Green**, 145 Marine Drive, Tel: 222294. **Sea Side**, 39/2 Juhu Beach, Tel: 6200293. **YWCA**, Madame Cama Road, Cooperage, Churchgate, Tel: 2020445. **YMCA**, 18, YMCA Road, Bombay Central, Tel: 890219; and 12 Wadehouse Road, Colaba, Tel: 2020079.

### Museums / Art Galleries

**Prince of Wales Museum**, Mahatma Gandhi Road, Fort, Tel: 244484/519. Open: 10 am-4.30 pm, art, archaeological and natural history exhibits. **Dr. Bhau Daji Lad Museum** (Victoria and Albert Museum), 91/A Dr. B. R. Ambedkar Road, Byculla, Tel: 377121. Open: 10.30 am-5.20 pm. Sundays: 8.30 am-5.20 pm, closed Mon, armory, sculpture, pottery, leatherwork, ivory, manuscripts, paintings, fossils, minerals. **Jehangir Nicholson Museum of Modern Art**. **National Centre for Performing Arts**, Nariman Point, Tel: 233838. Open: 11 am-7 pm, contemporary paintings. **Aakar Art Gallery**, Bhulabhai Desai Road. **Chemould Art Gallery**, M.G. Road, Tel: 244356. **Taj Art Gallery**, Taj Mahal Hotel, Tel: 2023366. Pundole Art Gallery, Hutatma Chowk, Tel: 298473.

### Post / Telegraph / Telephone

**General Post Office** (Poste Restante facilities), Nagar Chowk. **Central Telegraph Office**, Hutatma Chowk. **Foreign Post Office**, Ballard Pier. 24 hours counters at Santa Cruz / Sahar Airports.

### Restaurants

*CONTINENTAL:* **The Society**, Ambassador Hotel, Churchgate, Tel: 2041131. **Gaylord**, V.N. Road, Churchgate, Tel: 221250. **La Brasserie**, Oberoi Towers, Tel: 2043282. **Rooftop Rendezvous**, Taj Mahal Intercontinental, Tel: 2023366.

*BARBEQUE:* **Kandahar**, Oberoi Towers, Tel: 2043282. **Dhanraj Restaurant**, Link Corner Building, Bandra, Tel: 6423501.

*CHINESE:* **Chopsticks**, 90 Veer Nariman Road, Churchgate, Tel: 2049284. **Shangai**, 11-15 Ambedkar Mansion, Colaba, Tel: 2021304. **Chinese Room**, Kwality House, Kemps Corner, Tel: 8225068. **Shansui**, Centaur Hotel, Tel: 6126660.

*EXCLUSIVE:* **Trattoria** (Italian), Hotel President, Tel: 2150808,. **The Saladero** (salad specialities), Madame Cama Road, Tel: 2027989. **Prangan**, Golden Gage, Laram Centre, SV Road, Andheri W, Tel: 6281861. **The Outrigger** (Polynesian), Oberoi Towers, Tel: 2043282.

### Shopping

Areas for general shopping are Shahid Bhagat Singh Road, Mahatma Jyotiba Phule Market (or Crawford Market), D.N. Road, Bhuleshwar, Pherozeshah Mehta Road, Mangaldas Market, M. Karve Road, Jhaveri Bazaar, Linking Road, Bandra. The emporiums of Indian states, where handicrafts exclusive to a region are for sale, are concentrated in the World Trade Centre on Cuffe Parade.

### Excursions

**Elephanta Caves** (9 km) by motor launch. Famous for 7th-century rock cut cave temples. **Erangal** (35 km), **Ghodbunder** (93 km), **Gorai** (59 km) and **Juhu** (21 km) are beaches accessible from Bombay by suburban electric trains. The last is the most popular and has accommodation facilities. Numbering over 100, the **Kanheri Caves** (42 km) are noteworthy for their massive pillars, sculptures and stupas. Another site of Buddhist caves is **Karla** (100 km). The rock-cut *Caitya* of the 2nd century B.C. is most impressive.

The place for bird lovers is the **Karnala Bird Sanctuary** and **Fort**; 61 km en route to Goa it shelters indigenous and migratory bird species. The **Krishnagiri Upvan**, the Lion Safari Park (35 km), allows visitors to observe this creature in its habitat from closed vehicles. Regular trains run to Malad, from there roads lead to **Madh**, **Marve** and **Manori** beaches (45 km, 38 km and 40 km respectively from Bombay). Ferry services connect the last two. **Versova Beach** (29 km) is another sandy stretch on the Arabian Sea. All destinations can be covered within a day. An early departure is recommended. If you intend to take the suburban trains (cheap and convenient, but crowded), obtain details of departure and frequency of service in advance.

### Tourist Information

**Government of India Tourist Office**, 123 Maharishi Karve Road, Churchgate, Tel: 293144. Counters at Santa Cruz (Tel: 6149200) and Sahar (Tel: 6325331) airports.

**Directorate of Tourism**, Government of Maharashtra, Madame Cama Road, Opp. Life Insurance building, Tel: 2026713. **Maharashtra Tourism Development Corporation**, Express Towers, 9th Floor, Nariman Point, Tel: 2024482.

## MAHARASHTRA

India's third-largest state in area and population, Maharashtra stretches like a mammoth triangle over a substantial portion of the fertile Deccan peninsula. Its base runs north-south for nearly 720 km (447 mi) along the west coast, jutting out in a blunted apex towards the east, 800 km (497 mi) across central India. One of the foremost states in agricultural and industrial production, and also in the fields of education and culture, Maharashtra is often equated with its capital, Bombay. Without doubt, this island city accounts for more visitors to the state than any other place, but Maharashtra is more than just the Gateway of India. Its ancient culture has survived the British rule, and fosters a strong and vibrant literary heritage in Marathi, the predominant language. This common literature has nurtured a deep sense of nationality and unity among the Maharashtrians, whose ancestors defied the mighty Mughals under the leadership of their charismatic hero and king, Chatrapati Shivaji.

Maharashtra is first mentioned in the writings of the Chinese traveler Hsuan-Tsang (7th century B.C.); the origin of the name is still unresolved. One school of thought has it that the word is derived from the Sanskrit *rathi*, used to describe the skilful builders and chariot drivers who formed a fighting force (Maharathi) to conquer the original Naga settlers in the region that is now the modern state. Their language intermingled with the speech of these early inhabitants, becoming Maharashtri, and developing into Marathi by the 8th century A.D. The region was also influenced by traders and merchants from Central Asia and Greece, which probably explains the light eyes and fair skins of some Maharashtrians. Several Hindu kingdoms flourished in

the area – Satavahana, Vakataka, Chalukya, Yadava – only to give way to Muslim supremacy in the early 14th century A.D. Persian, the court language of the Muslims, greatly influenced the development of Marathi. By the middle of the 16th century, the region was once again fragmented into many little kingdoms, perpetually at war with each other. In the midst of this anarchy the popular leader and Maharashtrian hero, Shivaji, was born. With outstanding prowess and statesmanship, he established a Maratha empire that extended over western and central India, and also to the north and east, shaking the foundations of the Mughal empire. The kingdom fell to the British in the early 1800s, and was later reorganized according to language in independent India. So the British Bombay presidency became Gujarat in the north and Maharashtra in the south in 1956, with Bombay as its capital.

For the tourist, Maharashtra holds the promise of an interesting range of physical diversity. The rugged Western Ghats, a mountain range, fringe the west of the Deccan plateau, running almost unbroken from north to south, within 6 to 10 km (4-6 mi) of the Arabian Sea. The narrow Konkan coast is widest near Bombay, with little hillocks sprinkling its otherwise flat relief. Numerous hill stations have sprung up in the Ghats (literally meaning stepped embankments) which support a variety of wildlife in their forests - tigers, leopards, bison, antelopes, monkeys and game birds. The Bhima, Krishna and Godavari rivers, along with hundreds of fast-flowing streams, traverse the vast plateau,permitting the soil to yield such delicacies as the Ratnagiri Alphonso mango and the luscious Nagpur oranges. But it is Maharashtra's distinct cultural entity that is its greatest lure. The region's age-old artistic traditions are embodied in the ancient cave paintings and rock-cut architecture of Ajanta and Ellora, in its medieval

*Preceding page: At Kanheri. Right: Water is plentiful in the whole region.*

forts, in its classical and devotional music, and above all, in its unique theater, called the *tamasha.*

### Pune

**Pune**, where several institutions sustain all these timeless traditions, is Maharashtra's undisputed soul, even if Bombay is its heart. Pune is the erstwhile capital of the Peshwas and the birthplace of Shivaji. Best approached by road from Bombay (170 km or 105 mi), this city on the Deccan was preferred by the British to the island city because its climate is pleasant all year round. Rapid industrialization has taken its toll on what was once a pretty cantonment town. Even today, the army area is tranquil compared with the bustling old town, its quintessential bazaars making for fascinating stops along the way. Factories may have changed the air around the place, but not its old-world aura.

Within the city, the **Raja Dinkar Kelkar Museum** is the best place to visit. Set up by the man it is named after, the museum, which still houses its octogenarian founder, is the only one of its kind in the country. Kelkar, who saw the transformation wrought by modernity, could not accept that objects of utility were no longer works of art. His vast collection includes a fascinating array of brass lamps in every imaginable shape, ivory combs, miniature paintings, wooden doors, exquisite nutcrackers and kitchen utensils, collected over half a century. If you're lucky, he will tell you his story and take you on a guided tour. The range and beauty of the objects here is amazing.

The **Aga Khan Palace**, once the residence of the leader of a Muslim community called the Bohras, was later used by the British as a prison. Here, Mahatma Gandhi and his wife Kasturba were detained; she was never to leave, and a memorial in the grounds is dedicated to her. The Gothic-style **Deccan College** is considered the best in the region, and the **Film and Television Institute** draws talent from all over the country. This haven

83

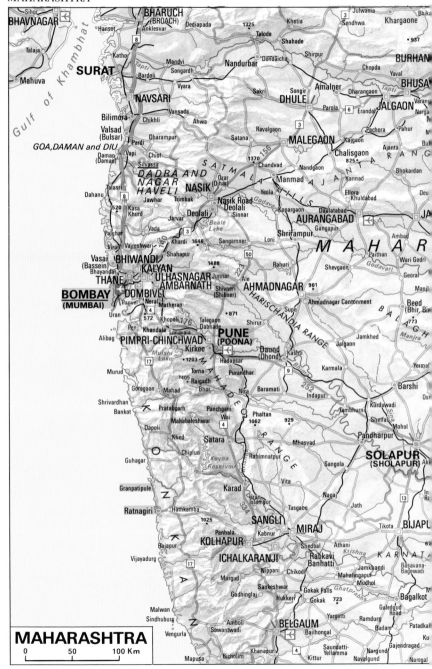

MAHARASHTRA

0    50    100 Km

for the film buff, with its impressive archives on world and Indian cinema, has given fresh impetus to new-wave cinema, and produced many fine actors and directors. The **Old Government House** which lodges **Pune University** is across the river from the **Shanwarwada Palace,** from where the Peshwas, who succeeded Shivaji and preceded British rule, administered the land. The palace was ravaged by a fire in 1827 and never quite restored, but it is an interesting reminder of 18th-century warfare, with menacing spikes on its gates to ward off elephants.

**Shinde Chhatri**, a Shiva temple, was built by a Maratha ruler and later extended in the southern European style to form an architectural curiosity. The **Pataleshwar Temple**, carved out of a single giant boulder in the 18th-century, the **Parvati Temple**, atop a hill on the city's fringes, and the "magical" levitating stone at the Muslim shrine of **Kamarali Darvesh** are important places of worship. Pune is also well known for its controversial **Rajneesh Ashram**, established by Bhagwan Shree Rajneesh. Westerners, in particular, have flocked to this ashram. **Simhagadh**, the Fortress of the Lion, is well worth the half-hour drive out of Pune. Three centuries ago, Shivaji's men scaled the steep walls of this majestic monument with the help of specially trained *ghorpads*, mongoose-like creatures commonly found in the wilds around here, and still treated with suitable reverence for their historic feat.

The **Torna, Rajgadh, Purandhar** and **Shivneri Fort**, the actual place of Shivaji's birth, are all within easy reach of Pune and afford a glimpse of military history. Otherwise, the city's **Empress Gardens** provide cool shady walks, and its theater, the *tamasha*, a worthwhile evening. The area's foremost performing art combines music, dance and drama, with a

*Right: The Ajanta Caves, ancient retreat of Buddhist monks.*

woman playing the role of narrator-cum-dancer, and clowns included for good measure.

Pune's distinctive cuisine is best tasted in a Maharashtrian home. Subtle and understated rather than elaborate, the food is vegetarian in Brahmin homes, though seafood is eaten in the coastal areas and the Kshatriya, whereas warrior castes are less restrained in their diets, eating anything from pork to game birds. The Irani restaurants, with their marble tables and bentwood chairs, serve Mughlai specialties and are run by Parsis, migrants from Persia many centuries ago. Try the legendary Shrewsbury biscuits at Kayani's: they are sold out even before they appear from the oven.

Maharashtra celebrates the usual range of Indian festivals, with much emphasis on *Ganesh Chaturthi*, when the elephant god is immersed in water amidst grand celebrations. *Pola* celebrates that beast of burden, the bullock, with races and decorations, whereas the *Hurda* folk festival celebrates the reaping of good crops.

All around Pune, the mountains beckon, dotted with lovely hill stations. **Mahabaleshwar**, at an altitude of 1,372 m (4500 ft), was discovered by Sir John Malcolm in 1828 and was a popular spot then as it is now, with its shimmering lake, and crisp air laden with the scent of strawberries in the spring. Panoramic points with quaint names and associations, **Arthur's Seat**, **Duke's Nose**, **The Dhobi** and **Chinaman's Waterfalls**, are all vantage points that afford spectacular views of the Ghats. **Panchgani**, 19 km (12 mi) before Mahabaleshwar on the winding ghat road, is a popular resort with boarding schools, though not as lovely as Mahabaleshwar. **Pratapgarh Fort**, 24 km (15 mi) from Mahabaleshwar, is imposing. Other hill stations in the region include **Lonavla** and **Khandala**, nestling in the steps of the Ghats. There is not much to see or do here, but the **Karla Caves**, 12 km (7.5 mi) from

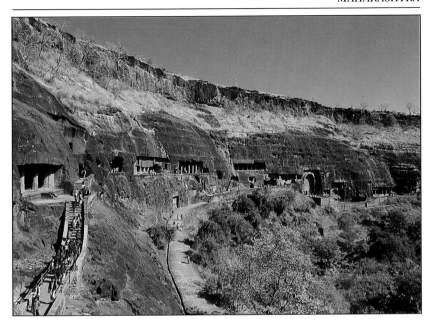

Lonavla and the **Bhaja Caves** still further up are Buddhist sanctuaries, some dating back to 200 B.C. The *stupa* and *vihara* architecture here is surprisingly well preserved: the view from the hill on which Karla is situated is breathtaking.

The closest hill station to Bombay is **Matheran**, 117 km (73 mi) away, via **Neral**. Getting there is fun, with an option of a circuitous toy-train, which chugs 21 km (13 mi) up a steep hill or an 11- km (7-mi) trek, which some enthusiasts insist is best attempted on a moonlit night. Inhabited more by monkeys than people, this popular resort was discovered by Hugh Malet in 1850, and literally means "jungle-topped hill." Shady walks in the woods, fine vantage points and horse-riding make a visit worth while. Do sample the *chikki*, a local sweet.

The capital of an erstwhile princely state, **Kolhapur** is also known as the Benares of the south, and is full of temples and palaces. This city, situated 395 km (245 mi) from Bombay, is the origin of the fine leather sandals called Kolhapuri *chappals*. It has a long tradition of wrestling, and a stadium for competitions. Visit the **Mahalakshmi Temple** and **Kotiteerth** built on a large lake. The **Shalini Palace**, built in the Indo-Saracenic style, and the **Old and New Palace** with its octagonal clock tower and museum suggest links with Europe. **Panhala**, 20 minutes away, is a pretty hill station with a historic fort, built in 1192, from where Shivaji masterminded his great escape. The **Pawala Caves** nearby are Buddhist.

Traveling west from Kolhapur is **Ratnagiri**, with a good beach, but better known for its delicious Alphonso mangoes. The beach at **Ganapatipule** (155 km or 96 mi) is beautiful and has only recently been developed into a resort. An old **Ganapati Temple** is built over a giant boulder on the seashore.

### Aurangabad

Named after the austere Mughal Emperor Aurangzeb, **Aurangabad**, 370 km (230 mi) from Bombay, is unfairly dis-

missed as a convenient base from which to explore **Ajanta** and **Ellora**. The city is strewn with relics from the Mughal era, notable is the **Bibi Ka Maqbara**, a poor imitation of the Taj Mahal, and Aurangzeb's attempt to show that he was not to be outdone by his illustrious father, Shah Jahan. The **Panchakki** once served as a grain mill, powered by a natural spring, and is also the tomb of a Sufi saint whom the last great Mughal revered. The Aurangabad caves, built in the Mahayana style, date from the 6th to the 11th centuries A.D., and are fine examples of this period. **Cave 3**, with its depiction of the Jataka tales, the well-preserved Buddha in **Cave 6**, and the lavish ornamentation of **Cave 7** are easily the most interesting in the cluster of twelve caves. Take along a torch if you'd like to examine the details. **Daulatabad** is 15 km (9 mi) from Aurangabad on the way to Ellora, with a fort on its pyramid-shaped hill. Once

*Above: The magnificent Kailashnath Temple at Ellora.*

considered invincible, with its slippery gravel pathways, spiked gates, menacing spiral staircases and dungeons which served as torture chambers, the fort is the venue of one of history's greatest follies. Mohammed bin Tughlaq, an eccentric Sultan of Delhi in the 14th century, was so impressed by the fort that he decided to move his capital here, and he named it the city of fortune. Thousands of his subjects died on the 1,100-km (684-mile) trail before he realized what a disastrous mistake he had made, and 17 years later he ordered them to move back.

### Ellora

The finest examples of cave architecture in the world are found in the hills at **Ellora** (ancient Elapur), honeycombed with over a hundred caves, 34 of which are most significant. Representing the Buddhist (**Caves 1** to **12**, A.D. 600 to 800) Hindu (**Caves 13** to **29**, A.D. 600 to 900) and Jain (**Caves 30** to **34**, A.D. 800 to 1100) religions, these caves testify that religious tolerance was a way of life in ancient India. The Vishvakarma Cave of the Buddhists, the Kailashnath Hindu temple and the Jain Indrasabha are real gems. They were literally carved out of solid rock to provide sanctuaries for monks.

Ellora was the capital of the Rashtrakuta rulers before they moved to Malkhed, and was probably an important place of pilgrimage long before the caves were built. It lay strategically at the junction of two major trade routes. The Chalukyas who ruled the Deccan between A.D. 550 and 642 and their successors, the Rashtrakutas (A.D. 757 to 973), were the patrons of these rock-cut marvels. The Buddhist caves belong to the Vajrayana sect of the Mahayana school, the Hindu caves are dedicated to Shiva, and the Jain caves are of the Digambara sect. The caves are not arranged chronologically, but should be explored thus to follow their development. **Caves 1, 5, 10** and **12** show the flowering of the Mahayana sanctuary. **Cave 1** is remarkable in its austerity, a *vihara* or shelter from the rain, where the monks lived and meditated. **Cave 5** is a typical Mahayana *vihara* with a shrine at the furthest end, carved pillars, cells, and a large central hall. The shrine here is guarded by two Vajrayani *boddhisattvas*, Padmapani, the lotus-holder, and Vajrapani, the sender of thunderbolts. Cave 10 is an interesting combination of *chaitya* (chapel) and *vihara*, with an imposing façade and two stories. The doorway is flanked by Apsaras, celestial beings, and the blending of wooden motifs and stone produces an optical illusion. **Cave 12** is a monumental *vihara* of three stories, almost baroque in style. A superb vantage point is the path between **Caves 15** and **16**, once an old trade route. The **Kailashnath Temple, Cave 16**, is the supreme masterpiece, hewn out of a monolith in the Dravidian style. Over 200,000 tonnes of stone were removed to carve the colossal temple,

which took over 100 years to complete, and is a treasure house of Hindu mythology. Shrines, pillars and panels adorn this complex, the most impressive of which is Ravana shaking Mount Kailasa, and the ultimate triumph of good over evil. **Cave 32** gives us an insight into the austere yet profusely carved architecture of the Jain style.

### Ajanta

Unlike Ellora, which seems to have been well known for much of its history, the 30 Buddhist caves at **Ajanta** lay deserted and forgotten for several centuries. These temples, hollowed out of solid rock, were excavated by Buddhist monks from the side of a horse-shoe-shaped ravine in 200 B.C., and rediscovered in 1819 by British soldiers.

The Ajanta murals and frescoes remain unmatched in the world of art, and are well preserved probably because they remained forgotten for so long. Of the 36 caves, five are *chaityas*, 25 *viharas*. The earlier group belong to the Hinayana sect (2nd century B.C.) the latter group, to the Mahayana Sect (A.D. 450 to 650). Numbered consecutively from the western entrance, the order bears no relationship to their dates. Although nearly every cave is fascinating, visit **Caves 10, 9, 12, 19, 24, 26, 2** and **1** in that order if the development of Buddhist rock-cut architecture is to be appreciated. The murals in Caves 1 and 2, painted with mineral colors, belong to the Golden Age of Indian art, the Gupta period (A.D. 320 to 650). Each mural tells a story: there is the birth of the Buddha, and stylized scenes from the Jataka tales.

### Nagpur and its Environs

**Nagpur** is India's orange-growing country. This erstwhile capital of the Bhonsle Marathas, the city on the banks of the River Nag, has an interesting **Cen-**

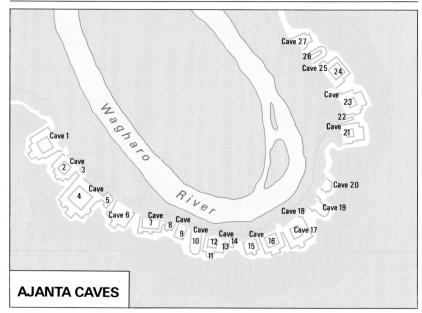

**AJANTA CAVES**

tral **Museum**, established in 1863, which displays tribal relics from the Gonds who ruled until the 18th century, and who still inhabit the region today.

Northeast of Nagpur is **Ramtek**, with temples built to commemorate the mythological visit of Rama and Sita when they were banished from Ayodhya.

About 80 km (50 mi) southwest of Nagpur is Wardha, the alighting point for **Sewagram**, where Mahatma Gandhi and his dedicated group of workers set up a "village of service." Established in 1933, Gandhiji's little abode is today a museum dedicated to the ideals of the man who formulated India's freedom. His disciple Vinoba Bhave's **Paunar Ashram** is 3 km away.

The **Nagzira Wildlife Sanctuary**, 115 km (71 mi) from Nagpur, has two perennial watering holes for animals, and is situated in lovely wooded isolation.

The **Nawegaon National Park** is 135 km (84 mi) from Nagpur, and has a pretty shrine amidst lush forests, on the banks of an 18th-century man-made lake. The **Tadoba** sanctuary with its thousands of crocodiles is well known, and the **Chikalda** hill resort jungles are full of fascinating wildlife.

Just two hours out of Bombay is **Nasik**, a holy city of 2000 temples on the gently sloping banks of the Godavari. Here some episodes of the *Ramayana* unfolded. Once every 12 years, the historic *Kumbh Mela* is held here. The steps that lead to the river banks are always crowded with religious devotees.

**Trimbak**, the revered source of the Godavari, is only 33 km(21 mi) away. The **Trimbakeshwar Temple** has exquisite carvings. The Hinayana Buddhist caves at **Pandu Lena**, 8 km (5 mi) from Nasik, date from the 1st century B.C. to the 2nd century A.D. All these sights are worth a visit.

The tourist circuit is usually confined to Bombay, Ajanta and Ellora. But Maharashtra has much more to offer the traveler who is ready to step off the beaten track and explore the less well known parts of this region.

## PUNE
### Accommodation
*LUXURY:* **Hotel Blue Diamond**, 11 Koregaon Road, Tel: 663775/Fax: 0212-666101. **Hotel Executive Ashoka**, 5 University Road, Shivaji Nagar, Pune 411005, Tel: 57391, 56463/51101.
*MODERATE:* **Sagar Plaza**, 1 Band Garden Road, Tel: 661880/661585/661534. **Hotel Amir**, 15 Connaught Road, Tel: 661840.
*BUDGET:* **Hotel Gulmohar**, 15 A/1, Connaught Road, Tel: 661773-5. **YMCA**, 6 Arjun Marg, Tel: 665004. **YWCA**, 5 Gurudwara Road, Tel: 660330.

### Festivals
Besides *Ganesh Chaturthi, Dussehra, Diwali* and Christmas, *Shiv Jayanti* (April/May), the birth anniversary of Shivaji, is celebrated in Pune.

### Museums
**Maratha History Museum**, Deccan College, Yerawad, Tel: 27231, open 11 am-5 pm, closed Sun, 1st and 3rd Sat and public holidays. **Raja Dinkar Kelkar Museum**, 1378 Shukrawar Peth, Natu Bag, Tel: 44466, open 8.30 am-12.30 pm, 3-6.30 pm. **Bharat Itihas Samashodhak Mandal Museum**, 1321 Sadashir Peth, Tel: 442581. **Ethnological Museum of Tribal Research**, 28 Queen's Gardens, Tel: 65941, open 10.30 am-5.30 pm, closed Sun, 2nd and 4th Sat of the month.

### Restaurants
*VEGETARIAN:* **Savera**, Opp. Railway Station, Tel: 227391. *CHINESE:* **China Town**, Blue Diamond Hotel, Tel: 663775. **Ming Court**, Hotel Regency, Dhole Patil Rd., Tel: 69411. **Suzie Wong**, Hotel Amir, Tel: 661840. *INTERNATIONAL:* **Golden Arch**, Hotel Executive Ashok. **Ashwamedha**, Blue Diamond Hotel. **Kwality**, 6 East Street, Tel: 664629. **Peshwa Inn**, Hotel Amir. **Khyber**, 1258/2 J.M. Road, Tel: 51933 **Oasis**, 595 Sachapir Street, Tel: 640857.

### Tourist Information
**Maharashtra Tourism Development Corporation**, Central Building, Sassoon Road, Tel: 668867/669169.

## AURANGABAD
### Accommodation
*LUXURY:* **Hotel Ajanta Ambassador**, Chikalthana, Tel: 82211/15, 82451-54, 82367, 84217, Fax: 02432-82367. **Welcomgroup Rama International**, R 3 Chikalthana, Tel: 83467-69. **Hotel Aurangabad Ashok**, Dr. Rajendra Prasad Road, Tel: 24520-29.
*MODERATE:* **Kathiawad Hotel**, Station Road. **Tourist Home**, Station Road.
*BUDGET:* **Youth Hostel**, Padampura Corner, Station Road, Tel: 3801. **MTDC Holiday Resort**, Station Road, Tel: 724713, 24259.

### Museums
**State Archaeology Museum**, Sonehri Mahal, Tel: 24269, open 10.30 am-5.30 pm, closed Sun. **History Museum** of Marathawada University, Tel: 24431, open 10.30 am-5.30 pm, closed Sun.

### Post / Telegraph / Telephone
**Head Post Office**, Juna Bazaar, Telegraph Office (24 hrs). **Nutan Colony Post and Telegraph Office**, Cantonment Railway Station. **Central Telegraph Office** (24 hrs), Kala Darwaza.

### Restaurants
*CHINESE / CONTINENTAL:* **Mingling**, Jalna Rd., Tel: 25991. **Albela**, Hotel Aurangabad Ashok.

### Tourist Information
**Government of India Tourist Office**, Krishna Vilas, Station Rd., Tel: 29817. There is also a counter at the airport. MTDC Holiday Resort, Station Road (East), Tel: 24713, 23299.

### Accommodation
**MAHABALESHWAR**: **Bellmont Park Hill Resort**, Wilson Point, Tel: 414. **Fountain Hotel**, Opp. Koyna Valley, Tel: PBX 227, 300, 425.
**PANCHGANI**: **Amir Hotel**, 188 Chesson Road, Tel: 211, 392.
**MATHERAN**: **Lord's Central Hotel**, Tel: 28. **Rugby**, Vithalrao Kotwal Rd., Tel: 291, 292.
**LONAVLA**: **Fariyas Holiday Resort**, Deluxe 29A, Tungarli, Tel: 2701-5. **Adarsh Hotel**, Shivaji Road, Tel: 2353. **Biji's Ingleside Inn**, New Tungarli Road, Off Bombay-Pune Road, Tel: 296352, 255132. **Span Hill Resort**, Tungarli, Tel: 3685.
**KHANDALA**: **Dukes Retreat**, Off Bombay-Pune Road, Tel: 2618293/94, 2613293. **Mount View**, Bombay-Pune Road, Tel: 2335.
**KOLHAPUR**: **Shalini Palace Ashok**, Rankala, A Ward, Tel: 28915. **Hotel Pearl**, New Shahupuri, Tel: 20451. **Woodlands**, Tarabai Park, Tel: 20941.
**SHOLAPUR**: **Ajanta Lodge**, Mechonochi Chowk, Tel: 26518. **Kinar Hotel**, 276 Plot No. 64, Hotagi Road, Tel: 6171.
**NASIK**: **Panchavat**i, 430 Vakilwadi, Chandakwadi, Tel: 75771-3. **Green View Hotel**, Trimbak Rd., Tel: 72231-3. **Samrat**, Opp. Indian Airlines Office, Tel: 77211, 78211.
**NAGPUR**: **Hotel Jagsons**, 30 Back Central Ave. Tel: 48611-14. **Blue Diamond**, 113 Desai Chowk, Central Ave., Tel: 47461-69. **Skylark**, 119 Central Ave., Tel: 44654-58.
**NAVEGAON NATIONAL PARK** (140 km from Nagpur): **Holiday Home, Tree Top Rest House**. Information: Divisional Forest Officer, Gondia, Rail-head Deolgaon (1 km).
**NAGZIRA WILDLIFE SANCTUARY** (140 km from Nagpur): **Rest House**. Information: Assistant Conservator of Forests Sakoli. Nearest town, Gondia (58 km); Rail-head: Gongle (20 km).

# GOA

If there is a tropical paradise on earth, this is it. Goa, no larger than a thumb print on the map, nestles on India's southwestern coast, between the states of Maharashtra and Karnataka. Few tourists leave the country without visiting this lush and beautiful territory, so much a part of India and yet so different. Goa's natural boundaries shielded it from the mainstream of history, the towering Sahyadri range cutting it off from the mainland, and the Arabian Sea flanking it on the west. Nature, too, has been more than bountiful. Little wonder then that the Portuguese explorers who came here looking for spices stayed on for 450 years. They endowed the predominantly Hindu land with an Iberian legacy, contributing a Latin flavor that is still very perceptible decades after the Portuguese heyday.

Goa is the only place in India that eluded British rule. The Portuguese had made themselves comfortable here 250 years before the British moved in; they outstayed the British by over a decade. The Portuguese came not merely as conquerors or colonizers, but as zealous missionaries who set about converting the original inhabitants to Christianity.

Strategically located on an Arab trade route, the port of **Gowapur**, near the mouth of the Mandovi river, has an ancient history, dating back to the 3rd century B.C. when it formed part of the Mauryan empire. Until the Middle Ages, several Hindu kingdoms held sway, including the Chalukyas of Badami (A.D. 580 to 750). The squabbling Hindu rulers were forced to unite in the face of the Muslim threat towards the end of the 13th century. Mohammad bin Tughlaq, Sultan at Delhi, came and went, leaving behind his minions to collect taxes on his behalf. In 1347 Hasan Gangu founded

*Left: The palm-filled region around Betul, Goa.*

the Bahmani kingdom, which lasted until 1526 under the rule of the Sultans of Gulbarga. Goa, wealthy because of its sea trade, soon became a favorite raiding ground for these Muslim rulers. Harihara II, ruler of the Hindu Vijayanagar kingdom, heeded the pleas of the Goans and sent his army chief, Madhav Mantri, to Goa from his capital, Hampi. For over a decade, Mantri was viceroy of a land several times the size of what the Portuguese ruled; he established a code of religious tolerance and set aside lands for Hindu temples which more or less still exist today. Strangely, there are no memorials to this remarkable man who saved Goa from the Sultans; he was truly one of history's unsung heroes.

Peace and prosperity marked the next century, with the little port at the mouth of the Zuari river dominating the trade of the wealthy Vijayanagar empire. When this town (called **Ela** today) became silted, Goa, at the mouth of the Mandovi, assumed importance, and was known for its trade in Arabian horses from Ormuz, which were much in demand .

In the 1470s Goa once again fell to the Muslims, this time at the hands of Mahmud Gawan of the Bahmani kingdom. The Bahmani kingdom itself was soon parceled out between three of its noblemen. Goa was won by Adil Khan, who founded the Adilshahi dynasty of Bijapur. But not for long; Alfonso de Albuquerque and his intrepid seamen were to change this little kingdom's fortunes like nothing else before. It was 1510, and Iberian Granada, the last bastion of the Muslim rule, had only just fallen to the Portuguese, whose Christian outlook allowed them to believe they were liberating the people. When Albuquerque's armada sailed into the placid waters of the Mandovi, he had spices, not conquest on his mind. His 23 ships and 1,000 men were not enough to capture India.

A commander of Vijayanagar's navy, Timoja (or Thimmaya), entreated the sur-

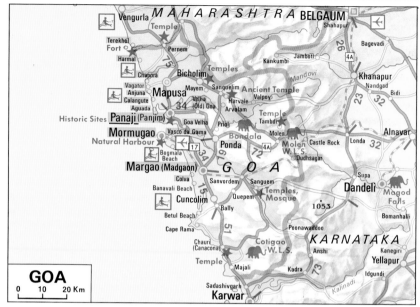

GOA
0    10    20 Km

prised Captain-General of the Indian Ocean to attack the flourishing town. And so he drove out Adil Shah and entered the city to the sounds of a fanfare. There was to be a counter-attack by the Muslims, resulting in bloodshed, but the Portuguese had finally established themselves.

Two churches bear testimony to this victory: **Our Lady of the Rosary** in **Velha Goa** and **Our Lady of the Mount**, a neglected monument on one of the highest hills in Goa. Albuquerque made no great attempt to convert the Hindus. He did, however, ban the practice of *sati*, not really prevalent in this area, and encouraged his men to marry the local women, both Muslim and Hindu. These were the earliest converts to Christianity in Goa.

Not content with being governor of Goa, Albuquerque left for greener pastures along the silk route to China. His last wish was to get a glimpse of Goa before he died; he barely made it. The man who gave Goa its name and made it Dourada, the City of Gold, was surely the first

to have been caught in its spell. Other nearby territories fell to the Portuguese almost without them lifting a finger: Daman, Diu, Salsette, Bassein, and of course, the group of fishing islands which they gave away as dowry to the British – Bombay. This was what came to be known as the Velha Conquistas (old conquests). The Novas (new) Conquistas were to take another two centuries, creating the united territory that is Goa, Daman and Diu today.

Wave upon wave of Christian orders descended upon this Jewel of the Orient, and were surprised to find religious tolerance instead of a barbaric society. Conversion wasn't as welcome as the Christian priests had thought it would be; there were only handfuls of Jews and Muslims: it was the Hindus who were to be tackled. Hindu temples were razed to the ground after special permission was obtained from the Viceroy in 1540; Goa's churches took their place. Hinduism became a crime; thousands fled their homes, preferring the nearby Muslim areas which, in retrospect, seemed less barbaric. The Hindus found ways to circumvent the laws, and even set up idols in the jungles of Ponda and Bicholim, outside the Portuguese jurisdiction. Even after being converted, Hindus stuck tenaciously to their rituals; today, Christianity in Goa is a mix of both religions.

In 1542, one of the two founding fathers of the Jesuit order, Francis Xavier, traveled to Goa. The Goans found in him a compassionate messiah, which to all purposes he was, despite the fact that he had played a crucial role in the Inquisition. Francis Xavier had no fondness for Goa and traveled southwards along the coast to Kerala. He died on the way to China; years later, a friend visited his desolate grave near the Canton river and found the body in perfect condition. It was brought to Goa and buried there 16 years after he died. In 1662, when St. Xavier was canonized, he was laid to rest at the **Cathedral of Bom Jesus** within a shrine of gold.

## Panjim

Much has changed in Goa since the 16th century when it was Ilha Illustrissima (illustrious town), the Rome of the Orient. Only the churches remain, as does the Latin-Iberian legacy. The town of **Panjim**, or **Panaji**, its capital, is small by Indian standards, but then much of Goa's population is rural. Situated on the southern bank of the Mandovi, the city center contains the **Church of Immaculate Conception**, with the inevitable square in front of it. Built in the baroque style in 1541, its balustraded sweep of stairway and its tall twin towers make it an impressive structure.

**Fontainahas**, with its cobbled streets and whitewashed Latin look, is an old residential area; other places of interest include the **Old Secretariat**, once Adil Shah's palace, **Campal**, and the **Strand** along the river.

## Velha Goa

The architectural genius of the Portuguese is manifested in the churches and the forts of **Velha Goa** (old Goa). Compared to the scaled-down look of most of the buildings of Nova Goa (Panjim), the Rome of the Orient offers a fascinating voyage through medieval architecture, magnificent churches, stately mansions and wide boulevards.

The **Basilica of Bom Jesus**, where the mortal remains of St. Francis Xavier are enshrined, is perhaps the best preserved and an important place of pilgrimage. A muted brick-red in color, the church's interior is remarkable for its simplicity, notwithstanding the heavily carved and gilded altars. Every ten years, an exposition of the saint is held.

Begun in 1562 and completed almost 100 years later, **Se Cathedral** is the largest building in Old Goa, impressive despite the fact that two of its towers were brought down by lightning in 1776. The **Cross of Miracles**, said to grow in size, is believed to have healing properties. Nearby is the **Church of St. Francis of Assisi**, which began as a mosque, and later became a church, with a substantial part of its flooring comprising elaborate gravestones dating back to the early 1500s. Today this interesting building is neither mosque nor church, but an **Archaeological Museum** housing Goan antiquities. Ancient stone inscriptions and two *sati* stones recall Goa's Hindu past. An enormous statue of Albuquerque was moved here from the Campal roundabout in Panjim. Originally part of a Hindu temple, the **Old Pillory monolith** stands outside a villa; it was used as a flogging stone for thieves and its present location denotes the old market place, unbelievable as this might seem. The **College of St. Paul** must have been a fine place of learning; the remains of its arch are more impressive than the **Viceregal Arch**, now a popular tourist spot.

The city, which was walled in, must once have been cluttered; today, there is enough room to admire the scale of the buildings that still exist. The **Church of St. Cajetan**, a miniature replica of St. Peter's Basilica in Rome, is near the ferry, as is the **Chapel of St. Catherine**. The **Convent of St. Monica** was one of the largest nunneries of the Portuguese empire. Past its austere towers is the **Church of Our Lady of the Rosary**, built in European and Indian styles to commemorate Albuquerque's victory in 1510. The first Portuguese lady to hazard the journey to India, Dona Catarina, lies buried here. The remains of **St. Augustine's Church**, perched high on a hill, can be seen for miles around. The solitary tower appears taller than its 46 meters.

A boat ride up the Mandovi will afford you more sights of Old Goa in an afternoon than you would have in two days

*Above: Working in the fertile rice fields of Goa. Right: A moment of leisure at Colva Beach, Goa.*

traveling by road. The trip starts at **Idalcao**, Adil Shah's palace, and takes you through lush countryside, dotted with quaint little houses. To the right is **Panjim** which, despite its rapid industrialization, has a relatively unspoiled look. Elegant mansions on the waterfront tell of the good years after the *Hidalgos* (Portuguese nobility) had left for good. **Velha Goa** looks different from the river, perhaps seeming more enchanting than it is in reality. The **Cabo Raj Nivas**, perched high on a cliff, was first a church, then a fort, and later became a nunnery before being designated the official residence of the Portuguese governor general in 1866.

The Portuguese amassed considerable wealth; they were also extremely worried about losing it, if their fortifications are any indication. What they feared most was an attack from the sea, and to prevent this, a chain of formidable embattlements was built along the coast. **The Fort of Reis Magos**, with its cannons trained towards the sea, now serves as a jail, just as it once did during the Portuguese rule.

Its neighbor, **Fort Aguada**, is something of a national monument; it once housed political prisoners and nationalist leaders who fought the Portuguese. A plaque here is dedicated to their memory. Aguada, where ships took on water in olden times, is also a prison today. It rises majestically atop a steep hill that thrusts out at a sheer angle from the sea.

Visitors may experience difficulty in obtaining permission to enter these forts, but the **Terekhol Fort** at the northern end of Goa is welcoming, and has a rest house. To reach it from the city center, you have to cross three rivers, two of them, the Chapora and the Terekhol, by ferry. The drive between is dense with betel nut and cashew trees; this is Pernem countryside.

Close by is lovely beach country, mile upon mile of unspoiled white sands, changing names as the road winds along: **Harmal**, **Arambol**, **Vagator**. Stop and see the private collection of the **Deshprabhus** of **Pernem**, the area's uncrowned aristocracy. Pottery from Ha-

rappan sites, solid silver furniture and exquisite European period furniture make this a rare collection.

### Temples

Though the Portuguese razed hundreds of Hindu temples to the ground, some survived their onslaught, and also that of time. The **Mangesh Temple** where legend has it that Parvati cried out to her husband Lord Siva to save her from a tiger, was shifted from its original site on the Zuari river to **Priol** in Ponda district. The **Shantadurga Temple** at **Kavalem** is distinctive for its elaborate *deepastambha* (lamp tower), and is dedicated to the goddess Parvati.

The temples of **Ramnath**, **Nagesh** and **Mahalakshmi** stand almost side by side in **Ponda**. They are shielded by jungles, a reminder that the Hindus lived in constant dread of being attacked because of their religion. The imposing **Tambde (Red) Surle**, stands on red earth which gives it its name. Built in the 12th cen-

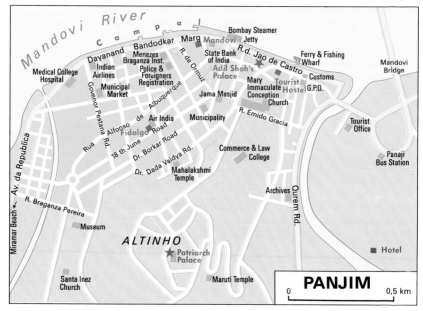

Mandovi River

Bombay Steamer
Jetty

Mandovi
Bandodkar Marg    Mandovi    R.d. Jao de Castro    Ferry & Fishing
Dayanand    State Bank    Wharf
Menezes    of India
Braganza Inst.    Mandovi
Indian    Adil Shah's    Customs    Bridge
Medical College    Airlines    Police &    Palace
Hospital    Registration    Mary    Tourist    G.P.O.
Municipal    Immaculate  Hostel
Market    Jama Masjid    Conception
Church

Albuquerque    R. Emido Gracia
de    Air India    Municipality
Alfonso    Fidalgo Road
Tourist
18th June    Office
Dr. Borkar Road
Commerce & Law
Dr. Dada Vaidya Rd.    College    Panaji
Mahalakshmi    Bus Station
Temple

R. Braganza Pereira    Archives    Qurem Rd.

Museum

ALTINHO    Hotel

Patriarch
Palace

Santa Inez    Maruti Temple    **PANJIM**
Church    0    0,5 km

tury, this rock-cut shrine stands in the middle of nowhere, one kilometer (half a mile) from civilization, and is by far the oldest temple in Goa. Buddhist and Brahminical rock-cut caves date earlier than this: there is one on the road from Ponda to Panjim. The **Arvalem Caves**, or the **Pandava Caves** as they are locally known, are not to be compared to Ajanta or Elephanta. In contrast, the **Rachol Seminary** is a palatial building with a definite atmosphere. It serves today as an evangelical school, much depleted in numbers since 1609, when it was built. Its collection of religious murals is priceless, its library one of the best in Goa.

The **Pilar Seminary** and its Carmelite building stand atop **Goa Velha** (not to be confused with Velha Goa), and the old Kadamba capital. Today, the building houses a **museum** which traces the region's history through a number of historical finds. In Ponda itself there is a

remnant of Goa's Muslim past - the **Saif Mosque**, which was built in 1560.

### Beaches

More people pay homage at Goa's beaches than at its temples. The flower children of the 1960 and 1970 first discovered Goa and its heavenly beaches; many of them never went back. **Calangute** was the hot favorite unil not so long ago; today **Anjuna**, **Chapora** and **Colva** (the nicest) are more in vogue.

The Goans, with their characteristic easygoing nature, turn a blind eye to the hippies. Relax and let live is the credo here. Industrialization and change are seeping into Goa's towns, notably **Margaon**, the second-largest town, **Vasco da Gama**, and **Marmagao**, one of India's finest natural harbors. However it still evades the villages, which are hard put to rid themselves of the sleepy Latin way of life. Siesta is still observed, there is always time to sit in the portico and chat, and Goa's natural wealth has in fact con-

*Right: Fisherfolk reaping the abundance of the sea, Calva Beach, Goa.*

tributed to her sagging economy. Four hundred and fifty years after the *Hidalgos,* with their swashbuckling ways and their ostrich plumes, left, the towns wear a deserted look, as the young are no longer content to spend their lives among the beauty of the casuarina groves. Thousands have left for the big cities, where they have meticulously retained their identity - once a Goan, always a Goan. And so some of the grand ancestral mansions with their hybrid architectural styles and their fabulous heirlooms lie deserted almost all year round; visitors to Goa wonder how anyone could bear to leave a place like this.

Many Goans have left for the more lucrative shores of the Gulf countries; they are now returning to try to cash in on Goa's enormous natural wealth, setting up fisheries and modern farms. Tourism also plays a crucial role in revitalizing the economy. The Goan may be Indian, but he is a Goan first, and though many can't afford to return, some are finding ways to do so.

Goa is lovely year-round, but the **Carnival** is a powerful crowd puller. By early February carnival fever grips young and old, transforming the sleepy roads into colorful revelry. Said to have originated as a pagan festival in Rome, it came to Goa via the Portuguese, and has now acquired a heady local flavor.

### Food and Culture

In Goa, music is the food of love, and life, but the sort that's eaten is equally important. Here "breaking bread" is a time- honored custom; even the poorest villager will embarrass you with his hospitality. Native Konkani food in Goa has borrowed the best of Arabic, Portuguese and southeast Asian influences, to produce a cuisine that is exotic and elaborate (see The Gastronomical Tour). The Goan also loves to drink as he loves to eat. Some of the best Indian wines are bottled here; though wine making has not assumed the proportions of a fine art, good full-bodied samples are available. The local brew, *toddy*, is best drunk fresh from the tree; *feni*, from cashew and coffee, is Goa's version of country liquor, very popular among the locals.

Goa's economy depends a lot on what are called cash crops, mostly coconut and cashew. Betel nut, pepper and fruit take up only 10 percent of the land that is under cultivation.

Music is as much a part of the Goan way of life as food and drink, and it is here that the divide between Christians and Hindus is most apparent. The music of the Goan Christian is in his blood, as it were, and most Goans can strum on a guitar or play a piano. Uniquely Goan, the music has spread beyond Goa's boundaries and into Bombay and other cities, where rock bands, as well as pop and jazz musicians, are invariably of Goan origin. The Goan *mandos*, lyrical folk songs, often extol the virtues of love and the sorrows, too. By contrast, Hindu or Indian classical music has no great tradition here. Four and a half centuries without patronage of any sort are difficult to recover from. Not surprisingly, religious and church music still forms a vibrant part of the people's lives.

The Goan forests are in absolute contrast to its beaches, but almost as exotic. More than a third of Goa's land area is covered by forests, and hopefully reforestation schemes will undo whatever damage has been wrought up to now.

Although the Ghats formed a daunting barrier, poachers and timber plunderers wreaked havoc before strict laws put them in their place. Initially Karnataka state, above the ghats, had more animals, but today the ecological balance has changed in Goa's favor, and animals have been known to wander into Goa. The main wildlife sanctuaries are the **Mahavir Sanctuary**, close to **Molem**, which is the largest and boasts 240 sq. km (93 sq. mi) compared to **Bondla's** meager eight, and yet the latter is more popular. It is more a jungle resort than a

sanctuary, the animals not being free to roam around unhampered, but with sufficient space not to resemble a zoo. Crocodiles, peacocks, deer, snakes, leopards and bison are the main attractions.

### Excursions from Goa

If you can bring yourself to leave Goa for excursions, **Dudhsagar Falls**, 100 km out of Goa on the rail route, is worth the effort. Dense forests suddenly give way to the sight of the thundering falls; look out for them if you approach Goa by train. The bridge across Dudhsagar cuts across the face of the falls, so you get a fabulous view.

Midway between Bombay and Surat, on the Gujrat coast, lies **Daman**, seized by the Portuguese in 1559 because they believed Bassein would remain secure that way. Bassein fell to the Marathas, but Daman belonged to the Portuguese till 1961, when they finally moved out, having overstayed their welcome by more than 200 years.

More Gujarati than Goan, this little town which, together with Diu and Goa, forms a union territory, had the dubious distinction of being a smuggler's paradise, at least until recently. From here foreign goods, including cheese and chocolate, clothes and gold were supplied to the rest of India after the British left.

Even today, innocuous sail boats are under constant customs surveillance. Rich mansions line the roads. Nearby is **Devka**, a little sea resort dominated by the Parsi community, but now quite desolate. The **Fort** at **Nani** (small) **Daman** looks as if it were designed purely for ceremonial entrances; its interior does not live up to the promise outside. The Convent in **Moti Daman** seems suspended in time. The **Somnath Temple** has been recently restored.

The little island of **Diu**, away from the tourist beat, is a pleasant surprise. It has changed little in the past 200 years.

## GOA
### Accommodation
*LUXURY:* **Fort Aguada Beach Resort**, Sinquerim, Bardez, Tel: (0832) 7501/07. **Majorde Beach Resort**, Majorde, Salcette, Goa 403713, Tel: 20025-26, 20321, 20204, 20126, Fax: 08342-20212. **Ramada Renaissance Resort**, Cobra Beach, Varca Village, Salcette, Margao, Goa, Tel. 08342/4, 23611/2, 5200/20. **Cidade De Goa**, Vainguirin Beach, Done Paule, Goa 403004, Tel. 3301/3308. *MODERATE:* **Hotel Aroma**, Gurha Rivara Rd., Municipal Garden Sq., Panjim, Tel: 43519, 44330. *BUDGET:* **Youth Hostel**, Miramar, Tel: 5433. **Tourist Cottages**, Farmaguid, Ponda, Tel: 2292.

### BOGMALO
**Hotel Oberoi Bogmalo Beach**, Dabolim Airport, Tel: (08345)-3291-5, 2191-2, Fax: 2510.

### PANAJI
**Hotel Fidalgo**, 18th June Road, Tel: 46291-99. **Tourist Hostel**, Tel: 3396, 3903. **Hotel Mandovi**, Bandodkar Marg, Tel: 46270-9, 44405-09.

### CALANGUTE
**Hotel Baia Da Sol**, Baga, Calangute, Tel: (083227) 6084/85, Panjim 5207. **Calangute Beach Resort**, Umatawad, Bardoz-Goa, Tel: 6063. **Concha Beach Resort**, Umtawado, Calangute Beach, Bardez/Goa, Tel: 6056/78, 87. **Tourist Dormitory**, Calangute Beach.

### COLVA BEACH
**Silversands**, Tel: (08342) 21645-6. **Sukhsagar Beach Resort**, Tel: 20224, 2188 Margoa Exch.

### Festivals
Goans are deeply religious people but what distinguishes them from other Indian communities is their exuberance. The no-holds-barred merrymaking evident here is unparaleled. *Jatras*, week-long fairs held at religious centers are numerous. *Bodgeshwar Jatra* (January) can be attended in Mapusa, the *Hanuman Jatra* (February) at Panaji and in the same month people flock to Mangueshi, 20 km from Panaji to celebrate *Manguesh Jatra*. Although the deities worshiped are Shaivite, the festivities are open to Christians as well. The 3-day *Carnival* (February/March), is a pre-Lent celebration with parades, masquerades and dancing, followed by somber rituals during Lent. Easter is celebrated with both reverence and gaiety. There is *Shigmo* (*Holi* or *Chitra Gulal*), the spring festival (March) of color; and *Novem* (August), when Christians take the first sheaves of harvested paddy rice to church to be blessed and offered in thanksgiving. A bullfight is the highlight of this fiesta. A festival for music lovers, classical this time, is *Dirdi* (November) held at Madgaon, 35 km from Panaji. The Kumbis perform *Zagor*, a dance drama on successive nights in Siolim to the accompaniment of folksongs. A feature

of Konkani drama is haunting interludes played on the *mando*. The post-Easter Feast of our Lady of Miracles (at Mapusa), the Procession of the Franciscan Third Order (following Lent) and the Feast of Jesus the Nazarene are accompanied by fairs. The patron saint of Goa is St. Francis, interred at the Basilica of Bom Jesus. The annual feast is in December and the exposition of the body is held once every 10 years. End of the year festivals include the Feast of Our Lady of Immaculate Conception and Christmas, both occasions for religious ceremonies, firework displays and exchange of gifts.

### Museums / Art Galleries
**Archives Museum of Goa**, Tel: 46006, Ashirwad Bldg., 1st Floor, Santa Inez, Panaji. 9.30 am-5.30 pm. closed Sat, Sun and publ. holidays. **Gallery Esperanca**, Opp. Merces Church, Vadi, Merces. 9 am.-12 noon, 2-6 pm, advance notice advised. **Archaeological Museum and Portrait Gallery**, Convent of St. Francis of Assisi, Old Goa, Tel: 45941. Open 10 am-12 noon, 1-5 pm, closed Fri.

### Post / Telegraph / Telephone
**Head Post Office**, Panaji, Tel: 43706. Sub-post offices in Margao, Vasco da Gama, Calangute, Mapusa and Colva.

### Restaurants
**Kamat Millan** (Vegetarian), Station Rd., Margao, Tel: 21235. **Little Chef**, Francisco L. Gomes Rd., Vasco Da Gama, Tel: 2122738. **Keni**, **Lucky Bar**, Mirman Beach.

### Shopping
Toys, figurines, candles, coir products, decorative pieces fashioned from seashells, cashew-nuts, "feni" - the local brew (2 bottles per head permitted) and fragrant soap are souvenirs to buy here. Emporiums are located at Panaji, Margao and Vasco Da Gama.

### Tourist Information
**Goa Tourism Development**, Corporation Tourist Hostel, Panaji, Tel: 43396/43903. **Directorate of Tourism**, Gov. of Goa, Tourist Home, Patto, Panaji, Tel: 45583/44757. Information counters: Tourist Hostel, Margao, Tel: 22513. Tourist Hostel Vasco, Tel: 3119. Dabolim Airport, Tel: 2644.

### Access / Local Transport
The nearest airport, Dabolim, 29 km from Panaji, is connected with Bombay and a few other Indian cities. International chartered flights also land here. The rail junction for Goa is Vasco Da Gama, connected by meter gauge to Miraj where three express trains from Bombay halt. Margao is a more convenient railhead for Panaji. A network of roads connect Panaji with major towns in India. Buses terminate/originate at the Interstate Bus Terminus, Panaji, Tel: 5620. Local transport comprises tourist cars, metered taxis and auto-rickshaws, motorcycles on hire and ferry services.

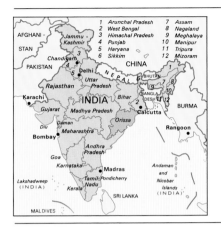

| 1 Arunachal Pradesh | 7 Assam |
| 2 West Bengal | 8 Nagaland |
| 3 Himachal Pradesh | 9 Meghalaya |
| 4 Punjab | 10 Manipur |
| 5 Haryana | 11 Tripura |
| 6 Sikkim | 12 Mizoram |

**ORISSA**

# THE DRAMA OF DEVOTION

## ORISSA

Orissa (155,842 sq. km or 60,170 sq. mi), on the eastern seaboard, has a lush and fertile coast which rises to the Eastern Ghats in the hinterland. This hilly area is among the poorest and most backward in the whole country, inhabited by numerous tribal groups that still retain distinct lifestyles. In contrast, the coastal region, in particular the delta of the Mahanadi (the "great river"), bears witness to Orissa's participation in the mainstream of political and cultural influences and also to its ancient tradition of seafaring. This was the Kalinga of yore, best remembered for a bloody battle in the 3rd century B.C. which is believed to have prompted the transformation of the Emperor Asoka into a peace-loving Buddhist. Two dynasties, the Kesari and the Ganga, who ruled Orissa from the 2nd to the 15th centuries A.D. gradually displaced the Buddhist and Jain influences which had penetrated the region. Both were Hindus, and vigorous patrons of art and architecture. They built temples that are exuberant expressions not only of religious fervor but of the beauty and abun-

*Preceding pages: Wheel of the chariot-like Sun Temple, Konark. Left: Stereo entertainment in the pre-television age, Orissa.*

dance of nature and the mythopoetic imagination. Ritual and worship at these religious centers gave birth to a variety of art and craft traditions that survived both Mughal and British domination.

### Bhubaneswar

**Bhubaneswar**, with its distinctive old and new city, is the capital. In the old city, nearly 100 temples survive of the more than 1,000 that were once built around **Bindusagar Lake**. According to legend, this lake contains water from all the rivers of India. The soaring 54-m (177 ft) spire of the **Lingaraj Temple** dominates the landscape. It was built in A.D. 1114 by the Kesaris, and is dedicated to Siva as Tribhuvaneshwara, the Lord of the Three Worlds. Its architecture is typical of Orissan temples in which the spire, which rises above the *sanctum sanctorum*, is preceded by porches, a dancing hall and one or more halls of offering. These are linked within but are discernible as separate sections from without. On the festival of *Shivaratri*, which is celebrated in February/March, thousands of pilgrims light lamps in a night-long ceremony of devotion.

**Mukteswar Temple**, built in the 10th century, has a beautiful stone arch at the entrance and a number of sculptures on

its outer wall. This arch is reminiscent of Buddhist votive architecture. Some of the sculptures depict stories from the *Panchatantra* tales; that of the monkey and the crocodile is particularly interesting. The **Parasurama Temple** has exquisite carvings and latticed windows. The 11th-century **Raja Rani Temple** has sculptures of graceful and sensuous female figures. The details of leaves, flowers and fruits are fine examples of the excellent craftsmanship of this region. **Brahmeswara Temple** is really a complex of temples with shrines at four corners, and sculpted façades (foreigners are allowed within). **Vaital** is a Tantric temple dedicated to the goddess Kapalini who is enthroned upon a corpse. Its barrel-shaped roof is an unusual feature.

Bhubaneswar has two interesting museums, the **Orissa State Museum** and

*Above: Sadhu savoring the quiet of his simple cave retreat. Right: A pata-chitra artist creating an image of Krishna and the gopis.*

the **Handicrafts Museum**. The former houses a rich and interesting collection of sculptures, rare palm leaf manuscripts, coins, copper plates, arms, Stone and Bronze Age tools, anthropological and geological specimens and musical instruments. The same complex houses the state academies of literature, fine arts, dance, music and theater.

The Handicrafts Museum on Secretariat Road has a large collection of Orissan handicrafts that include stone sculptures and brass castings, silver filigree work, *pata*-paintings as well as toys made of clay, wood and lacquer. Orissa's earliest paintings, about 1500 years old, are found in a rock shelter at **Sitabinji** in the Keorijhar district.

The painted ceilings and walls of Orissan temples depict various stories from Indian mythology. Similar stories are painted on cloth coated with a mixture of chalk and gum made from tamarind seed. Usually worked in bright primary colors, these paintings are known as *pata-chitra*. Most of the painters now live in **Raghu-**

**rajpur**, a village near Puri. Bhubaneswar also has a very interesting **Tribal Research Museum**.

### Excursions

Only 8 km (5 mi) from Bhubaneswar is **Dhauligiri**, which marks the site of the Kalinga war. There are eleven edicts of Asoka inscribed on rocks, dated as 3rd century B.C., the earliest known inscriptions in India. A *Shanti Stupa* (Peace Pagoda) is standing on the hilltop, and its white dome can be seen as one approaches Bhubaneswar. The remains of a city with fortifications and two elaborate gateways were unearthed at **Sisupalgarh**, 5 km (3 mi) northeast of Dhauligiri. The city is believed to have been a viceregal seat during Asoka's reign.

**Khandagiri** and **Udayagiri**, also situated on the outskirts of the city, are the caves that epitomize the ascendancy of Jainisim in Orissa. Their sculptural art of the 2nd century B.C. is demonstrated impressively in the colossal figure of Lord Mahavira on the Khandagiri hills and the exquisite rock reliefs on the Udayagiri hills. Emperor Kharavela's inscriptions are equally famous.

**Nandan Kanan**, 20 km (12 mi) from Bhubaneswar, has a wildlife and botanical garden, and is the home of the rare white tiger and white crocodile. **Cuttack**, the former capital of Orissa, is a commercial city, known for its extremely fine and delicate silver filigree ware. The Buddhist triangle of **Ratnagiri**, **Udayagiri** and **Lalitagiri** may be conveniently visited from Cuttack. In the middle of the 7th century there were over 100 Buddhist monasteries housing several thousand monks. The Chinese pilgrim Hsuan Tsang refers to the hill monastery of Pushpagin, identified by scholars as Lalitgiri or Udayagiri. Ratnagiri was a great center of Buddhism from the 5th to the 10th centuries A.D. On top of the hillock there flourished a *vihara* called Ratnagiri Mahavihara. A large number of structures, sculptures and inscriptions reveal that many Buddhist scholars of repute

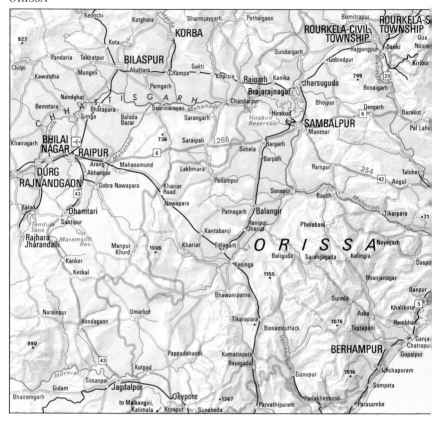

resided here, attracting monks from far-off places. This is one of the sites in India where Buddhism flourished almost to the 16th century. Besides the main stupa and a number of monasteries, eight brick temples in the Orissan style, dedicated to Manjusri and other Buddhist deities, have been found, as well as beautiful bronze images of Buddha.

## Puri

**Puri**, 60 km (37 mi) from Bhubaneswar, is the abode of Krishna as Jagannath, the Lord of the Universe. This seaside town on the Bay of Bengal is one of the four cardinal points of Hinduism. Here, the Lord Jagannath is enshrined with his sister Subhadra and brother Balabhadra. Together, they form a wide-eyed and attractive trinity. Their large colorful images in the temple are carved from wood, and are ritually replaced every 12 years. Small replicas are freely available. (This temple is not open to non-Hindus, but it can be viewed easily from the nearby Raghunandan Library.)

The main temple is a majestic structure of 65 m (213 ft), standing on an elevated platform. It was built in the 12th century by King Chodaganga to commemorate the moving of his capital from south to central Orissa. All the minute rituals are adhered to in this temple, in which all castes stand equal. More than 6,000 men serve as priests, wardens or pilgrim

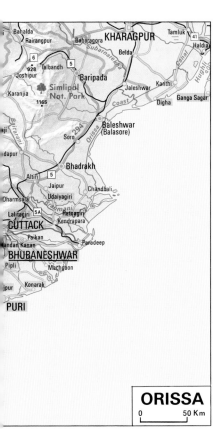

**ORISSA**

0 ⌞_____⌟ 50 Km

guides. Nearly 20,000 people are indirectly dependent on the temple for their livelihoods and thousands eat the food cooked in the temple kitchen.

The famous *Ratha Yatra*, the chariot festival, is an annual ritual held every June/July. The movable images of the deities are taken out on immense chariots, each supported by 16 wheels and drawn by thousands of people. Nearly five million pilgrims participate in this festival. (In the past, pilgrims caught up in the frenzy of devotion were known to have thrown themselves beneath the wheels of the moving chariot. This chariot was the origin of the word "juggernaut"). **Gundicha Mandir** is situated at the other end of Grand Road outside the

main temple. In commemoration of Krishna's journey from Gokul to Vrindavan, the chariot-drawn deities are taken to Gundicha Mandir. They remain there for a week and are brought back to the temple after ritual purification on the last day of the festival.

Puri also has a fine beach (see section on Beaches). **Pipli**, a village in the Puri district, is noted for its colorful appliqué work. Craftsmen who originally made canopies and umbrellas for the ceremonial appearances of gods and kings, have today expanded their varied repertoire to include tablecloths, handbags, cushion covers and dresses.

### Konark

**Konark**, the chariot temple of Surya, the Sun God, was built in A.D. 1238 by King Langual Narasimha Deva of the Ganga dynasty, during the golden age of Orissan art and culture. (Konark is derived from *kona*, or corner and *arka*, or sun). Though the main temple tower has now fallen, the audience hall stands as proof of the magnificent scale on which the temple was originally executed. The temple was conceived as a chariot. Its 24 giant wheels, which symbolize the division of time, are intricately carved on the spokes and axle-heads. The chariot is drawn by seven horses, and the three images of Surya receive the rays of the sun at dawn, noon and sunset. Huge figures of war elephants and lions, and those of horses trampling fallen warriors reveal the ancient mastery in sculpture.

Every aspect of life has been carved on the façades of the temple. Erotic images, as full blooded as those of Khajuraho, convey the sublimation of human love in a myriad of forms. In the early temples erotic sculptures were rare, but later, when the Tantric cult gained acceptance, they became a more common feature. According to authorities, they symbolize desire and creation, for it is held that

desire leads to creation. There are beautiful images of women playing musical instruments. Much of the sculpture is reflected in Odissi dance.

The Konark Temple, also known as the Black Pagoda, was conceived by an architect called Sibei Samantaray. It took 1,200 masons and sculptors 12 years to build it, at the staggering cost of the revenue of as many years. The **Archaeological Museum** at Konark shows a rare collection of sculptures.

### Other Attractions

The biggest inland lake in the country, **Chilika**, spreads over 1,100 sq. km (425 sq. mi) across the lengths of the Puri and Ganjam districts. It has numerous emerald green islands with a rich variety of aquatic fauna, and migratory birds in winter. Chilika's fishing catch includes mackerels, prawns and crabs. **Kalijai**

*Above: The Sun Temple, also known as the Black Pagoda, Konark.*

**Temple**, the abode of the presiding deity of the lake, is located on a small island.

**Gopalpur-on-Sea**, one of the ancient sea ports of Orissa, has in recent years developed into a well-known seaside resort. **Taptapani**, further inland, is a health resort with a hot sulphur spring. **Simlipal National Park** spreads at the foot of the steep hills in the Mayurbhanj district of north Orissa. It has a 2,750 sq. km (1062 sq. mi) sanctuary in which tigers, panthers and elephants roam.

The districts of Sambalpur, Sundargarh, Phulbani, Ganjam, Mayurbhanj and Cuttack are noted for their handloom textiles. The weavers have an inborn sense of color and texture. They tie and dye threads in a particular pattern and weave them into exquisite sarees and fabrics. **Rourkela**, in northern Orissa, is an industrial town with a large steel plant set up with West German help. South Orissa is rich in tribal life. These tribes are the Austro-Asiatic Mundas and the Tibeto-Burmese Bondas, concentrated around **Koratpur**, **Malkangiri** and **Kalimali**.

## BHUBANESWAR
### Accommodation
*LUXURY:* **Hotel Konark**, 86/A 1 Gautam Nagar, Tel: 54330/31. **Hotel Swasti** 103 Janpath, Unit 3, Tel: 404178/9, 404359. **Hotel Oberoi Bhubaneswar**, Nayapalli, Tel: 56116.
*MODERATE:* **Hotel Kalinga Ashok**, Gautam Nagar, Tel: 53318. **Hotel Prachi**, 6 Janpath, Tel: 402689, 402328, 402521, 402918. **Nilanchal Ashok**, Adjoining Raj Bhawan, VIP Road, Tel: 2968-80.
*BUDGET:* **Hotel Anarkali**, 110 Kharvel Nagar, Unit 3, Tel:5 4031. **Hotel Gajapati**, 77 Bhudhanagar, Tel: 51893. **Youth Hostel** (8km), Khandagiri Hill.

### Museums
**Orissa State Museum**, Tel: 52897, 10 am-5 pm, closed Mon and public holidays. Collection of Palmleaf and paper manuscripts, portraits, archaeological finds and costumes.

### Post / Telegraph / Telephone
Post Office, Old Town, Market Building, General Post Office, Tel: 51040.

### Restaurants
**Surya Restaurant**, Hotel Prachi, 6 Janpath, Tel: 402689, 402521. **Swosti Restaurant**, 103 Janpath, Unit 3, Tel: 404178/9.

### Tourist Information
**Government of India Tourist Office**, B 21, Kalpana Area, Tel: 54203. **Tourist Information Office**, Jayadev Marg, Tel: 50099. Information at the airport, Tel: 54006 and railway station, Tel: 54715.

## PURI
### Accommodation
*MODERATE:* **Hotel Prachi**, Baliapada Swargadwar, Tel: 2638. **Toshali Sands** (8 km), Puri-Konark Marine Drive, Tel: 2888, 2999. **Hotel Vijoya International**, Chakratirtha Road, Sea Beach, Tel: 3705-2. *BUDGET:* **OTDC's Panthanivas**, Tel: 2562. **South Eastern Railway Hotel**, Tel: 2063. **Puri Hotel**, Tel: 2114. **Pantha Bhawan (OTDC's)**, Mahodadhi Nivas, Tel: 2507. **Youth Hostel**, Chakrtirtha Road, Tel: 2424.

### Post / Telegraph / Telephone
Post and Telegraph Office, Tel:2057.

### Tourist Information
**Tourist Information Bureau**, Panthanivas, Tel: 2131. Also counter at railway station, Tel: 2519.

### Accommodation
**KONARK**: **OTDC's Panthanivas**, Tel: 31. **OTDC's Traveller's Lodge**, Tel: 23. Also private lodges and hotels. Alternately, stay at Puri (35 km).
**GOPALPUR-ON-SEA**: **Hotel Oberoi Palm Beach** (2 star), Tel: 23. Other hotels: **Golden House**, **Sea View Lodge**, **Youth Hostel**.

**CHILIKA LAKE: OTDC's Panthanivas** (at Rambha), Tel: 46. **Panthanivas** (at Barkul), Tel: Balugaon 60. **Ashok Hotel** (at Balugaon), Tel:8,9. **Hotel Chilika** (Balugaon), Tel: 68.
**CUTTACK**: **Hotel Ashok**, Ice Factory Road, College Square, Tel: 25708/9, 30091-94. **Hotel Anand**, Canal Bank Road, Ranihat, Tel: 21936. **Hotel Oriental**, Buxi Bazaar, Tel: 24249. OTDC's Panthanivas, Tel: 23867. **Hotel Trimurti International**, Link Road, Tel:2 2918. **Hotel Neeladri Mangalabag**, Cuttack, Tel. 23831, 32621.
**SIMLIPAL GAME RESERVE: Rest houses** at Joshipur, Nawana, Chahala, Gudgudia, Talbandha, Kanchida, Upper Barakmra Dhudru and Champa. These lie within 5 to 30 km of the Reserve. Reservation must be made through the Field Director, Simplipal Project Tiger, Baripada, district Mayurbhanj; or district forest officers of Karanjia and Baripada Divisions.

### Festivals
On *Mahashivaratri* (February/March), Shiva temples in Orissa hold special ceremonies which are particularly impressive in Bhubaneswar and Puri. *Ashokashtami* or the Car Festival of Lord Lingaraja (March/April) at Bhubaneswar is attended by thousands who join the procession of the chariot-borne Shiva image. The 21-day *Chandan Yatra* takes place in Puri and Bhubaneswar every year in April/May. Images of Lord Jagannath and other deities are taken in a stately cruise on the Narendra tank. It marks both the beginning of the Hindu calendar and the approaching summer. This is closely followed by *Shan Yatra* (Puri) when the gods are given a ceremonial bath. The grand festival of Orissa is the week-long *Rath Yatra* (or the Car Festival of Puri, June/July) when thousands of pilgrims pour in from all parts of the country. Another memorable festival is *Bali Yatra* (Cuttack, October/November) held on the bank of the Mahanadi river. After a dip in the river, adults and children alike float tiny boats in memory of the ancient seafarers who set sail from Orissa for Bali, Java and Sumatra.
During this festival, a lively fair takes place. *Dussehra, Durga Puja, Diwali, Ganesh Puja, Holi, Janmashtami and Ramnavami* are also celebrated in Orissa. An important tribal festival (celebrated by non-tribespeople as well) is the *Chaitra Parba* in April. Various folk performances are part of these celebrations.

### Shopping
Orissan handicrafts include silver filigree work, elaborately painted *patachitras* and sophisticated *ikat* textiles. Natural materials like *Sabai* grass, feathers, sea shells, ivory, cane clay, *solapith*, stone and horn are used to fashion objects. The exquisite Vichitrapuri sarees are almost collectors' items.

to Tumkur  Tumkur
Road
to Hyderabad

Sankey's
Sankey's Reservoir

Kempe
Gowda
Tower

**7**

Bellary  Road

Jayamahal  Road

Polo
Ground

**4**

XV. Cross Rd.

Venkatarangiengar

Mallikar –
junaswami T.

*MALLES-
VARAM*

Vill. Main

Road

Rd.

V. Cross Rd.

Vill. Main

Sankey's

Rd.

*SESHADRI-
PURAM*

Seshadripuram Main

Palace

Palace Cross Rd.

Maharaja's
Palace

*BENSON TOWN*

Nandidrug

Road

Cantonment
Stn.

Borebank

Coles  Road

Hanes Road

Tannery  Road

St. F. Xavier's
Cathedral

St. John's Church  Rd.  St. John's

Windsor Manor
Sheraton

Road

Road

Timmah

Lal M.

Jama M.

St. John's  Rd.

Ashok

Golf

Course

Old Butts

Rd.

Road

Rd.

Miller's

Rd.

Embassy

Chandni Chowk Rd.

Quadrant

Curzon
Hospital

West End

Queen's

Hospital

Parsi T.

Subahdar

Seshadripuram Main

Road

Bangalore
City Stn.

Racecourse

*Racecourse*

Tourist

Seshadri

Chattram

Rd.

Rd.

Cubbon

Road

Gen. Post
Office

YMCA

YWCA

Cavalry

Rd.

**4**

to Madras

Central
Bus Stn.

Magadi

Rd.

Vidhana Saudha
(Parliament,
Assembly Hall)

High Court

Palace

Post

Office

Rd.

University

K. Gowda Rd.

Central
College
Hostel

District Office

Cubbon

Tourist
Information

Govt.
Museum

Mahatma Gandhi

Rd.

Rd.

Tourist
Office

Brigade

Magrath

Rd.

Nilasandra

Broadway

Chikpete

Rd.

Public
Library

Park

Gov. of Karnataka Tourist Office

Grand

State Bank
of India

Hong Kong

Kasturba

Richmond

Residency Mark's

Shilton

St. Patrick's
Ch.

Hosur Road

Sudha
Lodge

Bhashyam

City
Market

Avenue

Nagartapete

Sri Narasimha Raja

Rd.

Rd.

Mission Rd.

Rd.

Rd.

Woodlands

St. Joseph's
College
Hostel

Langford

to Mysore

Mysore

Rd.

Victoria
Hospital

Fort

Rd.

Sir Puttanna Chetty

Rd.

Tipu's
Palace

Rd.

Central
Police Station

Lal Bagh Fort

National
Theatre

Wodeyar

Lal Bagh

Rashtriya Vidyalaya

Krumbiegal  Rd.

Kengal Hanumanthaiya  Rd.

Road

Bull Temple

Krishnarajendra

Nagasandra

Subrahman-
yaswami T.

Vanivilas

Rd.

Botanical

Albert Victor
Hall

Gardens

Kempe Gowda
Tower

Road

Hosur

Anjaneya T.

Rd.

Bugle Rock

Bull
Temple

*Krishna
Rao Park*

**7**

Anekal

to Krishnagiri

# BANGALORE

0        1 km

Hotel

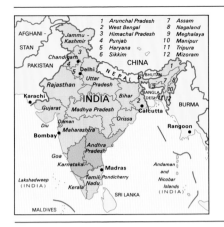

# PENINSULAR PANORAMA

**KARNATAKA**

**ANDHRA PRADESH**

## KARNATAKA

Karnataka (190,000 sq. km or 73,359 sq. mi), with a population of 37 million, was once known as Mysore State. The Western Ghats and the largely rugged terrain seem to have given rise to the term *Kalnadu*, "the territory with a rocky surface," in ancient times. Coastal Malnad, in the foothills of the Western Ghats, is known for its teak and rosewood forests, pepper, cardamom and arecanut. It is also one of the wettest regions in India. Up in the Ghats, **Coorg** district with **Mercara** as its main town, is a coffee growing area that is extraordinarily beautiful.

The presence of both large sandalwood forests and elephants has given the craftsmen of Karnataka great skill in ivory and sandalwood carving, which are the foremost handicrafts of Karnataka. The deep impression left by the Hoysala artists continues to this day in the skilful work of the ivory carvers of Karnataka.

The life of the people of Karnataka is molded by four major schools of thought that evolved through the centuries from the medieval period. They are the Vira Saiva; the Vaishnav faith, as propounded by the Dasamargins, the devotees and

*Preceding pages: Indian ladies at the Hoysala temple of Somnathpur, near Mysore.*

slaves of god Vishnu, especially in his Krishna and Rama forms; the Jain, mostly following the Digambara school; and Islam. The Karnataka ethos is essentially a blend of these four systems.

**Bangalore**, with its agreeable climate and flowering trees, is the capital of Karnataka, and a major commercial and industrial center. The **Assembly Building**, the gardens, **Tipu's Palace** and the **Museum** are among its attractions. Historically, it was ruled by the Gangas, Cholas and later Hoysalas, but Tipu is remembered affectionately for his valor, and his contribution to the recent history of the city. Bangalore has a well-known nature cure center. Not far away from Bangalore are the **Kolar Gold Fields**, the only big gold mine in India.

### Mysore

The palace city of Mysore, well known for its silk, is 170 km (106 mi) from Bangalore. Here, the fragrance of jasmine, sandalwood and incense permeate the air.

The focal point of the city is the **Maharaja's Palace** with its glittering interiors. The palace was built in the late 19th century, in the Indo-Saracenic style. Part of it is still used by the present royal family on festive occasions; part of it is a museum. The collection, which includes a golden

115

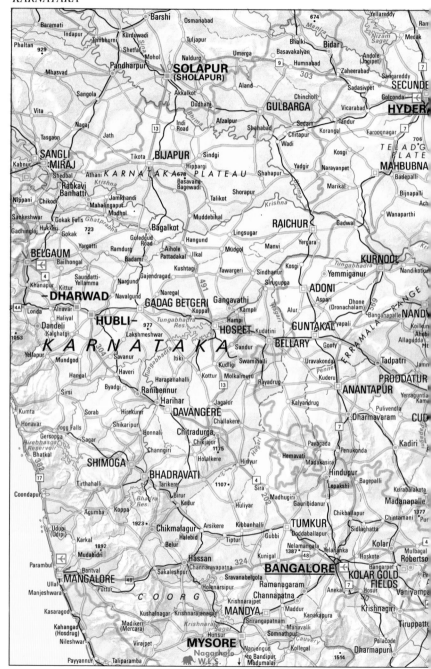

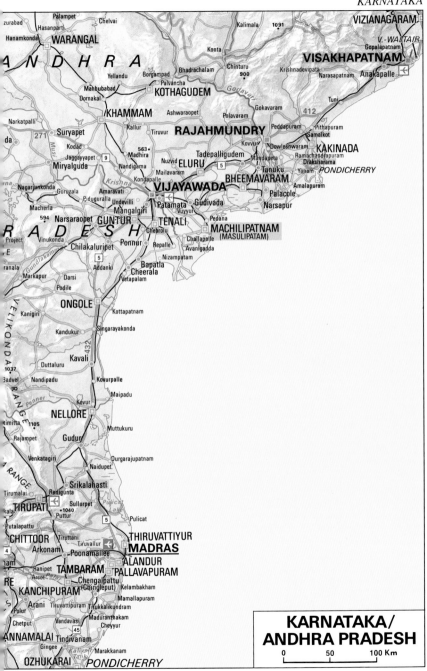

KARNATAKA/
ANDHRA PRADESH

0        50        100 Km

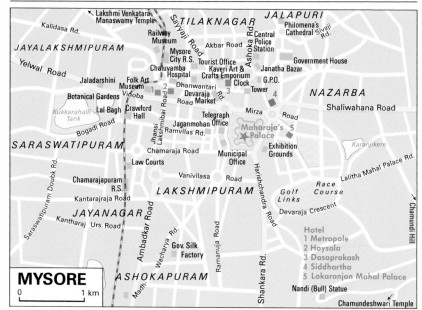

MYSORE

0      1 km

*howdah* that kings once used during processions, gives a taste of the splendid lifestyle of the Wodeyar rulers of Mysore. The ten-day festival of *Dussehra* (October), held with pomp in Vijayanagar times, has survived and is still a great attraction. A spectacular procession goes on parade, to the accompaniment of music, dancing and fireworks.

The Wodeyars of Mysore were devoted to the Goddess Camundesvari, enshrined in a hill called the **Camundi Hill** (13 km/8 mi). Halfway up the hill is the gigantic monolithic Nandi, the bull, ca. 5 m (16 ft) high. There is also a 12th-century temple dedicated to the goddess. About 20 km (12 mi) from Mysore is the **Krishnaraja Sagar Dam** (or **Brindavan Gardens**), a popular tourist spot.

Tipu Sultan was the terror of the British for nearly 20 years before he was killed by them in 1799. He had his capital at **Srirangapattinam**, 15 km(9 mi) from Mysore. Srirangapattinam is located on an island formed by the Kaveri river and has a temple dedicated to Vishnu in his reclining form. Tipu's fortress, **Darya Daulat**, and his summer palace emphasize his greatness. This palace, with ornate arches, has mural paintings depicting Tipu, his father Hyder Ali and many episodes connected with their lives. The tomb of Hyder Ali and the gardens are further places of interest.

For those interested in wildlife, **Nagarhole** (80 km/50 miles southwest of Mysore) and **Bandipur-Mudumalai** (80 km south of Mysore) are excellent sanctuaries for viewing elephants in particular. These moist deciduous jungles, famous for teak and rosewood, were once part of a gigantic forest tract belonging to the rulers of Mysore and Travancore.

### Sravanabelgola

This great center of Jain culture, noted for its colossal 20-m (66-ft) statue of

*Right: This star-shaped plan is unique to Hoysala temple architecture (Somnathpur - Keshava).*

Gommatesvara carved out of a single block of stone, is situated about 170 km (106 mi) from Bangalore. The Mauryan Emperor Chandragupta and the Jain monk Bhadrabahu came here in the 3rd century B.C, and ever since it has remained a pilgrim center for the Jains. The smaller hill contains over 100 memorials (7th to 9h centuries A.D.) to those Jains who chose to seek voluntary death.

Over the centuries Jain *bastis* (temples) were also built; some, like the **Chavundaraya Basti**, are of historic interest. By the end of the 10th century, importance had shift-ed to the top of the large hill, where the statue was erected in A.D. 980 by Chavundaraya, a minister to the Ganga king, to fulfil a dream had by his mother.

This great figure, visible from over 15 km (4 mi) away, was provided with an enclosure and railing in the 12th century. Once in 12 years the great Gommatesvara is given a ceremonial libation which attracts thousands of devotees from all parts of India.

On the west coast of Karnataka is another Jain center, **Mudbidri**, where a magnificent 1000-pillared Jain temple was built in the 15th century. For the past 2000 years or more Karnataka has remained the headquarters of the Jain faith in south India.

### Hoysala Extravaganza

The Hoysala temples are fascinating for their profuse and intricate carvings; no other group of Indian temples is as exuberantly carved. Between the years 1125 and 1225, the Hoysala rulers built over 100 temples. The most important ones are all located near Hassan and easily accessible by road from Mysore and Bangalore.

**Somnathpur**, 30 km (19 mi) from Mysore, is a good introduction to the group. The **Kesava Temple** dedicated to Vishnu was built by Somanatha, a Hoysala prime minister, in the 13th century. The Hoysalas built temples with single, twin or triple *sanctum* towers, the last two being a specialty. The Kesava Temple of Somnathpur has triple towers. The carvings from the base upwards, of majestic elephants, speeding horses and soldiers on the march create a tremendous sense of lively movement through space along the sacred clock-wise path. At eye level are the images of gods and goddesses bedecked with flowing garments and jewelry. These carvings complement the unique star-shaped layout of the temple. Usually ancient Indian art remains anonymous, but here the names of several artists are engraved.

**Hassan** (180 km/112 miles from Bangalore) forms a convenient base from which to visit the Hoysala temples at **Halebid** and **Belur**. Called Dvarasamudra or Dvaravatipura in ancient times, Halebid was the capital of the Hoysalas from the foundation of the empire in the 11th century until its fall in the 13th century. Here are Saiva, Vaishnav and Jain temples, most of them built in the 12th century. The most outstanding of these is the **Hoysalesvara Temple**, built by Ketamalla and his consort Kanchiyakka in A.D. 1125. It is even more elaborate than the temple at Somnathpur. The Hoysalesvara Temple had twin sanctum towers, though these have now disappeared. The sculpted figures include those of elephants, horses, swans, crocodiles and other animals and a row of musicians and dancers, topped by an impressive array of gods and goddesses. The stone used was of a soft variety that lent itself to intricate carving when originally quarried, and then later became hard. Experts consider that the Hoysalesvara Temple marks the height of artistic creation at the time.

There are over a dozen temples mentioned in records, and some of these still exist. They were obviously built by the same group of artists, whose chisels, it

seems, were never allowed to rest. Among these temples are the **Manikesvara Temple** (1136) and the **Kedaresvara Temple** on the western bank of the **Dvarasamudra Tank**. This temple had its tower until the 19th century, but vegetation and human neglect brought it down.

**Belur**, too, was a capital of the Hoysalas. The great Hoysala Vishnu Vardhana built the **Chenna Kesava Vishnu Temple** in A.D. 1117 and called it Vijaya Narayana. According to tradition, the king was a follower of the Jain faith, and was converted to Vaishnavism by the celebrated saint Ramanuja. This temple has a superbly carved entrance. Exuberant friezes of animals, riders, gods and goddesses appear here, too. The ceiling of the hall is exquisite, and so are the carved brackets. The names of artists are engraved, including that of Jakanachari, who was the architect of this temple.

### Hampi

**Hampi**, one of the magnificent ruined cities of the world, is a totally different experience for travelers. Here, the visual impact of the wildly beautiful landscape is as overpowering as the ruins. The town nearest to Hampi is **Hospet** (14 km/9 mi), on the site of the Tungabhadra dam. The history of this capital city of the Vijayanagar empire goes back to the age of the *Ramayana*. The dramatic site, with hills on both sides of the Tungabhadra river, is believed to be Kishkinda, the country of the monkey king. It is here that Rama met Hanuman, the great monkey, and Sugriva, the monkey king. The river site is called Pampatira, and the place has been considered sacred since time immemorial. It was raised to the status of a city, first named Vidyapuri, the city of learning. It was called Vijayanagar, the city of victory, around 1336, when two brothers, Harihara and Bukka, at the suggestion of the sage Vi-

*Right: The gopuram of the Virupaksha Temple, Hampi, stands in a boulder-strewn landscape.*

dyaranya, established this as their capital to defend the Hindu faith and institutions from the fierce onslaught of Islam. It did so admirably for 250 years, and the survival of the Hindu faith in the south owes much to Vijayanagar. Krishnadevaraya was acknowledged as the greatest among the rulers of Vijayanagar.

At the height of its glory Hampi was visited by travelers from Persia, Russia, Portugal and Italy, and they have left accounts of its splendors, "the like of which the eyes have never seen, and the ears have never heard." It was destroyed in 1565 by the combined forces of the Deccani Sultans, who mercilessly slew more than 100,000 inhabitants and pillaged the city for six months.

The remains of the ancient city are spread over a vast area of 26 km (16 mi), which now includes a number of villages. (It is advisable to hire a taxi from Hospet; bicycles are also available at Kamalapur village, near Hampi.) But the main ruins are found on the right bank of the River Tungabhadra. Recent studies have estab-

lished three well-defined zones: the sacred center on the rocky outcrop with a number of temples, some dating from the 8th and 9th centuries; the urban core with its fortifications separated from the sacred center by irrigation canals and a lovely valley of green fields; and the royal zone, consisting of the remains of palaces, audience halls, ceremonial platforms, tanks, watch towers and stables, within walled enclosures. The city was built in stages, but in accordance with an original plan. A number of monuments are worth visiting.

The **Vittala Temple** is an excellent example of the Vijayanagar school. A structure of particular interest is a small, perfectly proportioned chariot-like building, which originally had a superstructure. It once housed a Garuda, the eagle mount of Vishnu, to whom the main temple is dedicated. To the southwest of the temple is a lofty stone structure, called the king's balance. The rulers used to weigh themselves against gold and jewels which were then distributed to the learned and poor. A temple dedicated to Krishna was built by Krishnadevaraya in 1510. On the entrance tower are stucco figures, some of which portray the king, and battle scenes. Now in ruins, it is said to have been built by the ruler to house an image of Krishna, brought from Udayagiri in Orissa. Two other edifices deserve a visit: a huge monolithic Ganesh enshrined in a temple, south of Hemakuta hill, and the impressive image of Vishnu in his lion incarnation, Narasimha, with his consort Lakshmi. This sculpture was installed by Krishnadevaraya in 1528.

Nearer to the royal seat is the celebrated **Hazara Rama Temple**, with its scenes from the *Ramayana* and *Mahabharata*, and figures of dancers and fighters carved on the walls of the enclosure. In the royal zone, the most striking structure is the immense platform called the **Mahanavami Dibba**, or the royal seat, from where the king witnessed the *Mahanavami* celebrations. The platform affords an overwhelming view of the grand coloanaded halls, a recently exposed stepped tank of enormous dimensions, the aqueduct supported on stone pillars, the prince's quarters, the mint, the noblemen's quarters, the women's apartments and other remains unearthed recently. Close by are the **Lotus Mahal** and the elephant stable. Abdur Ruzzak, who was a witness to the *Dussehra* festival in 1443, wrote: "During three consecutive days from sunrise to sunset, the royal festival was prolonged in a style of the greatest magnificence. Fireworks, games, amusements went on. The throne which was of extraordinary size, was made of gold and enriched with precious stones of extreme value. In pursuance of orders issued by the king of Vijayanagar, the generals and principal personages from all parts of his empire presented themselves at the palace. They brought

with them a thousand elephants, which were covered with brilliant armor, and camels magnificently adorned."

The living center of Hampi is the **Virupaksha Temple**, dating to the 9th century, and still in use. Its lofty tower was built by Krishnadevaraya in A.D. 1510. The temple is dedicated to Siva who was the family deity of the Vijayanagar emperors. It remains a pilgrim center.

### Badami, Pattadakal and Aihole

In northern Karnataka is the 6th century capital of **Badami**, fortified by nature and the Chalukyan king Pulakesin I. A lake, nestling in the midst of rocky hills, lends an extraordinary beauty to Badami. On the face of the hill, which rises steeply at the southern edge of the lake, there are four caves in a row, scooped out of rock, in the tradition of architecture associated with later structures at Ajanta and Ellora. The caves have rectangular halls with shrines at the rear and a porch in front. The carvings on the brackets and the ceilings, and the great sculptures of the dancing Siva, of Vishnu measuring the universe, of Durga piercing the buffalo-headed demon and of Vishnu in his boar incarnation, are among the best in India. The first two caves are dedicated to Siva, the third to Vishnu and the fourth to Jain saints. The last, of inferior workmanship, is believed to have been excavated later than the others. The Vishnu cave bears an inscription, dating it to the late 6th century.

Across the lake is a group of temples, and the **Melegitti Sivalaya**, worth a visit, is on the hilltop. The **Museum** at Badami houses sculptures of interest, among which is a lovely image of a seated nude goddess with a lotus head. Such figures have been found all over India, dating from the first century B.C. to medieval times. Opposite the Museum is a boulder with the Pallava 7th century inscription of Mamalla I, relating to the sack of Va-

*Right: Mysore's maharaja palace in Indo-Saracene style, built in 1911/12.*

tapi (Badami). In the village is an old mosque and Tipu Sultan's treasury.

The cluster of temples at **Pattadakal** (30 km/19 miles from Badami) is situated on the banks of the Malaprabha river. The number of temples indicates that this was obviously once a place of tremendous importance. According to experts, this is where all the Chalukya emperors were crowned. The name Pattadakkal seems to suggest this too. All the temples here were raised by the Chalukya rulers; some are in the southern tradition, while others have northern curvilinear towers. A few temples are precisely dated.

The **Sangamesvara** was constructed in A.D. 750 by Vijayaditya. The **Virupaksha Temple** was built by Loka-mahadevi, the queen of Vikramaditya, to commemorate the king's victorious expedition to the Pallava capital of Kanchi. It is believed that Pallava artists, brought here after the conquest of Kanchi, worked on this temple, for it bears close resemblance to the Kailasanatha Temple of Kanchi. The name of the architect Sar-

vasiddhi Achari, who built the temple, is inscribed on the wall. This temple is the finest, with exceptionally beautiful sculptures, a Nandi Mandapa and an impressive courtyard. Its beauty is enhanced by the Malaprabha river, running close to its entrance. A view of the temples from across the river heightens appreciation of Chalukyan sensitivity to space and form.

**Aihole** (20 km/12 miles from Pattadakal) has numerous Jain and Hindu temples, which range in style from simple cave temples to free-standing structures. A few of these are well worth seeing. The excavated cave temple **Ravala Padi**, though simple externally, houses one of the finest groups of Siva sculptures which show the powerful deity dancing in the midst of eight mothers. The **Ladkhan Temple** is considered to be the earliest of the surviving structures because of its archaic plan and elevation. But the most impressive is the **Durga Temple**, apsidal in plan with a remarkable group of sculptures, mostly of Vishnu.

## Muslim Legacy

About 120 km (75 mi) north of Aihole is **Bijapur** which bears witness to the Muslim presence in the Deccan. The kingdom of Bijapur was founded by Yusuf Adil Shah in the 15th century. Bijapur has a distinctly Muslim flavor. The city is dotted with monuments that were raised by the rulers of Bijapur during the 16th and 17th centuries. They stand out in stark contrast to the more exuberant creations of the Hoysalas, but are no less beautiful in their islamic austerity.

The **Gol Gumbaz**, the mausoleum of Mohammad Adil Shah built in 1659, is famous for having the second largest dome in the world. This dome rises above an immense hall that is 1704 sq. m (2038 sq. yd) in area.

However, more beautiful than this majestic monument is the delicate **Ibrahim**

*Above: Keeping a place clean can be a full-time occupation (Brindaran Gardens, Mysore).*

**Roza**, built by Ibrahim Adil Shah II for his queen Taj Sultana. The **Jami Masjid** and the **Asar Mahal**, or the Hall of Justice, are other buildings of interest. A ruined citadel surrounded by fortifications is located in the heart of the city. The **Gagan Mahal** (1501) and the **Jal Manzil**, or water pavilion, within the citadel give an indication of the original scale and beauty of this place. Bijapur is also well known for the **Malik-e-Maidan**, a 55-tonne cannon used in historic battles. It bears inscriptions, one of them attributed to Aurangzeb.

**Gulbarga**, 150 km (93 mi) northeast of Bijapur, was the capital of the Bahmani kingdom in the 14th century. Within the ruined fort is the **Jami Masjid,** built in imitation of the great mosque at Cordoba, Spain. It is unique with its several domes. **Bidar**, 160 km (94 mi) further northeast, was also the capital of the Bahmani kingdom. Other impressive buildings within the 15th-century fort include the **Chini Mahal** and the **Turkish Mahal**. Both merit a visit.

## BANGALORE
### Accommodation
*LUXURY:* **Hotel Ashok Radison**, Kumara Krupa High Grounds, Tel: 269462/82. **Oberoi**, Mahatma Ghandi Rd., Tel: 573444, 567767/68. **West End Hotel**, Race Course Road, Tel: 264191/92, 269281. **Windsor Manor**, 25 Sankey Road, Tel:269898. *MODERATE:* **Blue Fox**, Mahatma Ghandi Rd., Tel: 587608. **Curzon Court**, Brigade Rd., Tel: 580716, 582997. **Woodlands**, 5 Sampige Tank Road, Tel: 225111.
*BUDGET:* **YMCA** (for families only), 57 Millers Road, Tel: 575885. **YWCA Guest House**, 86 Infantry Rd., Tel: 570997. **YWCA**, 32 Mission Road, Tel: 228574. **Youth Hostel**, 25 Gangadhara Chetty Road, Opp. Ajanta-Lakshmi Theatres, Tel: 611292, 569943.

### Museums / Art Galleries
**Government Museum and Venkatappa Art Gallery**, Kasturba Road, Tel: 564483. Open 9 am-5 pm, closed Wednesdays.

### Restaurants
*CHINESE:* **Blue Heaven**, Church St., Tel: 561796. **Copper Bowl**, 28 M.G. Rd., Tel: 565397. **Nanking**, Grant Rd. *CONTINENTAL:* **Blue Fox**, 80 M.G. Rd. **Casa Picolo**, Residency Rd. **Fiesta**, MSIL Complex, opp. HAL Airport. *MUGHLAI:* **Roomali**, Church St. **Royal Afghan**, Hotel Windsor Manor, Sankey Rd. **Kwality**, Brigade Rd. *SOUTH INDIAN:* **Amaravathi**, Residency Rd. **Brindavan Hotel**, M.G. Road.

### Tourist Information
**Government of India Tourist Office**, KFC Bldg., 48 Church St., Tel: 579517. **Government of Karnataka Tourist Office**, 9 St. Mark's Rd., Tel: 579139. Tourist Information at Bangalore Airport, Tel: 571467, and on M.G. Road, Tel: 572377.

### Access / Local Transport
*AIR:* Bangalore and Mysore, Belgaum, Mangalore and Bellary are serviced by airlines. Mysore is connected to Bangalore, Bellary, Hyderabad and Tirupati by Vayudoot flights. For Hampi, the nearest airport is Bellary (74 km) and for Aihole, Badami, Pattadkal and Bijapur it is Belgaun (189 km).
*RAIL:* Trains run from Mysore to Arsikere, Bangalore and Hassan. Bangalore is connected by rail to nearly all the important cities in the country.

## MYSORE
### Accommodation
*LUXURY:* **Lalitha Mahal Palace Hotel**, T. Narsipur Rd., Tel: 26316.
*MODERATE:* **Metropole**, 5 Jhansi Lakshmibai Rd., Tel: 31916, 31967. **Dasaprakash Paradise**, 105, Vivekananda Rd., Yadavagiri, Tel: 25555, 27777. **Quality Inn Southern Star**, 13 Vinobha Rd., Tel: 27217-21.

*BUDGET:* **Arathi**, Ooty Rd., Tel: 20377. **Indra Vihar**, opp. Mysore Zoo, Tel: 20232. **Kiron Lodge**, Shyam Sundar Theatre Complex, Tel: 24753. **Siddhartha**, 73/1 Government Guest House Road, Nazarbad, Tel: 26869.

### Museums / Art Galleries
**Folklore Museum**, University of Mysore, Manasa Gangotri, Tel: 22525. Open 10.30 am-5.30 pm, closed on 2nd Sat and Sun. The **Jayachamarajendra Art Gallery** is part of the Museum. **Rail Museum**, K.R.S. Road. Open 10 am-1 pm, 3-5 pm, closed Mon. Railway engines, coaches and signals.

### Restaurants
*CHINESE:* **Chiang**, Shyam Sunder Theatre Complex. *VEGETARIAN:* **Dasaprakash**, Gandhi Square. **Yatrik**, Opp. Zoological Gardens. **Indra Bhavan**, Sayyaji Rao Road. *CONTINENTAL:* **Gun House Imperial**, Bangalore-Nilgiri Road.

### Tourist Information
**Tourist Information Bureau**, Old Exhibition Bldg., Irwin Rd., Tel: 22096. **Archeological Survey of India**, Mysore Palace Complex, Tel: 22672.

### Festivals
**January-February-March-April**: *Car Festival* at Srirangapatnam (16 km from Mysore). *Banashankari Temple Festival* near Badami. *Purandaradasa Aradhana* near Vittala Temple (Hampi). The *Virupaksh Temple (Hampi) Car Festival.* (The same site celebrates the marriage of Lord Virupaksha and Pampa in **December**). Also in Pattadkal (29 km from Badami). *Siddheswara Temple Festival* (Bijapur). *Car Festival* of Ramalinga Temple at the banks of Malaprabha river (Aihole). The *Karaga* festival is celebrated in Bangalore. Annual *Car Festival* at Chennakesava Temple (Belur). **September-December:** The 10-day *Dussehra Festival* (Sept-Oct) is held in Mysore. A *Float Festival* and a *Car Festival* are celebrated at the Chamundeswari Temple (atop Chamundi Hills, 13 km from Mysore) during *Dussehra.* The *Groundnut Fair* takes place in November at the Bull Temple (Bangalore).

### Accommodation
**BIJAPUR: Hotel Mayura Adil Shahi** (KSTDC), Anand Mahal Road. Tel: 934, 401.
**BADAMI: Hotel Mayura Chalukya** (KSTDC), Ramdurg Road. Tel: 46.
**HOSPET** (for visits to Hampi): **KSTDC Bungalow**, Tungabhadra Dam Site.
**BELUR: Hotel Mayura Velapuri** (KSTDC), Tel: 9.
**HASSAN: Hotel Hassan Ashok**, B.M. Road. Tel: 8731. **KSTDC Guest House**, Tel: 8406 and **Traveler's Bungalow**, Tel: 8437, on B.M. Road.
**HALEBID: Tourist Cottages** and a **Traveler's Bungalow**. Alternately stay at Hassan (31 km) or Belur (16 km).

# ANDHRA PRADESH

Andhra Pradesh (275,000 sq. km or 106,177 sq. mi) lies in the heart of the geographically ancient Deccan. The state can be broadly divided into three main regions: Telengana, which covers the hilly areas north of the river Godavari; the deltaic tract spanning the estuaries of the Krishna and Godavari; and the hinterland, where the rocky plateau is split by hot dry valleys. Telegu, which came into its own in the 4th century A.D., is still the main language of the people, although since the advent of Muslim rule in the 14th century, Urdu is also spoken by a section of the people who follow Islam.

Telegu is a Dravidian language, with a greater admixture of Sanskrit than either Tamil or Kannada. Hailed as a sweet language by eminent poets, it has a particularly musical quality. The geographical location of Andhra has to a large extent determined its history and culture, allowing the people to benefit from traditions of both the north and the south. Despite its strong Dravidian base, Andhra was once a major center of Buddhism, and more recently of Muslim rule.

## Hyderabad

**Hyderabad**, the capital of Andhra, rose to prominence in the 17th century when the fourth Qutb Shahi ruler, Muhammad Quli Qutb Shah, created a new capital near Golconda and named it after his queen, Hyder Mahal. In 1687, Golconda was captured by the Mughal emperor Aurangzeb. Confusion followed the death of the emperor, and in 1725 his viceroy, Asaf Jah, set himself up as Nizam. Using Hyderabad as his seat of power, he ruled over a vast area which included parts of Karnataka and Maharash-

*Preceding pages: The Qutb Shahi tombs at Hyderabad.*

tra. The city gradually replaced Delhi as the center of Muslim India, and drew a steady stream of fortune seekers from other parts of the Muslim world. A 19th century traveler likened the city to a "flower bed crowded with men and women in bright dresses and with a fine, cheerful air of independence, more Arab than Indian.... Many men carry swords in their hands; one can see elephants and camels in the streets besides carriages and men on horseback."

The sixth Nizam, Mahboob Ali Shah, enthroned in 1869, was known to be one of the richest men in the world, and eccentric too, fulfilling such whims as having his clothes laundered in Paris. He had his own stock of tigers and more than 1500 km (932 mi) of private railways, facilities which impressed kings and dukes who came here from all over the world.

Closely associated with the British, the Nizam alone among the Indian princes was granted the title of His Exalted Highness by them. While most of the princely states voluntarily joined the Indian union after independence, the eighth and last Nizam had to be forced to do so.

Hyderabad became the capital of Andhra Pradesh when the states were reorganized on a linguistic basis. The twin cities of Hyderabad and Secunderabad are separated only by the **Hussain Sagar Lake**. **Secunderabad** was originally a cantonment area, where the British Residents lived.

The most prominent landmark of Hyderabad is the **Charminar**. This ceremonial archway was built by the founder of the city to commemorate the end of the plague in 1593. Rising to 60 m (197 ft), it affords fine views of the city. Its architecture is typical of the Qutb Shahi style. Nearby is the main mosque of the city, the **Mecca Masjid**. It was begun by Qutb Quli Shah in 1614 but was completed only in 1687, and is one of the biggest mosques in the world. The **tombs of the Nizams** of Hyderabad are close by.

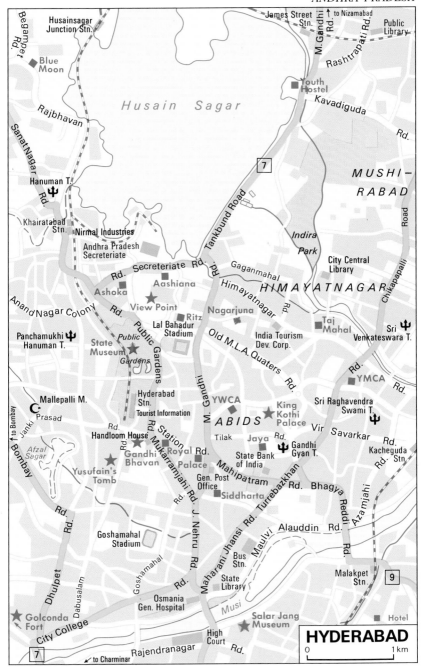

Begampet Rd.

Husainsagar Junction Stn.

James Street Stn.

M. Gandhi Rd. ↑ to Nizamabad

Public Library

Blue Moon

Rajbhavan

*Husain Sagar*

Youth Hostel

Kavadiguda

Rd.

7

MUSHI–RABAD

Sanat Nagar Rd.

Hanuman T.

Rashtrapati Rd.

Road

Khairatabad Stn.

Nirmal Industries

Andhra Pradesh Secreteriate

Tankbund Road

Indira Park

City Central Library

Secreteriate Rd.

Rd.

Gaganmahal

HIMAYATNAGAR

Chikapapalli

Ashoka

Aashiana

Himayatnagar

Rd.

Anand Nagar Colony

Rd.

View Point

Ritz

Nagarjuna

Taj Mahal

Sri Venkateswara T.

Panchamukhi Hanuman T.

Lal Bahadur Stadium

Old M.L.A. Quaters

India Tourism Dev. Corp.

State Museum

Public Gardens

Rd.

YMCA

Rd.

Mallepalli M.

Prasad

Hyderabad Stn.

Tourist Information

M. Gandhi

YWCA

ABIDS

King Kothi Palace

Sri Raghavendra Swami T.

Vir Savarkar

Rd.

↑ to Bombay

Janki

Afzal Sagar

Rd.

Handloom House

Station Rd.

Mukarramjahi Rd.

Royal Palace

Tilak

Jaya

Rd.

Gandhi Gyan T.

Kacheguda Stn.

Rd.

Azamjahi

Bombay

Yusufain's Tomb

Gandhi Bhavan

State Bank of India

Mahipatram

Rd.

Bhagya Reddi

Rd.

Gen. Post Office

Siddharta

Turrebazkhan

Rd.

Maharani Jhansi Rd.

Alauddin Rd.

Dhulpet

Goshamahal Stadium

Goshamahal

J. Nehru Rd.

Maulvi

Bus Stn.

Malakpet Stn.

9

Dabusalam

Osmania Gen. Hospital

Rd.

State Library

Musi

■ Hotel

Golconda Fort

City College

Rajendranagar

High Court Rd.

Salar Jang Museum

**HYDERABAD**

0   1 km

↙ to Charminar

7

At the top of a hill, 4 km (2.5 mi) from the Charminar, is the **Falaknuma Palace** (now a museum) built during the time of the sixth Nizam. It is said that several shops in Europe were emptied to adorn its extravagant interiors. However, the city is more famous for the **Salar Jung Museum**, named after a great lover of antiquities. When Salar Jung I bought the Benzoni sculpture, "The Veiled Rachael", in 1867, he started one of the largest collections of objets d'art in the world. It grew over the course of three generations to a staggering 35,000 objects which include Marie Antoinette's dressing table, Nur Jahan's jeweled dagger and a selection of Deccani miniature paintings, textiles and manuscripts.

The **Osmania University** is an important center for the study of Urdu, Arabic and Persian. The bazaars of Hyderabad are fascinating to wander through, especially in the area around the Charminar. *Ikat* textiles, Poccampalli and Venkatagiri sarees, *bidri*-ware (silver, finely set in bell-metal), stone bangles and lacquered Kondapalli dolls are among the specialties.

The city has also been famous for its pearls since the time of the Qutb Shahi rulers. The main pearl market is at **Patherghatty Road**. Initially, pearls were brought from Basra for grading, but now they come mainly from Japan. Not surprisingly, the city has a number of antique shops. It is also associated with an evolved cuisine, and the excellent quality of its seedless grapes. A tribe of gypsies, known as Banjaras, frequent the city. Originally, Banjaras supplied provisions to medieval armies. Though their means of livelihood have changed they continue to dress in an exotic manner.

**Golconda** (11 km) was the capital of the Qutb Shahi dynasty, founded by the Turkoman Sultan Qutb Quli Shah. He was the governor of Telengana under the

*Above: The Charminar, Hyderabad's landmark and city center. Right: The solid bastions of Golkonda Fort near Hyderabad.*

Bahmani kingdom, when, in 1512, he declared himself independent and established Golconda as his capital. It remained the capital until the founding of Hyderabad. Though a few structures date to earlier Hindu dynasties, most of the monuments in and around the formidable **Golconda Fort** belong to Qutb Shahi times. Here, the last Qutb Shahi king held out against Aurangzeb for seven months, before being defeated through treachery. The mosques, pavilions and tombs are characterized by large ornamental façades, bulbous domes and minarets decorated with stucco work. Experts discern Iranian features in their design and execution, especially in the delicately patterned colored tiles and intricate mother of pearl inlay.

Of the many tombs, that of Abdullah Qutb Shah is the best. Golconda is also famous for the diamonds it has yielded, among them the Orloff, the Regent and the historic Kohinoor diamonds. It is worth setting aside half a day for a visit to this historic fort.

### Warangal

**Warangal** (120 km/75 miles northeast of Hyderabad) was known as Ekasilanagar in ancient times. It was the capital of the Kakatiya dynasty from the 12th to the 14th centuries, after which it came under the control of the Tughlaqs of Delhi. There are two remarkable groups of monuments here, including some temples and an interesting fort. At **Hanmokonda** is the 1000-pillared temple that was erected around A.D. 1160 by Pratapa Rudra. It consists of a triple shrine of great magnitude, built over a platform, and connected to a common central hall. Interestingly, the three shrines are dedicated to Siva, Vishnu, and Surya, the sun god. The hall with 300 richly carved pillars is most fascinating. The other interesting monument at Warangal is the **Fort**, with four ornamental gateways of remarkable beauty. But a far more beautiful temple is the **Ramappa Temple** at **Palampet** (60 km/37 miles). This temple is reminiscent of the Hoysala extrava-

ganza at Belur. The carved figures of elegantly poised dancing girls recall the great heights to which the art of dance was taken in the Kakatiya court. It is here that Jaya, a minister to the Kakatiya ruler, wrote *Nrittaratnavali*, a treatise on dance which has survived to this day. The figures at the temple seem to illustrate the forms and poses outlined in the book.

### Vijayawada

**Vijayawada** is one of the major towns of Andhra Pradesh. In medieval times it was called Rajendra Cholapuram, after Rajendra I. The town is surrounded by many hillocks, the most prominent being the **Kanaka Durga Hill** and the **Sitanagaram**. The goddess Kanaka Durga and Lord Mallesvara Siva are held in great esteem by the people of Andhra. Recently,

*Above: The water buffalo is an ever-present feature of the Indian landscape. Right: A temple elephant collecting donations by blessing devotees with his trunk.*

a remarkable panel, assigned to the third century, depicting a row of gods and goddesses, a *linga* and a standing goddess with lotus head, was found on the Kanaka Durga hill, which takes the artistic history of this region back to a much earlier date than had been estimated.

Vijayawada and its neighborhood boast some cave temples like the Pallava caves of Mamallapuram, on the north bank of the river at **Mogalrajapuram** (3 km/1,5 miles east of Vijayawada), in Vijayawada and at **Undevilli** in the Guntur district, where Vishnu is enshrined in his reclining form. They seem to have been excavated in the 6th century, and the soft rock has left the sculptures in a weathered condition. Most of the caves are Saivite, the **Akkanna Madanna** cave at Vijayawada is considered the earliest of them.

### Nagarjunkonda and Amaravati

**Nagarjunkonda** and **Amaravati** were two of the finest Buddhist centers of the

ancient world, flourishing between the 3rd century B.C. and the 3rd century A.D. Amaravati, which had, among other Buddhist structures, a superbly carved marble stupa (first century A.D.), was pillaged by building contractors in the 1890s. The parts that escaped destruction are now housed in the Madras Museum, and in the Victoria and Albert Museum in London.

Further up the Krishna river is **Nagarjuna Sagar**, about 170 km (106 mi) from Hyderabad and Vijayawada. A valley surrounded by hills on three sides was called **Nagarjunkonda** after the great Buddhist philosopher Nagarjuna, who lived in the 2nd century A.D. As Vijayapuri, it was the capital of the Ikshuvaku dynasty which was to displace the Satavahanas in the 3rd century A.D., and who ruled this region for over 150 years. The Iskhuvakus were Hindus, and they built temples to Siva, Vishnu and Kartikeya. Excavations have revealed a well-laid-out capital with a palace surrounded by ramparts and an impressive bathing

ghat. It had a residential area, a shopping complex and an amphitheater which could accommodate 1000 spectators. Experts consider that this was probably inspired by Roman tradition. It encloses a rectangular area for music and dance. There was also a public assembly hall and a burning ghat.

However, Nagarjunkonda is better known for its Buddhist past. This site, one of the greatest archaeological sites in the country, was first discovered in 1926, and excavated over a long period of time. Before the waters of the gigantic **Nagarjuna Sagar Dam** (the largest masonry dam in the world) could submerge this area, a massive salvage operation was undertaken and a considerable part of the remains was removed and reassembled in a museum on top of the hill.

There were more than 30 Buddhist establishments in Nagarjunkonda. The **Mahachaitya**, built by queen Chandasiri, contained one of the relics of the Buddha. There was a great monastery, and smaller ones housing monks of different Buddhist sects. Some of the *chityas* (prayer halls) housed images of the Buddha, while others, following the Hinayana school, enshrined symbols of the Buddha. The sculptures, dating mostly from the 3rd and 4th centuries A.D., and relics found here are displayed in the island museum, where the site has been reconstructed. Besides Brahminical and Buddhist finds, Nagarjunkonda has yielded finely sculpted and inscribed pillars, called *Chayasthambhas,* which were erected as memorials to dead kings, queens, artisans or religious persons.

## Masulipattanam

The coastal town of **Masulipattanam** is renowned for its *Kalamkari*, a hand-painted textile. This textile was one of the greatest attractions for 17th-century western traders who knew it as chintz, and for which there was a great demand. The cotton has to be treated initially with mordant before applying color. As a *kalam* (pen) is used in this technique, it came to be called *Kalamkari*. The colors used are vegetable dyes. From very early times Masulipattanam produced the finest examples of this cloth. The Mughal Emperor Aurangzeb had the interiors of his tents tastefully decorated with chintz from Masulipattanam. Persian traders of the 17th century placed their orders with the artists of Masulipattanam. Many European experts in the 17th and 18th centuries observed and documented the creation of these textiles, and many western museums count *Kalamkari* textiles from Masulipattanam among their priceless exhibits. Though technology has greatly changed much of the way of life, there are still families of artists in Masulipattanam who produce *Kalamkari* textiles in the same traditional way their forefathers

*Right: A charming and colorful Banjara tribal woman.*

did. The designs are traditional, often depicting scenes from popular epics like the *Ramayana* and *Mahabharata.*

Further up the coast from Masulipattanam, mostly near **Rajahmundry**, developed the concept of *Pancaramas* – five temples – dedicated to Siva. These temples are located at **Amaravati**, **Draksharama**, **Samalakot**, **Bhimavaram** and **Chebrolu**. Beyond the port of **Visakhapatnam** is the **Srikakulam** district, which was part of ancient Kalinga (Orissa). The **Madhukesvara Temple**, dating from the 8th century, is the most important one in the district, and closely resembles the temples at Bhubaneswar.

## Srisailam

Known as Srisailam, Sriparvatam or Sri Kailasa, this sacred hill (130 km/81 mi from Kurnool) has been a pilgrim center for Saivites of different orders from time immemorial. It is referred to in the *Mahabharata* and all the great legends (*Mahapuranas*). Srisailam was also a center of Buddhism in ancient times; the Chinese travelers Fa Hsein and Hsuan Tsang associated this place with the famous Buddhist philosopher Nagarjuna. The temple on the hill, dedicated to Mallikarjuna, was extolled by the Tamil Saivite saints in the 7th century. In the past, all the great rulers of the region have paid personal visits to this hill and left offerings, especially the Vijayanagar emperor Krishnadevaraya. The Chenchu tribes of Andhra consider Mallikarjuna their own special deity. Located in the Kurnool district of Andhra, this picturesque hill rises on the southern bank of the Krishna river, known here as the Patala Ganga, the "Ganga of the nether region."

The **Ahobilam Hill**, 140 km (87 mi) southeast of Kurnool, is dedicated to Vishnu in his lion incarnation, Narasimha. The hilltop shrine has an image standing in a natural cleft in the rock, and is considered a self-manifest deity. The

shrine at the foot of the hill houses Narasimha with his consort, Lakshmi. According to the Hindu faith, Narasimha is a powerful deity, capable of bestowing success in all our endeavors. The temple was used for worship even before the 10th century. In the 14th century, the Kakatiya ruler had a metal image consecrated to carry in processions.

### The Hinterland

**Hemavati**, in the Anantapur district, is generally not included in the itinerary of most tourists, as the village is somewhat difficult to reach. Hemavati was the capital of the Nolamba Pallava dynasty, a branch of the Pallavas that rose to prominence in the 9th and 10th centuries A.D. Though the number of monuments

left by them is limited, the quality of their workmanship is excellent. Their temples are not great from the architectural point of view, but the sculptures are marvelous works of art. The exuberant Hoysala style seems to have received its inspiration from this school.

**Lepakshi**, near Anantapur, is known for the best Vijayanagar murals of the 16th century. The paintings are preserved in the **Virabhadra Temple**, built in the middle of the 16th century. It has three shrines, connected to a central hall, where paintings depict scenes from the epics and portraits of the builders.

### Thirupati

The religious ethos of Andhra Pradesh is enshrined in **Thirupati**, dedicated to Vishnu as Venkatesa. This most celebrated pilgrim center can easily be reached from Madras, by air, rail or road. The temple has been in existence for over 2000 years, and is referred to in the Tamil epic *Silappadhikaram*. The hill is be-

*Above: A flower-laden bridegroom at a Muslim wedding, Hyderabad. Right: Hyderabad is also famous for its wonderful pearls.*

136

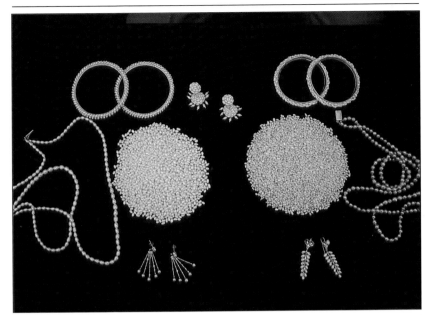

lieved to be the glorious mythical mountain Meru, and said to represent seven peaks. Here, Vishnu is adored as "the Lord of Seven Hills." There are two temples, one at the top of the hill, the other at the foot of the hill; the former is more venerated. Epigraphs from the time of the Pallavas have been found, and the Cholas are known to have contributed to the temple. However, the Vijayanagar rulers were those most closely associated with it. The superstructure was covered with gold in A.D. 1570 by the royal priest of the Vijayanagar ruler, an act that has often been repeated.

Most of the structures, such as the entrance towers and the pillared pavilions, were built in the Vijayanagar age. The Vijayanagar emperors lavished an enormous amount of wealth and jewels on it, and arranged festivals and details of worship that continue to this day. The Vijayanagar emperor Krishnadevaraya, who paid two visits to this temple, donated large quantities of jewelry and gold. In fact, he even issued a special gold currency, bearing the figure of Lord Venkateswara on one side and his own name on the other.

Ramanuja, the great Vaishnavite reformer, is intimately associated with Thirupati. The temple now houses a museum. The architecture and sculpture is splendid, however, it is the faith of the people that is powerfully manifested here. The Thirupati Temple is the richest Hindu temple in the country, and devotees offer their hair here as an act of devotion, making it a major center for the export of hair.

Not far from Thirupati is the village of **Gudimallam**, famous for the earliest *linga* (first century B.C.) in its phallic form, which is still worshiped today.

**Srikalahasti**, 30 km (19 mi) from Thirupati, is an ancient Saivite center between two steep hills, on the banks of the river Swarnamukhi. The *linga* in the *sanctum* is the personification of one of the five basic elements, the wind. This place is particularly associated with Kannappan, an ancient hunter, who was devoted to Siva.

## HYDERABAD / SECUNDERABAD
### Accommodation
*LUXURY:* **Hotel Banjara**, 13 Banjara Hills, Tel: 222222. **The Krischan Oberoi**, Road No. 1, Banjara Hills, Hyderabad 500034, Tel: 22212, Fax: 223079.
*MODERATE:* **Ritz Hotel**, Hill Fort Palace, Tel: 233571. **Hotel Ashoka**, 6-1-70 Lakdikapul, Tel: 230105. **Hotel Nagarjuna**, 3-6-356/358 Basheer Bag, Tel: 237201. **Hotel Taj Mahal**, 4-1-999 Abid Road, Tel: 237988.
*BUDGET:* **YMCA**, Tel: 57850. **YWCA**, Tel: 53996. **Secunderabad Youth Hostel**, 5-4-203 Near Sailing Club, Secunderabad, Tel: 70087.

### Museums
**Salar Jung Museum**, Dar-ul-Shifa, Tel: 43211. Open 10 am-5 pm, closed Fri, public holidays. **Museum of Indian Art**, 1-2-214 Gagan Mahal Road, Tel: 61561. Open by appointment. Collection (private): miniatures, bronzes, terracotta, ivory. **Site Museum**, Qutb Shahi Tombs Complex, Golconda. Open 10.30 am-5 pm, closed Fri and public holidays. **State Museum**, Public Gardens, Tel: 32267. Open 10.30 am-5 pm, closed Mon and public holidays.

### Post / Telegraph / Telephone
**General Post Office**, Abid Rd., Tel: 57978. **Head Post Office**, R.P. Rd., Secunderabad, Tel: 72683. **Central Telegraph Office**, Abid Road and Mahatma Gandhi Road (Secunderabad).

### Restaurants
*INTERNATIONAL:* **Broadway**, Abid Rd., Tel: 230075, 231142. **The Country Club**, Begumket, Hyderabad, Tel: 212000 **Three Aces**, Abid Road, Tel: 222480. **Golden Gate**, 4-1-970 Abid Road, Tel: 232485 (with bar). **Manu Café**, 4-1-873 Tilak Rd., Tel: 233180. *VEGETARIAN:* **Daawat**, Hotel Basera, Tel: 823200. **Samtrupti**, Hotel Sampurna International, Tel: 90165.

### Festivals
The Muslim festival of *Id*, following the month-long fasting during Ramzan is celebrated in Hyderabad. Prayers are offered at mosques all over the state. The *tazia* processions on *Muharram* commemorate the martyrdom of the Prophet's grandsons. *Makar Sankranti* (January) is a three-day harvest festival when every household displays its collection of dolls. It is also the occasion for the *Batakamma* or *Bonalu* festival, exclusive to women. On the following day, *Kanumma*, cattle are worshiped statewide. Andhraites celebrate their new year on *Chaita Sudda Padyami* (March/April) and the birth of Lord Ram (*Ramnavami*) in April. The Hindu shrines scattered across the state are also sites of festivals. The 10-day *Kalyana Mahotsavam* is observed at Srisailam during *Mahashivratri*, the festival dedicated to Siva and celebrated in February/March.

### Shopping
Handicrafts include *Kalamkari* fabrics, silver filigree (from Karimnagar), *nirmal*-work on wood, lacquered toys (from Kondapalli), embroidered, mirror-worked bags and dresses of the Banjara tribespeople, handwoven textiles from Venkatagiri and Pochhampalli;,crochet work, *Himroo* silks and *bidri*-ware. Pearls, carpets from Warangal and ivory inlaid in wood can be bought at bargain prices. Main shopping areas are around the Charminar, Abid Rd., Basheerbagh, Sultan Bazaar and Nampally in Hyderabad; M.G. Road and Rashtrapati Road in Secunderabad. Also visit **Nirmal Industries**, Khairatabad, and **Handloom House**, Mukkaram Jahi Road.

### Tourist Information
**Government of India Tourist Office**, 2nd Floor, Sandozi Bldg., 26 Himayat Nagar, Tel: 66877. **Department of Tourism**, Government of Andhra Pradesh, 5th Floor, Gagan Vihar, M.G. Road, Tel: 557531-32. Counters at Begumpet Airport, Tel: 77192. Hyderabad Railway Station, Tel: 221352, and Secunderabad, Tel: 70144-5.

### Access / Local Transport
*AIR:* Indian Airlines connects Hyderabad to major cities in India, and to Jeddah in the Middle East. Vayudoot flies to Rajahmundhry, Ramagundam, Thirupati, Vijayawada, Visakhapatnam and Warangal. *RAIL / BUS:* Nagarjunsagar, Srisailam and Amravati are connected by bus. Macherla (29 km) and Kazipet are the convenient rail-heads for Nagarjunkonda and Warangal respectively.
*TOURS:* The Andhra Pradesh Tourism Travel Development Corporation organizes conducted tours to nearly all tourist centers and sights in the state and those outside it.

### Accommodation
#### VIJAYAWADA
**Kandhari International**, Labbipet, Bunder Rd., Tel: 471311. **Mamta Hotel**, Eluru Rd., Tel: 61251.

#### AMARAVATI
**Hotel Neelam**, Bandnera Road, Tel: 72647/73039. **Kazipet, Tourist Rest House**, 6 km from Warangal. (APTDC), Tel: 6201.

#### NAGARJUNKONDA
**Vijay Vihar Guest House,** Hill Colony. **River View Rest House** (Right Bank). **Tourist Annexe**. **Tourist Cottages** are also available.

#### VISAKAPATNAM
**Hotel Sun-N-Sea**, Beach Rd. **Hotel Palm Beach**, Waltair. **Hotel Marina**, Beach Road. **Park Hotel**, Beach Road, Visakhapatran 530023, Tel. 54181.

#### THIRUPATI
**Bhimas Deluxe Hotel**, 34-38 G. Car Street, Tirupati, Andhra Pradesh 517501, Tel: 20121 (4 lines). **Hotel Mayura**, 209, T.P. Area, Tirupati, A.P. 517501, Tel: 20901, 22866.

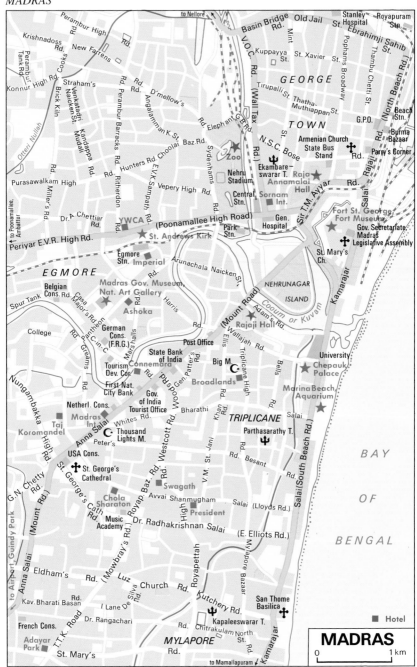

MADRAS

0        1 km

■ Hotel

# BASTION OF TRADITION

**MADRAS**
**TAMIL NADU**

## MADRAS

Madras, the fourth biggest city in the country, is the capital of Tamil Nadu. Originally consisting of several hamlets, later integrated into one city, it has witnessed phenomenal growth in the past few decades. Despite this, Madras has a relatively peaceful atmosphere, and its ambience is totally different from that of Bombay, Delhi or Calcutta.

The present city of Madras encompasses several ancient settlements of historic interest, and temples that are known to have been sanctified by the visits of Saivite saints and Vaishnavite Alvars in the 7th and 8h centuries A.D. **Thiruvan-miyur** in south Madras, **Mylapore** and **Triplicane** in central Madras and **Thiru-vorriyur** in the north are among the well-known settlements that have occupied pride of place in the religious and cultural history of Madras celebrated in literature. Except for Triplicane, which is a Vaishnavite center, the other three are Saivite centers of great fame. From about the 4th century A.D. to the 9th century, this region was ruled by the Pallavas, whose patronage is evident in lithic records that

*Preceding pages: Harvesting the crop near Madras. On top of the ancient lighthouse, Mahabalipuram. Detail of a carved gopuram.*

have been found in the city. Some of the Pallava kings assumed the title "rulers of Mylapore." Besides Saivism and Vaishnavism, Buddhism and Jainism also flourished under the Pallava dynasty.

Towards the end of the 9th century, the imperial Cholas captured this region. They made many rich endowments to several temples, and also built new ones in Mylapore and in various other parts of the city. These ancient settlements were administered by the Cholas under a well-defined territorial system and received great attention and riches. **Egmore** (where the **Madras Museum** is located) and **Puliyur**, where the modern film industry thrives, are examples that are recorded in the Chola epigraphs. In the 14th century, the city region came under the control of the Vijayanagar kingdom and remained so until the British rose to power much later in the 18th century.

Around 1520, the Portuguese established a trading center, and the Jesuits had begun to convert people to Christianity. According to tradition, St. Thomas visited this site. A little to the north of Madras is **Pulicut**, where the Dutch established a trading center and fortified it at the beginning of the 17th century. The Dutch and the Portuguese, rivals in trade, frequently fought among themselves. To keep them in check, at the

beginning of the 17th century the Nayak governor, under the Vijayanagar Emperor Damarla Venkata and his brother, built the town **Chennapattnam**, named after their father, Chennappa.

On the coast to the north of the River Coovum, there existed a hamlet called **Madras Kuppam**. The British, who failed to establish themselves at Pulicut because of Dutch opposition, thought it prudent to establish a separate trading center of their own at **Madraspatnam**. They obtained permission from the Vijayanagar ruler Venkata, and settled there in 1641. Francis Day, an employee of the company, took great interest in establishing this as a British settlement and **Fort St. George** was raised in 1641. The place became famous as Madraspatnam. Both settlements, Chennapatnam and Madraspatnam, existed side by side, the former inhabited by the local people, the latter by the British.

*Above: Cinema poster at Madras, film capital of the south.*

**Fort St. George**

Originally the Fort was square in plan, with a warehouse and some residential buildings. Immediately to the north of the Fort lived native artists, painters and weavers, in the area then known as Black Town. Rich Armenian merchants also lived in the vicinity, and their sojourn is commemorated not only by the name **Armenian Street** but also by the **Armenian Church** built in the 17th century.

Fort St. George was later remodeled and enlarged, with beautiful streets, residences and bastions. It has since been a center of administration, and today the **Madras Legislative Assembly** and the **Government Secretariat** are housed within the Fort. **St. Mary's Church**, situated within the Fort, was the first Anglican Church to have been built in India (1680). Robert Clive was married here. Opposite the church is Clive's house, where he lived in 1753 with his wife. It now houses the **Archaeological Survey of India**.

The **Fort Museum** of colonial history is also within the precincts. It traces the history of Fort St. George and displays the armory, coins, medals and other artifacts used by the British and their contemporaries. It also has excellent paintings of the British nobility and of life in old Madras. A tall marble statue of Lord Cornwallis with the two captive sons of Tipu Sultan graces the entrance.

The **Kapalisvara Temple** at Mylapore, dedicated to Siva as Kapalisvara, dates from earlier than the 6th century A.D. It was originally located on the seafront, where the **San Thome Cathedral** and the Bishop's residence now stand. In the 16th century the temple was destroyed by the Portuguese and rebuilt at its present location.

The temple now consists of the *sanctum* of Lord Siva and his consort, the Goddess Parvati, and a number of other deities, situated within an enclosure, and preceded by an entrance tower (built in 1906) in the east and the temple tank in the west. Regular festivals are held in the temple, the annual festival in March-April being the greatest in the city.

Millions of devotees throng the vicinity to see the deities taken out in procession around the main streets. The tall tower (*Gopuram*) symbolizes the temple and is the dominating feature of all temple towns and villages in Tamil Nadu. The **Parthasarathi Temple** at Triplicane is old, but was rebuilt in 1564, as it had suffered damage at the hands of the Portuguese. It is dedicated to Krishna as the charioteer of Arjuna.

The ancient **Siva Temple** at **Thiruvanmiyur** has many Chola structures and inscriptions. From here, the Pallava group of monuments at **Mamallapuram** (Mahabalipuram) is barely a 40-minute drive along the coast. In all these temples, non-Hindus are not permitted beyond a certain point, but one can still obtain a clear view of most rituals, which are best seen in the early morning and evening.

Rituals apart, temples are an interesting place to just observe people.

## Museums

The **Madras Government Museum** and the **National Art Gallery** are situated on **Pantheon Road**. The Madras Museum is known for its exquisite collection of more than 2000 South Indian bronzes and the Amaravati marbles.

Originally part of the Madras Literary Society, the Central Museum, Madras, as it was known then, came into existence in 1850. It was moved to the present site in 1854, on which a building called the Pantheon used to stand. Built towards the close of the 18th century, the Pantheon was a great hall situated in the midst of a big garden. It was used as a dining hall, ballroom and theater by the Europeans. Sadly, the original Pantheon building no longer exists though the road still bears its name. Three great buildings of architectural value - the **Museum Theatre**, the extension hall and the **Connemara Public Library** were built within the compound in 1896.

The present museum has several sections, but four galleries, the Hindu Sculpture Gallery, the Amaravati Gallery, the Bronze Gallery and the National Art Gallery, constitute the main attractions. The **Hindu Sculpture Gallery** gives a view of the evolution of sculptural art under the Pallava, Chola and Vijayanagar rulers. The **Amaravati Gallery** houses over 100 Buddhist sculptures from the Amaravati *stupa*, dating from the 2nd century B.C. to the 2nd century A.D.

The delicacy with which the human forms are delineated, and the perfection attained in the use of the chisel are remarkable. Indian art reached its zenith under the Amaravati school, and what is displayed here is representative of the best of Indian art. A model of the Buddhist *stupa* that was originally adorned by these sculptures is also on display.

In the **Bronze Gallery,** some of the impressive bronze masterpieces made in the south are on display. The Madras Museum possesses the richest collection of South Indian bronzes in the world. The Ardhanarisvara (half male and half female form of Siva) from Thiruvenkadu, Nataraja images, the delightful Parvati bronzes, some of the Buddhist bronzes from Nagapattinam and Jain bronzes form the precious collection. But the breathtaking Nataraja, on seeing which the famous French sculptor Rodin went into raptures, and the best sculptures of Rama, Lakshmana, Sita and Hanuman (of the epic *Ramayana*) ever made in bronze can be seen at the **National Art Gallery**, adjacent to the Bronze Gallery.

The National Art Gallery building is a landmark in the city of Madras, built in memory of Queen Victoria in 1902, and then called the Victoria Memorial Hall. Besides the Nataraja and Rama group of bronzes, the gallery houses paintings by some of the foremost artists of India.

"The Abode of Arts" or **Kalakshetra** is an ornament to the city of Madras. It was established by a woman of great vision and zeal, Rukminidevi Arundale, who dedicated her entire life to the arts. The institution is situated in the ancient settlement of Thiruvanmiyur, in the midst of trees and lovely flower gardens, and imparts a traditional education to students of dance, music and painting. It has an extraordinary theater, where in the month of December Kalakshetra holds its annual ballet festival. During the festival, the *Ramayana* and other poetic creations are enacted.

In this part of the city, on the southern banks of the River Adyar, is the **Theosophical Society**. Established by Annie Besant, the Theosophical Society has the most beautiful garden in the whole of the city and serves as a center for Theosophists from all over the world.

All year round concerts are held in Madras, and in December and January the famous Music and Dance Festival takes place. Great musicians and dancers perform before a most knowledgeable audience, and there are also lecture demonstrations of music and dance.

*Bharata Natyam* and Carnatic music occupy pride of place, but all schools of Indian dance and music are thoroughly enjoyed during this festival. There are several associations, called the *sabhas*, organizing such festivals, but the **Music Academy** holds the most honored place. But that is not all. Men, women and young children throng nearby temples in their hundreds in the early hours of the morning on all 30 days of this Tamil month and recite the songs of Saivite and Vaishnavite saints.

### Other Sites of Interest

The **San Thome Cathedral** on the coast is associated, according to one tradition, with St. Thomas, and dates back to the time of the Portuguese in the 16th century. Rebuilt later, the cathedral is the most impressive in the city. The Bishop's house is located next to it.

The **Little Mount** near Saidapet and the **St. Thomas Mount** on the way to Madras airport are also centers of Christian faith.

Two other churches of interest are **St. George's Cathedral** and **St. Andrew's Kirk**. The Nawabs of Arcot held the city for some time after the fall of the Vijayanagar empire. There are several Islamic buildings – mosques and palaces – that bear witness to the Muslim contribution to the city. The **University** building is particularly interesting in this respect. Victorian and Georgian buildings have also survived here and there.

**Rajaji Hall** is approached from the main arterial road, called **Mount Road**. The **Guindy Deer** and **Snake Parks** are worth a visit. The fine 13-km (8 mi) long **Marina Beach** is a popular recreation ground, though unsafe for swimming.

# MADRAS
## Accommodation

*LUXURY:* **Taj Coromandel**, 17 Nungambakkam High Road, Tel: 474849, Fax: 044 470070. **The Trident**, 1/24 G.S.T. Road, Tel: 2344747, Fax: 2346699. **Welcome Group Chola Sheraton**, 10 Cathedral Road, Tel: 473347, Fax: 044 478779. **Welcome Group Park Sheraton**, 132 T.T.K. Rd., Alwarpet, Tel: 452525, Fax: 044 455913.

*MODERATE:* **Blue Diamond**, 934 E.V.R. Periyar Salai, Tel: 6412244. **Dasprakash**, 100 Poonamallee High Rd., Tel: 8255111. **Kanchi**, 28 Commander in Chief Rd., Egmore, Tel: 4711000. **Madras Hotel Ashoka**, 33 Pantheon Road, Egmore, Tel: 8253377. **New Victoria**, 3 Kennet Lane, Egmore, Tel: 8253638. **New Woodlands**, 72-75 Dr. Radhakrishna Rd., Mylapore, Tel: 473111. **Swagath**, 243-244 Royapettah High Road, Tel: 868466.

*BUDGET:* **Ganpat**, 103 Nungambakkam High Rd., Tel: 471889. **Maris**, 9 Cathedral Rd., Tel: 470541. **Peacock**, 1089 Poonamallee High Rd., Tel: 39081-10. **Silver Star**, 5 Purusawalkam High Rd., Tel: 664414. **YMCA**, Royapettah, 14 Westcott Rd., Tel: 811158. **Youth Hostel**, Indira Nagar, Adayar, Tel: 412882. **YMCA**, Vepery, 74 Ritherdon Rd., Tel:32821. **YWCA Guest House**, 1086 Poonamallee High Rd., Tel: 39920, 39986.

## Museums / Art Galleries

**Government Museum and Art Gallery**, Pantheon Rd., Egmore, open 8 am-5 pm, closed Fri and national holidays. **Fort Museum**, South Beach Rd, open 9 am-5 pm, closed Fri and national holidays.

## Post / Telegraph / Telephone

**General Post Office**, Rajaji Salai, Tel: 512011. **Post and Telegraph Office**, Anna Salai, Tel: 848832.

## Restaurants

*CHINESE:* **Chunking**, 67 Anna Salai. **China Town**, Cathedral Road. **Golden Dragon**, Taj Coromandel. **Sagari**, Chola Sheraton.

*VEGETARIAN:* **Hotel Dasprakash**, Poonamallee High Rd. **Matsya Udupi Home**, Halls Rd., Egmore. **Gopika**, Hotel Peacock, Poonamallee High Road. **Raintree**, Connemara Hotel, Binny Road (South Indian). **Dakshin**, Park Sheraton. Restaurant in the **New Woodlands Hotel**.

*NON-VEGETARIAN:* **Buhari**, 53 Anna Salai. **Jewel Box**, Hotel Blue Diamond, 934 E.V.R. Periyar Salai. **Bilal**, Mount Road. **Navayuga**, Dr. Radha Krishnan Road.

## Tourist Information

**Government of India Tourist Office**, 154 Anna Salai, Tel: 88685/6. Information counters at the international and domestic arrival lounges of the airport (Domestic, Tel: 431686). **Government of Tamil Nadu Tourist Office**, 143 Anna Salai Road, Tel: 840752. Also information counters at the airport (domestic) and the central railway station, Tel: 33351. **State Information Centre**, Government of Tamil Nadu, Government Estate, Tel: 845293. **ITDC**, Commander-in-Chief Road, Victoria Crescent.

## Access / Local Transport

Madras, the state capital is well connected by air, rail and road to all the major cities in India. Airlinks also exist with some southeast Asian cities. There are regular passenger liners from Madras to the Andaman and Nicobar Islands.

Coaches, tourist and metered taxis, auto and cycle rickshaws are the modes of local transport generally available all over the state. In major towns and cities a bus service provides connections to all the important places in the city and its vicinity. Madras city is also served by economical, fast and frequent suburban electric trains.

## Shopping

The main shopping area is **Anna Salai**. Aside from bookstores and departmental stores the state's handicrafts are sold in the emporium on this road. Other shopping areas include **Parry's Corner** and **Burma Bazaar** which consists of 500 little shops. Items include silk, banana fiber baskets, coir mats and cane furniture. There are wood carvings and inlaid wood decorative pieces to choose from. Bronzes, stone carvings and brassware are other specialties of the state.

## Festivals

Considering the number of churches and temples that dot this coastal city, it is not surprising that religious festivals are frequently celebrated.

Among the important religious celebrations is the *Kapalisvara* Temple Festival, known as the *Aruvathumoovar* festival, held in March/April every year. This temple, dedicated to Siva, also enshrines bronze statues of 63 Saivite saints, canonized for their devotion. These 63 bronze images are carried in a colorful procession on the eighth day of the ten-day festival. The Adhispurisvar temple celebrates a 15-day festival. There is a tradition that associates Durga, enshrined in the northern side of the temple, with Kannagi, the heroine of the ancient Tamil epic *Silappadhikaram*. On the last day of this festival the *pandal* (ceremonial canopy) is burned as a symbol of Kannagi burning the city of Madurai. (See p. 36 for the story of *Silappadhikaram*).

An important Christian festival takes place at Little Mount on the fourth weekend after Easter, at the Church of Our Lady of Health. The festival is a unique combination of religious fervor and gaiety, and resembles a medieval religious fair. Madras is also famous for its *Music and Dance festival*, held in December/January.

### TAMIL NADU

Tamil Nadu, at the southern extreme of the Deccan peninsula, offers a visual feast of magnificent ancient temples and the vivid experience of active temple cities, associated not only with religion but with highly evolved expressions of the creative mind. Tamil Nadu is also where traditions are cherished, respected and tenaciously adhered to as a part of daily life by all people, resulting in a distinctive lifestyle.

The profusion of sophisticated architecture and sculpture to be seen here is among the finest in India, and, in some cases, the world. It is set against the serene backdrop of lush paddy fields, the Eastern Ghats, the Nilgiri Mountains (where tea and coffee are grown), and the sea. **Uthagamandalam (Ooty)** and **Kodaikanal** are two fine hill stations, rising to over 2,500 m (8,200 ft). The former, especially, retains a strong flavor of the British Raj. The **Mudumalai Wildlife Sanctuary**, famous for its elephants, is contiguous with Bandipur in Karnataka. The coastline of Tamil Nadu is dotted with charming fishing villages and towns where European settlers first established trading centers in the 17th century.

### Mamallapuram

**Mamallapuram** (or Mahabalipuram), 45 km (28 mi) from Madras, offers the combination of superb monuments, a fine beach resort and good sea-food. It is the birthplace of the great 5th century Vaishnav saint Bhutattalavar, and has since remained a pilgrim center. But its importance lies mainly in the group of rock-cut monolithic temples and other structures, excavated during the reign of the Pallavas and renowned the world over. There are four types of monuments: rock-cut monolithic temples, excavated cave temples, open air rock sculptures and structural temples.

About 4 km (2,5 mi) before Mamallapuram is the **Tiger Cave**, an excavated cave shrine that has an aureole of tiger heads. In the heart of Mamallapuram is the magnificent open air rock sculpture known as **Arjuna's Penance**, which is believed to represent a story from the *Mahabharata*. In this story, Arjuna, an exiled Pandava prince, goes to the Himalaya to perform severe penance in order to obtain from Siva a celebrated Pasupata weapon that will enable him to conquer the Kaurava princes.

A natural cleft in the center of the immense rock is supposed to be a celestial river descending to earth. On the two wings of the rock are carved gods, saints and sages, men and women, birds and animals and a herd of elephants led by a majestic tusker, all converging on the center to witness the act of Arjuna doing penance, and Siva giving him the celestial weapon. This is a creation of supreme and unsurpassed artistic expression, pulsating with life.

Nearby are the **Ganesa Ratha**, a monolithic temple, the **Varaha Cave** with its excellent sculptures, and the exquisite **Krishnamandapa** depicting the scene of Krishna lifting Mount Goverdhan to protect his cowherds. At the far end of the village are the **five rathas**, monolithic temples, named after the five Pandava brothers, the heroes of the *Mahabharata*. Each temple, graced with sculptures, represents a different type of architecture. On the way back from the *rathas* it is worth visiting the **Mahishasuramardini Cave** with its two superb sculptures – the first, of the Goddess Durga seated on her lion mount, vanquishing the arrogant buffalo-headed demon, is considered the jewel of Pallava sculptural art; the second is of Lord Vishnu reclining on a serpent. The lighthouse opposite the cave was built recently. At the top of the rock is a temple from where one has a panoramic view of the entire village.

**TAMIL NADU**

0        50 Km

On the seashore is a group of three temples, collectively called the **Shore Temple**. Two of these are dedicated to Siva, and the third, sandwiched between them, is dedicated to Vishnu. The dramatic location of this temple and its pyramidal structures have fascinated poets, art lovers and historians.

Mamallapuram served as the port of the Pallavas and was named after the great Pallava king Mamalla, who ruled in the mid-7th century A.D. A conspicuous feature of this place is that most of the monuments remained unfinished. There are two prevalent theories about the origin of the monuments. The first holds that they were created by a succession of rulers spanning 100 years beginning with Mamalla around A.D. 630. The second and more accepted view is that these

*Above: Arjuna's Penance, Mahabalipuram, one of the most elaborate reliefs in all India.*
*Right: Durga slays the buffalo-headed demon, Mahishamardini Cave, Mahabalipuram.*

monuments were the creation of a single ruler, Rajasimha (A.D. 700-730), a man of unlimited imagination, a great lover of art and also the builder of the wonderful Kailasanatha Temple of Kanchi.

**Kanchipuram**

Situated 70 km (44 mi) from Madras on the Madras-Bangalore highway, **Kanchipuram** is one of the seven sacred cities of India. According to tradition it was the most attractive city of ancient India, and often referred to as the "golden girdle of the world." It was one of the greatest centers of learning in the pre-Christian era and important for all Indian religions. It served as the capital of ruling dynasties from the pre-Christian era almost to the 18th century, when Madras gained prominence. The great Pallavas, who ruled from the 3rd to the 9th century A.D., were followed by the Cholas who retained Kanchi as their northern capital. It was a great center of Buddhism and under the rule of Asoka, the Mauryan

emperor (3rd century B.C.) built a Buddhist stupa here. There were over 100 Buddhist monasteries here sheltering around 10,000 Buddhist monks. Dharmapala (6th century A.D.), a Buddhist teacher from Kanchi, later became the head of the famous Nalanda University. Another great Buddhist thinker, Bodhi Darma (A.D. 520), who was the son of the king of Kanchipuram, went to China and founded *Dyanamarga* Buddhism, which is called *Chang* Buddhism in China and *Zen* in Japan.

The city of Kanchipuram has three divisions: Siva Kanchi, Vishnu Kanchi and Jain Kanchi, based on the dominant faith of each part. There are over 100 temples in active worship in the city. Though a number of temples here are over 1400 years old, it would be advantageous to start with the **Kailasanatha Temple,** the earliest surviving structure and the most beautiful. Built by the Pallava ruler, Rajasimha, it is laid out according to canonical texts, and is the only temple in the whole of India to retain all of its

classical components without any alteration. The eight little shrines in line with the entrance were built by the queens of Rajasimha. The rectangular temple at the entrance was built by the son of Rajasimha and houses a *linga* in the *sanctum.* Behind this shrine is the magnificent courtyard with a row of smaller cellular shrines housing images of Siva in his benign and terrifying aspects, and secondary deities. Behind the courtyard stands the majestic *sanctum* tower.

There are eight smaller Pallava temples in the city, all built in the 8th century. Among these is the **Vaikunta Perumal Temple**, built by Pallava Nandi II. Dedicated to Vishnu, it has three *sanctums*, one over the other. In the surrounding enclosure sculptures narrate the history of the Pallava dynasty from its legendary ancestors to the exploits of the builder.

The great Siva temple of **Ekambaranathan**, has been in active worship for over 1300 years. Its several concentric enclosures, built of granite, were added

through the centuries by successive rulers and nobles. The tallest entrance and enclosure were built around A.D. 1525 by the great Vijayanagar emperor, Krishnadevaraya. The temple has a sacred mango tree, believed to be over 2000 years old.

The Vishnu temple of **Varadaraja**, at the other end of the town, has a 16th-century pillared pavilion famous for its exuberant workmanship.

Those interested in Jain art can visit Jain Kanchi (**Thirupparuthikunram**) across the dry river bed. This settlement dates to the 6th century. The 18th century Jain paintings on the ceiling of the main pavilion depict Jain cosmology and scenes from the life of the Tirthankarar.

The **Kamakshi Temple**, dedicated to the Goddess Kamakshi who is the presiding deity of the city of Kanchi, and the **Subrahmanya Temple** are other important centers of Kanchi, which was also the home of Sankaracharya, the great exponent of Advaita philosophy. The pontiff of the monastery is venerated for his wisdom and piety.

### Pondicherry

**Pondicherry** is on the seacoast, 115 km (72 mi) from Kanchipuram. This former French colony, established in the 18th century, was returned to India in 1954, and is now a Union Territory. Pondicherry is a different experience from the other towns of Tamil Nadu. Traces of French influence are evident in the streets along the waterfront, in official buildings around **Government Square**, in the Gothic-style **Sacred Heart Church**, and rather vividly in the uniforms worn by policemen. Pondicherry is better known for its **Sri Aurobindo Ashram** and **Auroville** (10 km or 6 miles), developed as an experiment in international living.

*Left: A bronze image of Shiva as Natraj, the Cosmic Dancer.*

From Pondicherry it is convenient to proceed to Chidambaram via **Cuddalore**, which was a European trading center. **Panrutti**, on the outskirts of Cuddalore, has a Siva temple, **Thiruvadigai**, which is the best example of a Pallava brick temple. Here, the Saivite saint Appar embraced Saivism and started his religious movement.

### Chidambaram

**Chidambaram**, known as the "City of the Cosmic Dancer," is 50 km (31 mi) from Cuddalore. Even as one approaches this sacred city through green paddy fields, four lofty towers rising into the sky seem to draw the visitor into this rich center of religion, philosophy and the arts, which also served as the most inspiring source of Saiva thought for over 2000 years. Here Nataraja, the Lord of Dance, is enshrined, represented by the powerful bronze image known throughout the world as the most perfect synthesis in metal of art, literature and science. The dance of Nataraja is called *Ananda Tandava*, the blissful dance.

The **Chidambaram Temple**, situated in the middle of the town, is surrounded by four broad "chariot" streets. Four *gopura* or entrance towers, one on each main road, lead the visitor into the temple enclosure. The towers, the enclosure and the paved space were built by Vikrama Chola and his son Kulottunga Chola II in the 12th century. The northern tower was rebuilt by Krishnadeva Raya of Vijayanagar around A.D. 1525. His figure and those of the four architects who designed the tower have been carved here. The towers were designed according to canonical texts and built of granite up to the ceiling, with the structure of seven storeys in brick and mortar. The niches carry images of minor deities in the lower courses and manifestations of Siva in the upper courses. There is a 1000-pillared hall in the northeastern part of the enclo-

sure which is a 12th-century Chola structure. A minister to the Chola Emperor of that time wrote a literary masterpiece on the lives of the 63 Saivite saints in this hall, which is recited to this day.

The main image of Nataraja is within a rectangular shrine, covered with copper tiles and gold. It is called "The Golden Hall" and is, conceptually, the center of the universe, where the cosmic dance takes place. The four Vedas, the Upanishads, the six branches of knowledge, the 18 Puranas, and all other canonical texts and devotional hymns are identified with one or other parts of this temple, which thus symbolizes the totality of Indian knowledge, and also the body, enshrining the cosmic dance of Lord Nataraja as its soul. The temple is also held as the Yogic body and the dance as the Supreme Bliss. The thinking consciousness of all human beings is called *chid*, which, according to the Saiva philosophy, is immeasurable,

*Above: Detail of a staircase at the Brihadis-vara Temple, Tanjore.*

expanding with knowledge like the immense sky, *ambaram*. The word *chidambaram* thus stands for the ever expanding consciousness, and the supreme knowledge that dawns on it is Nataraja.

At another level the universe is said to be projected into space, sustained in space, and dissolved into space. The human mind, however, is shrouded; it regains its natural poise by the removal of ignorance, achieved through the grace of God. These acts of creation, sustenance, dissolution, concealment and bestowal of grace are different acts of the omnipotent Siva, and are called "the five acts", symbolically represented by Nataraja: the little drum in his right hand represents creation; the right hand showing the gesture of protection represents sustenance; the fire in the left hand signifies dissolution; the right leg planted on the back of the dwarf, concealment; and the lifted leg and the left arm pointing to it symbolize God's grace. The encircling aureole of fire represents cosmic space and the light of knowledge.

The Brahmin priests, traditionally called "the 3000 Dikshitas," perform daily rites following the Vedic tradition and also conduct festivals. The Chola Emperors held Nataraja as their family deity and were crowned in his immediate presence. The temple of the goddess Sivakami, the consort of Nataraja, located within the temple complex, was built in the Chola period and has a remarkable series of dance sculptures. Close to the Nataraja shrine is the temple of Vishnu in his reclining form, called Govindaraja. The sight of Nataraja being worshiped is an unforgettable one (foreigners are allowed inside the temple).

The annual festival held in December/January is the most impressive. In recent times, in February/March, leading dancers from all parts of India congregate and dance in the temple as an offering to Nataraja. The Natyanjali dance festival lasts for five days.

### En Route to Tanjore

60 km from Chidambaram, on the Madras-Tanjore highway, is **Gangaikonda-cholapuram**. Situated about 1 km off the main road, the monumental temple called **Gangaikonda Cholisvaram** was built by the Chola Emperor Rajendra I in A.D. 1020. It rises to a height of over 60 m (197 ft) and is built entirely of granite. It is not the entrance tower but the *sanctum* tower that is large here, next only to the awe inspiring temple of Tanjore, built 20 years earlier. This temple was built by Rajendra Chola to commemorate his great conquest up to the Gangetic plain, the northernmost victory ever achieved by any south Indian king. The temple has beautiful stone sculptures, the outstanding ones being of Nataraja, Siva and Parvati garlanding a devotee, and of Saraswati, the goddess of Learning. The *linga* in the *sanctum* is one of the biggest in the south. The temple also houses some remarkable bronzes of the Chola age.

The emperor also built a capital here, with imposing palaces and fortifications. This mighty capital controlled the entire destiny of the south for nearly 250 years. From here, the Chola commanders set out to conquer overseas territories like the Srivijaya kingdom, Malaysia, Singapore, Sumatra, Java and other islands. It was the capital of the Cholas until the fall of the dynasty towards the end of the 13th century. The remains, now called "the palace site," can be seen about 1 km to the southwest of the temple.

Once the home of intellectuals, especially Brahmins, **Kumbakonam** may be called the second capital of the Tanjore district. Situated on the fertile banks of the Kaveri, the town is associated with art and literature, music and dance, and, above all, with the proverbial shrewdness of its people.

The town has several temples of which the **Nagesvara Temple** is perhaps the finest. Though small, it houses some superb sculptures of the 9th century, representative of the Pallava Chola transition. Two figures of women carved in stone are unparalleled in Tamil art. Along the base of the temple run miniature panels of remarkable workmanship, portraying the story of the *Ramayana*. Another temple of interest is the Vishnu temple of **Sarangapani**, sanctified by the visits of several Vaishnav saints.

Not far from Kumbakonam is the village of **Swamimalai**, renowned for its **Subrahmanya Temple**. It is also important for connoisseurs of Indian art, for here live a few families of artists who pursue the traditional art of bronze casting. The skill of the Chola artists who lived 1000 years ago still lives in the delicate fingers of the Swamimalai artists. Here, one can see the lost wax (*cire perdue*) process of bronze casting and buy small bronzes made by these artists.

On the outskirts of Kumbakonam is **Darasuram**, ancient Rajarajapuram, with a remarkable 12th-century Chola

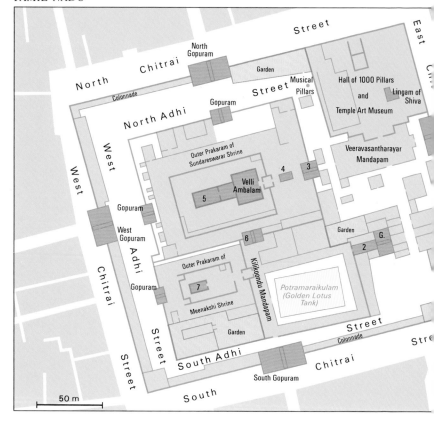

temple. Certainly the best of that age, this Siva temple deserves attention simply for its beauty alone.

### Tanjore

**Tanjore** (**Thanjavur**) represents the acme of grandeur and perfection attained by the imperial Cholas in the fields of administration, architecture, the arts and philosophy, all culminating in the **Brihadisvara Temple** built in A.D. 1000 by Rajaraja Chola I. It is perhaps the greatest temple ever to have been erected in India. This temple is overwhelming in its boldness of conception, its perfect symmetry and the finesse with which it has been built. The pyramidal central tower, rising

to over 70 m (230 ft), has a dignity and majesty that bears witness to the vision and devotion of its builder, Rajaraja.

The stone sculptures, great pieces by themselves, are nevertheless submerged in the magnitude of the architecture, as tiny parts of embellishment. The inner walls around the *sanctum* carry Chola frescoes of supreme beauty, depicting manifestations of Siva and scenes from the lives of saints. The paintings that have survived show the mastery of the Chola artists in delineating emotion and delicate movements. Dance, as performed by Siva, and specified in Bharata's treatise, is portrayed in 108 poses sculpted on the inner wall of the first floor around the *sanctum*.

Avanimoola

Street

Pudhu Mandapam
(Thirumalai's Choultry)

of
ya

Entrance

of Vinayaka

## MEENAKSHI TEMPLE
## — MADURAI —

G. = Gopuram — Gateway Tower
Mandapam — Pillared Hall

1  Ashta Shakti Mandapam
2  Mudali Mandapam
3  Gopura Nayak Gopuram
4  Kambathadi Mandapam
   and Nandi Mandapam
5  Sanctum Sanctorum of Sundareswarar
6  Nadukattu Gopuram
7  Sanctum Sanctorum of Meenakshi

epigraphs, left by the founder, as this one. Most of these are inscribed on the walls and pillars of the temple in the beautiful Tamil script.

The inscriptions record the names of the founder, and those members of the royal family who made gifts to the temple. They also give an insight into the administrative set up of the temple, the rituals and festivals that have been conducted here, the number of bronze images consecrated, the enormous amounts of jewelry donated to adorn these images, as well as the names of singers, musicians, dramatists and 400 accomplished dancing girls, who offered dance as a part of the rituals. Over 100 bronzes, donated by Rajaraja and others, are no longer to be seen in the temple; only one survives, a superb example of bronze art, and this is the image of Nataraja still being worshipped. Do not fail to look at this graceful bronze, in a small shrine to the north of the entrance.

Tanjore is also famous for two other institutions - the **Tanjore Art Gallery** which shows more than 100 Chola bronzes of outstanding merit, including the world famous Vrshavahana Siva and his consort Parvati from Thiruvenkadu; and the **Sarasvati Mahal Library** known for its interesting collection of rare and illustrated manuscripts. These two institutions are housed in the **palace**, built by the Nayaks in the 16th and 17th centuries, and subsequently enlarged by the Maratha rulers. The tradition of the Maratha school of painting, known as Tanjore painting, still survives in the town to this day. It is also famous for the art of making musical instruments. The stringed *veena*, made by the traditional craftsmen of this town, are widely recognized for their excellent quality.

### Along the Coast

The coastal road south of Chidambaram passes through villages of historic

It is an experience to see the interior of the tower, not only for the handling of space by the architect but also for its geometric perfection. The name of the architect who designed and erected this magnificent edifice is mentioned in inscriptions as Rajaraja Perum Taccan.

The *sanctum* enshrines a big *linga*, appropriate to the magnitude of the temple. The front hall, originally two-storied, seems to have suffered in later times and was later rebuilt in the 17th century. The big Nandi (bull) in a pillared pavilion also dates to the 17th century. The two entrance towers, much smaller in size than the *sanctum* towers, were also built by Rajaraja whose name they bear. Perhaps no other temple in India is as rich in

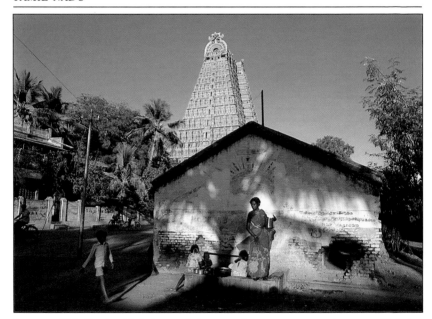

interest. **Sirkali**, the birthplace of the Saiva saint Sambandar, with its great temple of Siva, leads on to **Poompuhar**, a port town where the River Kaveri joins the sea.

This was an ancient and important international port called Kaberis Emporion in the writings of classical geo-graphers of the west (first century A.D.). A colony of Roman Greeks existed here in the first century A.D. It was also a great center of Buddhism which was frequented by monks from the Far East. About 2 km from this village is **Thiruvenkadu**, a great center of bronze art that has yielded over 30 superb bronzes of the Chola period.

Further south is **Karaikkal**, a French settlement, and **Tranquebar**, where the Danish East India Company built a castle – the **Danesborg Castle**– in A.D. 1620

*Above: Carved gopuram of the Srinangam Temple at Thiruchirapalli. Right: Hall of the Thousand Pillars in the Srirangam Temple.*

under an agreement between Christian IV, the King of Denmark, and Raghunatha Nayak, the King of Tanjore. The Danesborg Castle and the main city, as founded by the Danes, still survive.

Another Dutch settlement, **Nagapattinam**, was also a great center of Buddhism. Not far away from here is **Nagore**, with its famous Muslim shrine, and **Velankanni**, a Christian settlement.

**Thiruvarur** is 24 km (15 mi) inland from Nagapattinam. The **Siva Temple** is one of the biggest temple complexes in the south. Three great music composers of the 18th and 19th centuries, called the "music trinity" and considered the fathers of present day classical music traditions, all came from this place.

### Thiruchirapalli

**Thiruchirapalli** (Trichy in its shortened form), 55 km (34 mi) west of Tanjore, retains the atmosphere of an ancient village. Deriving its name from a tall hillock on the banks of the River Kaveri,

Trichy has another landmark, the lofty **St. Joseph's Church**. There are three groups of monuments of special interest. The **Siva Temple** on the hill is over 1300 years old and can be reached by a steep flight of steps.

A little further up is a cave temple excavated in the early 7th century by the famous Pallava emperor, Mahendra I, who, an inscription records, went into poetic ecstasy on reaching the summit of the hill and seeing the course of the River Kaveri with its fresh waters, and banks covered with green gardens of flowers and coconut groves. A **Ganesh Temple** has since been built on the summit.

From there, one can see the **Temple of Srirangam**, the abode of Lord Vishnu in his reclining form. Situated on an island formed by the Rivers Kaveri and Kollidam, this temple, according to legend, dates to the epic age.

Ramanuja, the Vaishnav saint, passed away at this site and is closely associated with the temple. In the 1000-pillared hall the 4000 Vaishnavite systems of the Al-

wars are recited to the accompaniment of dance by a family of devotees called Arayars.

The **Horse Court**, a great attraction, is a landmark in sculpture and architecture. But the earlier shrine of Krishna as Venugopala, built in the 13th century, also displays sculptures of remarkable beauty in its niches. The *Vaikunda Ekadasi* festival, celebrated here in the month of December, is famous.

### Madurai

**Madurai**, famous for its **Meenakshi Temple**, is the epitome of south Indian temple cities, alive and bustling with pilgrims and religious preoccupations. It has occupied a vital place in the history of Tamil Nadu for over 2000 years.

It was the capital of the Pandyan rulers, who were great patrons of Tamil learning. Later royal records refer to the establishment of the Tamil Sangam (the association of Tamil poets) by the Pandyas at Madurai. The city was successively ruled

by the Pandyas, the Cholas, and then the Pandyas again until the beginning of the 14th century, when it fell into the hands of invading Muslims.

The Hindu kingdom was eclipsed for nearly 70 years, after which it was re-established by the Vijayanagar rulers. In the mid-16th century, they founded the Madurai Nayak dynasty which ruled the region until the mid-18th century. The central *sanctums* of both the Lord Sundaresvara and the Goddess Meenakshi were rebuilt by the first of the Nayak in the 16th century.

Subsequently, his grandson added many imposing structures, the most notable of which is the 1000-pillared hall, exhibiting some of the most delightful sculptures of the age. During this period of time most of the other great entrance

*Above: Profusely carved towers of the Mee-nakshi Temple at Madurai. Right: Kan-niyakumari, or Cape Comorin, the southern-most tip of India.*

towers (*gopura*) were erected. From 1550 to 1650, in a span of a hundred years, the temple grew to its present size and shape. There are four lofty *gopuras*, and all of them are profusely carved.

The sacred tank inside the temple, called the golden lotus tank, is held in great veneration. The inner corridors of the temple serve virtually as a bazaar, selling flower garlands, objects used for rituals and household utensils. The entire city revolves around the temple, and the life of the people revolves around Goddess Meenakshi.

The most outstanding Nayak ruler of Madurai was Thirumalai Nayak, who ruled between A.D. 1623 and 1659. He systematically beautified the city and erected a magnificent palace for himself, which still survives. He gradually reorganized the temple administration and instituted several festivals, the most important being the *Chitra* (April) festival which is celebrated to this day.

In the nearby village of **Thirupparankunram**, Thirumalai arranged spe-

cial worship in the temple dedicated to Subrahmanya. His contribution to the temple of Alagar Koil, the temple of Lord Vishnu, was equally great. He arranged for a magnificent festival for Lord Alagar (on April full moon, in the Tamil month of *Chitra*) when the deity was brought in a procession to Madurai to the accompaniment of music and dance.

This lively festival is still held today with great enthusiasm. People celebrate, dressed in colorful 17th-century costumes, lavishly bedecked with garlands, and are accompanied by joyous singing and dancing throughout the night, a sight which transports spectators back to the 17th century.

### To Cape Comorin

**Rameswaram** is situated on an island in the Gulf of Mannar. According to ancient traditions, it derives its name from Lord Rama, who consecrated a *linga* made of sand to expiate the sin of killing Ravana. The glory of the **Rame-swaram Temple** is symbolized in its corridor which extends to over 1 km.

The Rameswaram corridors were built by the Sethupatis in the 17th century. Rameswaram is also a great pilgrim center for the Sikhs, since the temple was visited by Govind Singh.

Interestingly, the Tamil priests from Rameswaram went to the Far East in the 16th and 17th centuries, and they serve there to this day as royal priests in Thailand, using Tamil verses for the coronation ceremony of the Thai kings.

Further down the coast is **Kanniyakumari** (Cape Comorin) poised on the tip of the peninsula, from where sunrise and sunset are both spectacular. Here, the waters of the Arabian Sea and the Bay of Bengal mingle with the Indian Ocean.

An important pilgrimage center dedicated to the Virgin Goddess, Kanniyakumari also has a **Vivekanda Memorial** situated on the Vivekananda Rock off the coast. The **Church of Our Lady of Ransom** is located in the picturesque fishing village.

## Accommodation

### MAMALLAPURAM
#### (Mahabalipuram)

*LUXURY:* **Golden Sun Hotel Beach Resort**, 59 Covelong Road, Tel: (04113) 245, 246, (en route to Mahabalipuram from Madras). **Temple Bay Ashok Beach Resort**, Tel:251-257. **Silversands Beach Resort**, Covelong Road, Tel: 228, 283, (en route to Mahabalipuram from Madras). **Tamil Nadu Tourism International Beach Resort Complex,** Tel: 235, 268.

*MODERATE:* **VGP Golden Beach Resort**, East Coast Road, Injambakkam, Tel: 412893, (en route to Mamallapuram).

### PONDICHERRY

*LUXURY:* **Hotel Pondicherry Ashok**, Chinnakalapet, Pondicherry 605104, Tel. 460, 468, Fax: 91(0)4113-280.

*MODERATE:* **Seaside Guest House** (at the Aurobindo Ashram), 10 Goubert Ave., Tel: 26494. **Hotel Mass**, Maraimalai Adigal Salai, Tel: 5977, 3262. **Ram International**, West Blvd., Tel: 5471. **Grand Hotel D'Europe**, 12 Rue Suffern.

*BUDGET:* **Youth Hostel**, Solai Nagar, Tel: 3495. **Government Tourist Home**, Uppalam Road, Tel: 3376/7/8, and Indira Nagar, Tel: 6145.

### CHIDAMBARAM

**Hotel Tamil Nadu (TTDC)**, Railway Feeder Road, Tel: 2323. **Star Lodge**, 101 South Car Street, Tel: 2743. **Hotel Raja Rajan**, 163 West Car Street, Tel: 2690. **Hotel Sharda Ram**, 19 V.G.P. Street, Chidambaram, Tel: 2966, 2496 (5 lines).

### KANCHIPURAM

*BUDGET:* **Sri Ram Lodge**, 19-20 Nellukkara Street, Tel: 3195/6. **NCS Lodge**, 461-A/B Gandhi Road, Tel: 3054.

### MADURAI

*LUXURY:* **Hotel Madurai Ashok**, Alagarkoil Road, Tel: 42531. **Pandyan Hotel**, Race Course, Tallakulam, Tel: 42470-42479. **Taj Garden Retreat**, 7 Thiruparam-Kundaram Road, Pasumali, Madurai 625004, Tel: 22300, 88102/3/6, 88256.

*MODERATE:* **Hotel Tamil Nadu (TTDC)**, Alagarkoil Road, Tel: 42451. **Hotel Tamil Nadu (TTDC)**, West Veli Street, Tel: 31435.

*BUDGET:* **YMCA**, Dindigul Road, Tel: 33649. **YWCA**, Vallabhai Road, Tel: 24763.

### TIRUCHIRAPALLI

*MODERATE:* **Hotel Sangam**, Collector's Office Road, Tel: 25202. **Hotel Aristo**, 2 Dindigul Road, Cantonment, Tel: 41818, 40004. **Hotel Tamil Nadu (TTDC)**, MacDonald Road, Cantonment, Tel: 25383.

### RAMESWARAM

**Hotel Tamil Nadu (TTDC)**, Tel: 277l. **Hotel Alankar**, Tel: 216. **Hotel Maharaja**, Tel: 271.

### THANJAVUR

*MODERATE:* **Hotel Tamil Nadu**, Gandhi Rd:, Tel: 57, 601. **Ashok Traveller's Lodge**, Vallam Rd., Tel: 365. **Ashoka Lodge**, 93 Abraham Panditar Rd., Tel: 594.

### OOTACAMUND

*MODERATE:* **Hotel Savoy**, Tel: (0423) 4142/44. **Hotel Dasaprakash**, Tel: 2434/5, 3613.

*BUDGET:* **Southern Star Ooty**, Havelock Road, Tel: 3601/9. **Fernhill Palace**, Fernhill Post, Tel: 2055, 3097. **Lakeview**, West Lake Road, Tel: 2026, 3580-82. **Hotel Maurya Sudarshan**, Tel: 2577. **Hotel Tamil Nadu (TTDC)**, Tel: 2543/4.

### KODAIKANAL

*LUXURY:* **Kodai International**, Lascot Rd., Tel: 649, 793, 767. *MODERATE:* **Carlton**, Lake Rd., Tel: 4260/63. **Holiday Home**, Golflinks Rd., Tel: 257. **Sornam Apartments**, Fernhill Rd., Tel: 431. **Sterling Holiday Resorts**, Gynthane Rd., Tel: 4037, 4060/65. **Tamil Nadu TTDC**, Fernhill Rd., Tel: 481. *BUDGET:* **TTDC Youth Hostel**, Tel: 481. **YHAI Youth Hostel**, Greenlands.

### Festivals

It is not unusual to find a festival on every calendar date in Tamil Nadu. The true spirit of *Pongal* (January), a harvest festival, can best be experienced in the rural areas. Just as the Kapalisvara Temple in Mylapore, Madras celebrates its annual festival (*Arupathumoovar* in March) so do the many other important shrines in Tamil Nadu. Major festivities to look out for are: *Music and Dance Festival* (December-January) in Madras; *Thyagaraja Music Festival* (January) in Thanjavur; *Festival of Our Lady of Health* (August-September) in Velankanni; *Masai Magam* (February/March) in Pondicherry; *Float Festival* (January/February) in Madurai; *Chitrai* (April/May) in Madurai. The *Float Festival* is held in the Vandiyur Mariamman Theppakulam. The deities of the Meenakshi Temple are placed on floats and pulled across the brilliantly lit waters of the tank till they reach the temple at the center. During *Chitrai,* Madurai celebrates the Meenakshi Sundaresvar *Kalyanam* (marriage). The idol of Meenakshi's brother is brought from Alagar, and the festival lasts 10 days. The highlights of *Pongal* are bullfights and bullock-cart races.

### Shopping

**Thanjavur** is famous for copper plates inlaid with brass and silver, silk carpets, bell-metal crafts, papier maché dolls, silk carpets and items made of pith. **Kanchipuram** has earned a name for handloom silk. **Madurai** is known for cotton textiles produced here. Leather goods and handicrafts made of rosewood, sandalwood, seashells and ivory are the specialties of Madras. There are several emporiums exclusively devoted to silk, woodcraft or ivory.

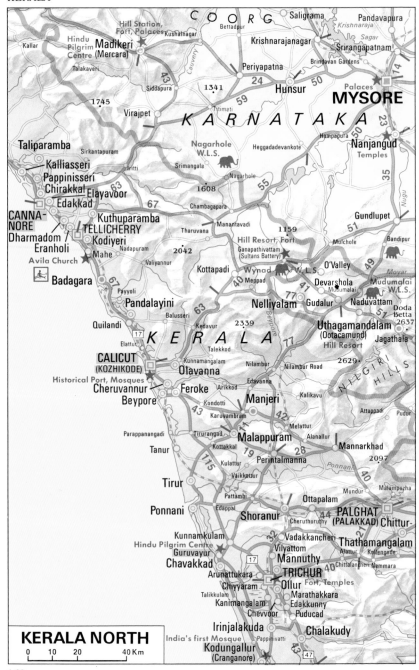

**KERALA NORTH**

0    10    20         40 Km

# A CELEBRATION
# OF LIFE

**KERALA**

## KERALA

Kerala is an explosive experience. It is the smallest of the big southern states of India, packed closely with people (25.4 million in 38,900 sq. km/15,019 sq. mi or 655 per sq. km) in a narrow strip of land between the mountain ranges known as the Western Ghats and the beaches of the Arabian Sea. It clings like a banana leaf to the southwestern coast of the Indian peninsula and receives the full fury of the monsoon winds that lash the coast for three months starting in early June.

Rich in experience but young in age; the modern state of Kerala was created in 1956, when the states were reorganized on a linguistic basis, and the Malayalam language became the official tongue for Kerala. The speakers are called Malayalis, and nothing infuriates them more than to be told that to outsiders their musical language sounds like a tin drum full of stones being shaken together.

After the monsoon, the red earth of Kerala swells with the floodwater of her 44 rivers and fills the countryside with the green of rice fields, banana plantations, coconut and arecanut (this bears a

*Preceding pages: Pilgrims at Brihadisvara Temple, Tanjore. A catamaran and fishermen, Kerala coast.*

hard round nut that is chewed with betel leaf). In the misty highlands are the commercial estates that produce rubber, tea and coffee. Threading its way tenaciously through all this is a climbing vine that bears small green berries with an acrid taste. Pepper! It was the flourishing pepper trade that put the Kerala coast on the map of the ancients.

After the season of rains comes the season of celebration. The principal festival is *Onam*, in the month of *Chingam* (August-September). Children gather masses of wild flowers with which women create carpets of increasingly complex designs until the tenth day of *Onam*, when there is a grand feast.

All festivals in Kerala start with a ritual bath and end with a feast. On the final day of *Onam*, the people of Kerala honor their mythical ruler with feats of valor. There are also boat races that pitch one village against the other.

The most famous ones are at **Aranmulla**, **Haripad** and **Alleppey**. The men race their beautifully decorated "snake boats," swaying to the rhythmic cries of the cox and urged on by spectators lining the banks. There are displays of the Kerala martial arts, *kalaripayatu* and *panthukali*, in which two opposing teams standing in a line toss a leather ball filled with coir to one another. The young girls per-

form a circular dance, clapping their hands and laughing happily while singing together.

By way of contrast, the second major festival of Kerala is *Vishu* which is celebrated in the privacy of every home just before the beginning of the planting season in February. It involves an elaborate ritual which indicates the fortunes for the year ahead.

Just because of these two pastoral festivals and the verdant countryside, Kerala should not be mistaken for a simple agricultural state. In 1957, shortly after it was formed, it created headlines by becoming the first state ever to vote democratically for a Communist government. Since that time the Communists have been in and out of favor, but the visitor cannot fail to notice the red flags that wave like the

*Above: Exquisite mural of Lakshmi, Goddess of wealth, Mattancherry Palace, Cochin. Right: Kerala's Christians are regular church-goers.*

pennants on a castle at the entrance to almost every village. In cities, the processions and political rallies are the noisiest, gaudiest ever.

Everyone partakes with good spirits, the marchers, the spectators and even the police, just as they enjoy the traditional temple processions, called *padayani*, when a gorgeously arrayed image of the Goddess Bhagwati is paraded.

This is just one of the several contradictions which coexist in modern Kerala, where many diverse customs have combined to impart a unique character. A brief glimpse of these different aspects may help towards a better understanding of modern Kerala.

**Early History**

By the early part of the Christian era, three great kingdoms, the Chera, Chola and the Pandya, had established themselves in southern India. Though they moved their borders frequently, it is generally thought that the Cheras ruled

from the region roughly occupied by Kerala today. Some feel that even the name Kerala is an echo from the Chera empire.

By the 12th century the kingdoms of the Kulashekaras and the Ays, who had dominated the intervening centuries, had broken up into innumerable smaller principalities and separate kingdoms.

The caste system, brought by the Aryans, had begun to exercise a vicious hold on the people. In Kerala, the Brahmins were known as the Namboodris. The mythical Parasurama himself is said to have divided the land, which he retrieved from the sea, between them.

The Nairs were the fighters, and the Ezhavas, who were supposed to have come from Ceylon, bringing, so the story goes, the coconut tree with them, were the cultivators.

One explanation for the dominance of the Namboodris in Kerala, at a certain point of history, is that whenever there was a war, the lands were made over to them, declared sacred so to speak, and *hors de combat*. Not only did the Brahmins slowly begin to control most of the property, but since it was the Nairs who went to war, they lost a great majority of their men. (And this perhaps explains why, until very recently, the Nairs had a matriarchal society).

In course of time the merchant class was filled by the Christians, the Muslims (called Moplahs in Kerala), and the Jews.

### The Advent of Christianity

Christianity was introduced in the first century A.D. The tradition, supported by a quaint church with pillars carved in the Hindu style at **Malankara**, is that St. Thomas landed there in A.D. 52 and established seven churches starting at **Kodungallur**, the old Muziris, that continued to be the major port. He is credited with having first converted a group of Namboodri Brahmins.

The number of Christians on the Kerala coast was further strengthened in

A.D. 345 by the arrival of Syrian immigrants belonging to seven tribes from Baghdad, Nineveh and Jerusalem, under the leadership of Knayi Thomas (Thomas of Cana). The Kerala Christians used the Syriac liturgy, which was in a dialect of Aramaic, the language of Jesus Christ.

### Islam

The Arabs had been in command of all the important shipping routes until the Portuguese came. They discovered the monsoon winds that brought their hardy *dhows* with their billowing sails to the famed spice coast. The result was that Islam first entered India through Kerala, and on silken wings rather than with the flaming sword.

The tradition is that in A.D. 664 two Muslim leaders named Malik-ibn-Dinar

and Sharaf-ibn-Malik landed at Cranganore with a party of scholars and their families, and were made welcome. The first mosque was apparently built at **Cranganore,** and others followed.

The older mosques in Kerala today are all but indistinguishable from the architectural style of other temples, with their pitched roofs and gables, except that the carved figures were replaced by stylized flowers, and elaborate geometric forms were introduced as decoration.

A good example of the austere elegance of Islam, combined with the exuberance of Kerala, is to be seen in the **Muchchandipalli** at **Calicut**. An interesting twist to the saga of the Muslims of Kerala in recent years has been their part in the Middle East oil rush.

In the 1970s, large numbers of the Gulf Indians came from Kerala. Their Middle East affluence is to be seen in the rows of taxis and jeep-taxis that line the main street of every town, as well as in gaudily decorated "modern" buildings, mosques and hotels.

*Above: A toddy tapper at work on the Tree of Life. Right: A spice trader in the Jewish town of Chochin. Far right: In a Jewish synagogue, Chochin.*

### The Jews

The Jews first came to India almost 2000 years ago. One group migrated to Cranganore in the first century A.D. and lived happily until the arrival of the Portuguese. By this time the Arabs, too, were feeling threatened in that their pepper-trade monopoly was under attack from all sides.

When the Jews complained that the Arabs were adulterating the pepper that they exported, the Arabs made this a pretext for massacring members of the community and looting their property. It was at this point that the Raja of Cochin gave them some land in his territory.

Unfortunately, this was close to the Portuguese, who lost no opportunity in harassing them. However, by the time the Dutch came the Jews were again prosperous. There exists a vivid historical account of the Zamorin (a corruption of Samuris) of Calicut receiving Vasco da Gama on his first visit to the coast in 1498. The Portuguese wanted permission

to build a factory, trading rights and of course the pepper, which was the main reason for having undertaken the difficult journey around the Cape. Neither the Zamorin nor the Portuguese adventurer were prepared to trust one another. The Portuguese sailed out of the Zamorin's grasp and made overtures to another prince, the Kolathiri, at Cannanore further north.

This ruler had his own reasons for wanting to cock a snook at the Zamorin. He was accommodating, and Vasco da Gama sailed home with enough cargo to pay the cost of his expedition 60 times over. Two years later, Pedro Alvarez Cabral made the same journey, landing first at Calicut, and then sailing down to Cochin where as usual he found the Raja of Cochin chafing under the overlordship of the Za-morin of Calicut.

Two years later, Vasco da Gama had not only managed to get a trading monopoly in pepper but had started to build the Fort at Cochin, which was to remain in foreign hands for the next 450 years.

During the early stages of the Zamorin's struggle with the Portuguese, his success in battle was provided by his Muslim admiral, known as Kunjali Maraikar, which became a collective title for a whole series of captains. For two decades, the Kunjali Maraikars kept the Portuguese fleet on the move, attacking them, and then escaping all the way from the Straits of Malacca to the Andamans and Ceylon. Finally, however, the Zamorin was forced to capitulate. The legend of the Maraikars lingers on in the songs that the fishermen sing as they brave the waves and put out to sea.

The Portuguese presence gave a lasting flavor to several areas of Kerala society. Today their legacy may be seen in small things, such as the cashew nut that the Portuguese are said to have brought to Kerala, along with fruits such as the guava, the custard apple and the papaya. They are credited with having established the cultivation of pepper on a scientific basis, as well as the commercial exploitation of the coconut tree by creating a demand for coir.

On a larger scale, the innumerable churches that are to be seen almost everywhere in Kerala were inspired by the Portuguese forms of ecclesiastical architecture, although they were unable to foist their dour version of Roman Catholicism on the independent-minded Keralites.

All through the early part of the 17th century, the Portuguese tried to reform the church and introduce the Latin Mass, until a rumor reached the Christians at Mattancherry, Cochin, that the Syrian Patriarch had been forcibly detained at Madras. This led to a mass revolt. They each held a rope that had been tied to a cross in the old church at Mattancherry and took "The Oath of the Coonan Cross" that they would remain free of any Latinizing influences.

The Church, as it is now in Kerala, has formed itself into five main branches: the Nestorian Church (mainly in Trichur and

*Above: Red is the other color of Kerala, the strong-hold of Indian Communists.*

174

Ernakulam but with a congregation in Trivandrum, too); the Roman Catholic Church; the Jacobite Syrian Church, also known as the Orthodox Syrian Church; the Anglican Church that is now a part of the Church of South India; and the Marthoma Syrian Church. The Syrian Christians, among the most dynamic and well educated of the communities in Kerala, are concentrated in Kottayam.

There are a number of old churches in this area. The **Cheriapally Orthodox Church** at **Kottayam** is one of the more interesting ones, with lively murals around the altar. The love of the Kerala craftsman for dramatic situations and profuse carving has given a certain Baroque splendor to some of the other churches, where St. George and the dragon are given an interesting prominence. Protestantism came to Kerala in the 17th century under the influence of the Dutch, who, followed by the English, replaced the Portuguese as the new colonizers. Today, 24 percent of the population are Christians.

### Modern Kerala

When the modern state of Kerala was established, it was at first an amalgam of princely states and provinces. In the north there was Malabar, which had formed part of the Madras province under the British. At the center was Cochin and further south the important state of Travancore, which extended to Cape Comorin. The rulers of Travancore had their headquarters at what is now the Padmanabhapuram Palace. The former British outposts at Fort Cochin and Anjengo were smoothly incorporated, while Mahe, a tiny French protectorate, remained a part of French Pondicherry, which has now become a Union Territory.

**Trivandrum** was made the state capital. **Cochin**, which has a superb natural harbor, became the main commercial center, incorporating the town of **Ernakulam** on the mainland as a convenient base. Some of the old ports, which had received orders from the court of the biblical Solomon for teakwood, ivory, gold and peacock feathers, and provided the Egyptians with the spices that were needed for embalming the royal dead, and much later sent shiploads of pepper to the Romans, still exist. Kerala still provides up to 40 percent of the world's pepper. **Cannanore** and **Calicut** (calico was made here) from where fine cotton goods sailed both east and west, are still known for their textile industry, Cannanore being especially associated with "seersucker," cotton fabric.

**Alleppey** is known for its coir; **Quilon**, another ancient port, is famous for cashew nuts, while **Kottayam**, further inland, is a center for rubber, teak, tea and coffee. **Palghat**, which is strategically located in the wall of the Western Ghats, is a very picturesque town and is known as the rice bowl of Kerala.

High up in the mist-covered mountains of Kerala are the tea estates at **Munnar**, **Peermade**, and further north, the **Wynad** region. There are the famous temple towns of **Trichur**, **Guruvayur**, **Vaikom** and **Kodungallur** or Cranganore (the ancient Muziris), at which temples more often than not carry signs that say "For Hindus only".

Besides these, there are hill stations and game sanctuaries such as **Thekkady**, **Ponmudi**, **Malampuzha Dam**, and **Idukki**. With its long, sea-facing profile, Kerala has some fine beaches, the best known of which is **Kovalam**. Kerala has a rich tradition of dance and has made a unique contribution to theater with its form of dance-drama, *kathakali*.

Kerala has also produced some outstanding film makers and writers, and has the highest rate of literacy in India. Industrially, Kerala is rich in minerals. The first cement factory, using seashells, was started at Kottayam. Kerala also boasts a refinery and an atomic power station.

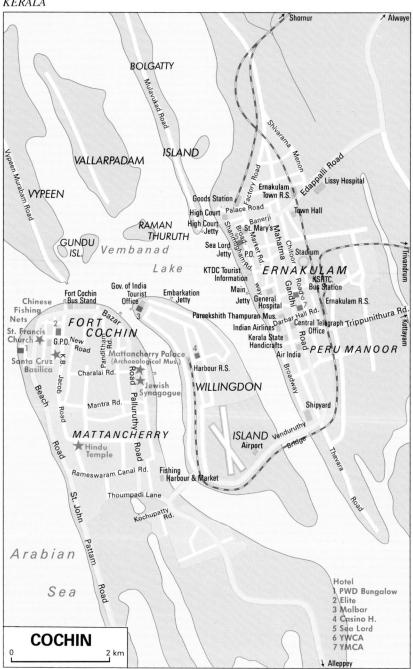

**COCHIN**

0        2 km

Hotel
1 PWD Bungalow
2 Elite
3 Malbar
4 Casino H.
5 Sea Lord
6 YWCA
7 YMCA

## Cochin

To the modern visitor, **Cochin** offers all the attractions of Kerala in a concentrated package. One of the best ways of getting to know what is available is to make use of the excellent services provided by the **Kerala Tourism Development Corporation (KTDC)**. They have arranged two excursions by ferry boat that explore old and new Cochin, at **Bolgatty Island** (where the British Residents used to stay in solitary splendor in a house that has now been turned into a guest house), and **Gundu Island** (where coir mats are made). The **Tourist Office** is next to the **Malabar Hotel** on **Willingdon Island**. Though the tour officially starts from the jetty on the mainland at **Ernakulam**, visitors may also board the boat from the Willingdon Island tourist jetty.

The atmosphere at **Fort Cochin** is quaint and infectious. The spirit of the Portuguese, the Dutch and the English lingers in the narrow streets and the architecture of the houses as it does in the fine old **Church of St. Francis**, where Vasco da Gama was buried in 1524. Fourteen years later his remains were taken back to Lisbon, Portugal, but his tombstone still marks the spot where he was once buried. The church itself (the oldest to be constructed by Europeans in India) stands as a record to the changes of historical necessity. It was first a simple wooden structure built by the Franciscan monks who came with Pedro Alvarez de Cabral, who followed in the tracks of Vasco da Gama.

When the Portuguese felt that they had a hold on the land, they rebuilt the church in stone. Almost a century later the Dutch took over and it became a Protestant church. In 1795, the British turned it into an Anglican church, and now it is run by the Church of South India. Visitors are shown how the hand-operated fans or *punkahs*, pulled by servants sitting outside, moved in waves over the pews, cooling the congregation. A fascinating register, which visitors may examine, has records of births and marriages dating to the colonial era. The **Basilica of Santa Cruz** is also worth a visit.

The early morning ferry stops at **Mattancherry** (Cochin), popular among sailors for its bright-eyed "Mattancherry Mamas" but better known to tourists for its palace which contains some smaller masterpieces of mural painting. The **Mattancherry Palace** is an interesting slab of a building, two stories in height, with a massive, square, tiled roof associated with the Dutch style of roof design, in contrast to the Portuguese tradition of slender roofs over individual rooms. It is also called the **Dutch Palace**, because although it was originally built by the Portuguese as a peace offering to the Cochin Raja of that time, whose palace they had destroyed, it was later renovated by the Dutch. Part of it serves as a **Museum** that displays artifacts, including palanquins, used by the Rajas. Wall paintings decorate the bedrooms and private cambers. They portray traditional themes from the two epics, the *Ramayana* and the *Mahabharata,* in a manner that reflects the lush countryside of Kerala. The use of color is particularly subtle.

From the Dutch Palace to the **Jew Town** is a only a small step but the atmosphere changes, all is very neat and quiet and the air is filled with the aroma of spices. This was once an affluent quarter dominated by the "White Jews" of Kerala (as opposed to the Black Jews who had their own synagogues). The White Jews handled the spice trade. Now the tiny Jewish community in Cochin has dwindled to 30 persons as the younger generation has migrated to Israel.

The **Clock Tower** dominates the narrow lane that leads to the **Synagogue**. It was built in the 18th century by the famous Ezekiel Rahabi who used to trade pepper with the Chinese. He also in-

stalled the quaint blue and white porcelain floor (which makes you feel as if you are standing in a soup plate when you walk into the synagogue) by importing the hand painted tiles, no two of them alike, from China. There are two pulpits; one of them may be used by the women, who are very independent here. The Synagogue, known as the "Pardesi" or foreign synagogue, is a wonderful sight during feast days, when the sacred scrolls are displayed in huge carved silver cylinders topped with golden crowns and the walls are covered with rich brocade hangings, the special oil-filled chandeliers are lit inside and a tall tree-shaped lamp of lights (the *menorah*) is kept burning at the entrance outside.

Other attractions at Cochin include the **Museum of Kerala History and its Makers** with a one hour sound and light show that touches upon the highlights of

*Above: Not the rope trick, but a fisherman winding up for the day. Right: Large Chinese fishing nets at rest at Cochin.*

Kerala history, using cleverly sculpted models.

In the evenings, there is a speeded up version of *kathakali*, the dance-drama of Kerala. Traditionally, such performances take place over a cycle of ten nights in a special hall within a temple complex. Dance, music, song, discourse – both comic and serious – and drama are combined to bring alive well-known sequences from the epics. The story is of secondary importance. The skill of the actors lies in creating a mood, or feeling, that will enable the audience to react and respond in sympathy, anger, and finally understanding. To most people, therefore, a quick display of *kathakali* hardly makes sense. It is nevertheless interesting to watch the dancers lie in a state of suspended animation, while the elaborate *kathakali* make-up is applied, and to watch their transformation from human beings into gods. Those who are more interested may visit the school of dance at **Cheraturuthy**, near Palghat, where the **Kerala Kalamandalam** was established

by the poet Vallathol to preserve the traditional dance-dramas of Kerala.

For the indolent there is no better place to observe the variety of Cochin than from the seclusion of the **Malabar Hotel**, on the fingertip of **Willingdon Island**, where it points towards the Arabian Sea. Willingdon Island is sandwiched between two channels of water that separate it from the busy city of **Ernakulam** on the east and Cochin on the west. The most spectacular sunsets can be seen here: as the sun slowly sinks, it appears to fall into the gigantic Chinese fishing nets that hover against the skyline. These nets are a delicate reminder of the ancient links with China and may be seen elsewhere, for instance in the backwaters of Quilon.

The Chinese came to pick up luxuries such as ivory, gold and pearls, for which the coast was famous, and also pepper, mahogany and camphor wood. The Chinese had their own fort near Calicut called "Chinnakotah" and have left a number of traces in the daily life of the Keralites, for instance the *Chinnachatti* or round metal *wok* with handles.

Willingdon Island is indeed a gift from the sea. It has been dredged from the seabed during the widening and improving of the natural harbor of Cochin. The role of island creator was played by the British marine engineer Sir Robert Bristow. He has left a lively account of his feat, which, given the time and age he lived in, – between the two world wars –, was an engineering miracle.

## Temple Towns

Kerala has some of the rarest temples in India, built in a style that is unique and profoundly pleasing. Some of them are circular structures with conical copper-tiled roofs. Others have been set out with a marvelous understanding of the use of space, both covered and uncovered to create a feeling of harmony that is echoed in the use of carved wooden gables and pillars to support the pitched roofs with their tapering finials. While most of these

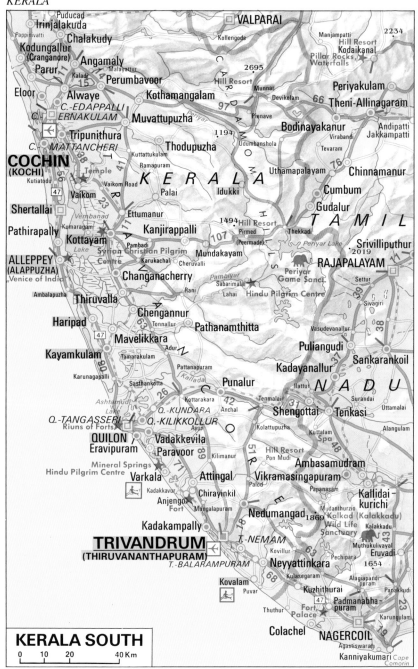

**KERALA SOUTH**

0   10   20        40 Km

architectural masterpieces are unfortunately out of bounds for non-Hindus, it is still possible to enjoy the activity that takes place just outside a temple. A visit to temple towns such as **Trichur** (74 km/46 miles north of Ernakulam) and **Guruvayur**, still further, is worth the trip, if only for this reason. Trichur is also where the grand *Pooram* festival takes place at the **Vadakkamnathan Temple** in April-May.

Everyone can see this festival, because a movable image of the main deity is brought out to witness a competition between two rows of magnificently arrayed elephants whose owners brandish brilliantly decorated parasols set on top of bamboo poles. The crowd roars its approval for the best side, and the musicians deafen everyone within earshot. The climax of the festival is when night sets in and the sky is filled with fireworks. For exotica and pageantry, there are few festivals in India that can match *Pooram*.

**Towards the Mountains**

Cochin may also be used as a base for one of the mountain retreats nestling in the mist-covered slopes of the Western Ghats. **Kaladi** (48 km/30 miles northeast of Cochin) is a famous place of pilgrimage and the birthplace of Adi Shankara, who preached the philosophy of Advaita or non-dualism in the 8th century A.D. **Munnar** (137 km/85 miles from Cochin) is surrounded by tea gardens and breathtaking scenery. The hillsides are covered with carefully tended tea bushes. The planters live in gracious old bungalows, meeting up in the British era planters' clubs, where it is sometimes possible to get overnight accommodation. By contrast, the **Periyar Game Sanctuary** is a very busy wildlife resort, centered on a huge artificial lake. The road to Periyar passes through **Kottayam**, an important commercial town dominated by the Syrian Christian community of Kerala.

There are interesting churches in Kottayam, especially at **Cheriapalli** and **Valiapalli**. The town, situated on the eastern shores of the immense Vembanad Lake, is linked by boat to Alleppey. Kottayam can also form the base for a fascinating journey into the interior of the backwater country, to genuine backwater islands such as **Kannaidy** and **Pulinccano**. **Kumarakam** is a pleasant tourist resort on the outskirts of Kottayam, set in the midst of a rubber forest.

The road to Periyar passes through plantations of rubber, teak, coffee and tea, and spices may be obtained in a small town called **Kumily**, just outside Periyar. The highlight of a visit to Periyar is a guided tour of the lake with a sight of the birds and animals that come to the edge of the water for a drink, particularly in the early morning. The elephants and deer are always around despite the noise made by boatloads of people. Professional guides also lead trekking parties into the surrounding jungle.

Since Periyar is on the border between Kerala and Tamil Nadu, it is customary to continue on the same road to Madurai and the other temple cities of Tamil Nadu. Some visitors prefer to go back to Cochin, for a very interesting drive towards Trivandrum.

All along the road to Alleppey people can be seen working at the thriving cottage industry of coir making. **Shertallai,** in particular, is an important center. The fiber is made from the husk of the coconut and is but one product of the "tree of life," as the coconut palm is known in Kerala. No part of this tree is wasted, and its innumerable uses include the medicinal. In fact, there is a whole science of oil massage in Kerala, done for therapeutic purposes. At **Shoranur** there is a center for oil massage therapy and natural medicines for which Kerala is well known. The Arya Vaidya Sala at **Kottakal** preserves and promotes the knowledge of the alternate system of medicine that used to

rest in the hands of traditional doctors, or *Vaidyars,* who had a deep knowledge of herbs and medicinal plants, which might well have been a legacy from the ancient forest dwellers.

The gymnasiums or training schools for the martial arts, called *kalaris* (such as the C.V.M. Kalari in Trivandrum), use coconut oil for massage, to keep the muscles of the trainees supple.

### Backwater Country

**Alleppey**, wedged between the Arabian Sea and the Vembanad Lake (which stretches all the way to Cochin), and crisscrossed by canals, was once known as the "Venice of the East." A weed, called *African payal*, has clogged many of the canals but the town still retains a charm that is worth experiencing. It is fa-

*Above: Coconuts, still indispensible to the lifestyle of Keralites. Right: Christian religious procession at Trivandrum beach.*

mous for its boat race. On the road to Quilon there are interesting temples at **Ambalapuzha Haripad**, and a palace at **Kayamkulam**.

Alleppey and Quilon are at the center of the famous backwaters. Quilon is at the edge of the vast **Ashtamudi Lake**. Though the backwaters may be seen at Cochin itself, there is nothing to compare with the beauty and dreamlike quality of the backwaters of Quilon. Most people prefer to take a one-way trip by boat from Quilon to Alleppey, or from Alleppey to Changanacherry, for instance, and then to pick up a taxi or bus to the next destination. The idea of using the backwaters as a quick transport system was started by Tipu Sultan, the so-called Tiger of Mysore, who had his eye on Kerala in the course of his stormy career, but it was the British who perfected the canal systems. The beauty of this area is unique and unforgettable, a lotus eater's land, silent, with shining stretches of water filled with lotus and lilies, and marshy tracts where water birds wade. Roads are replaced by

canals, and graceful boats are the only mode of transport. A journey through the backwaters (the total area covers 3,200 sq. km or 1,236 sq. miles) affords a glimpse of a people for whom water is a way of life. Houses built on narrow strips of land reveal the owners' personal beliefs, for the doorways are variously adorned with a crucifix, a photograph of the holy city of Mecca, Lenin, or the Narayana Guruswami who proclaimed that all men are equal and all life sacred in the eyes of God. Nature has wrapped this diversity in a harmonious embrace which does not leave the visitor untouched.

### Trivandrum

**Trivandrum**, the capital of Kerala, is a charming, friendly town with an undulating landscape where large public buildings are surrounded by lovely gardens. Formerly the capital of the Travancore Maharaja, it has wide avenues, a well-kept **Zoo**, a **Botanical Garden** and a museum. Most fascinating today is the **Napier Museum** which is situated in a strange building with an elaborate roof, a combination of colonial and traditional architecture. The Maharajas of the past were wealthy and indiscriminate collectors of souvenirs which they liked to display to their awestruck subjects. Besides such items, there is a good bronze and ivory section, a display of the traditional jewelry of Kerala, and a model of a temple. Even more interesting is the adjacent **Sri Chitra Art Gallery** with its extensive southeast Asian art collection and special sections devoted to the Himalaya paintings of the Roerichs, father and son, that have aroused much admiration. There are also paintings on mythological themes by Raja Ravi Varma, a prince and native son of Kerala.

Trivandrum is also famous for the **Padmanabhaswamy Temple**, built in the Dravidian style, but again this is only accessible to Hindus. The biggest attraction for the visitor to Trivandrum is the fabulous beach at **Kovalam**, just 11 km (7 mi) away (see the section on Beaches).

KESAVADA-SAPURAM

↖ to Quilon

47

to Nedumangad ↗

Avenue

Quilon Road

MUTTADA

Kavudiyar Palace

KAVUDIYAR

KUMARA-PURAM

PATTAM

Main Central

NANDANKOD

Kowdiar

★ Pattam Palace

Ullur Todu

Kollur

★ Botanical Gardens, Zoo

★ Raj Bhavan

★ Chitra Art Gallery

Kanaka Kunnu Palace

Rd.

Mascot

Rd.

★ Napier Museum

★ Vellayambalam Palace

Rd.

Christ Church of India

✝ University Hostel

Public Library

Rd.

Senate Hall

✝ St. Joseph's Cath.

Taj

Tagore Centenary Theatre

Cotton Hill

General Hospital

University

✝ St. George Syrian Ch.

Rd.

Statue Rd.

Secreteriate

Anayara Rd.

Sankumukham Rd.

✝ St. Anne's Ch.

Central Telegraph Office
Central Bank of India

G.P.O.

Central Stadium

YMCA

Tourist Information

Hospital

CHAKKA

Petta Stn.

VANCHIYUR

Press Rd.

Residency

Chettikulangara Rd.

M Gandhi Rd.

Tourist Office

Bus Stn.

Aristo

Killi Ar

Karali

Parvati Puttam Ar

PERUNTANI

Aratt Rd.

Thakaraparambu Rd.

Central Stn. Rd.

Taikkad

Central Stn.

Ajanta

Power House Road

FORT

☪ Padmanabhaswamy Temple

Chalai

Bazar

to Nagercoil ↗

Rd.

Sanku-mukham

Road

★ Bhajanapura Palace

☪ Chala Juma M.

Lucia Continental

CHALA

Aerodrome

Srivaharam Ambalam T.

Sastam Kovil

Kochchiravila Rd.

Kovalam Rd.

Nedumkad

**TRIVANDRUM**

0        1 km

■ Hotel

The local beach is at **Shakhamukham**, near the airport. It is not advisable to swim at Shankhamukham, but a visit to the picturesque fishing village nearby is very interesting.

Because of the reorganization of the country on a linguistic basis, the star attraction of Kerala architecture is now a part of Tamil Nadu, 55 km (34 mi) south of Trivandrum on the Cape Road. This is the fabulous palace of **Padmanabhapuram**. It was the ancient capital of the old Travancore or Venad State from the 16th to the late 18th centuries.

It is forever associated with the name of King Marthanda Varma, who not only dedicated himself to reconstructing the Sri Padmanabha temple at Trivandrum, but encouraged the development of the arts and literature in spite of having to face severe political uprisings throughout his rule. It was also as a result of his ad-

*Above: Elaborate make-up creates this mask, worn by a Kathakali dancer.*

ministrative acumen that the center of power shifted to Trivandrum.

**Padmanabhapuram Palace** is set in a wild and beautiful landscape backed by hills. The palace, built of wood, is a supreme example of the sophisticated and pleasing nature of traditional Kerala architecture. Such perceptions of space and form, more reminiscent of the architecture of southeast Asia, are unique in the whole of India.

The high degree of architectural skill and the innate elegance of the Kerala builder and artist can be admired in all their austere charm at Padmanabhapuram Palace. One need only mention one room, the Council Chamber, where the King would meet his advisors, to illustrate the rare and touching charm of the palace.

The chamber has black polished floors that shine like mirrors, wooden walls that lean out to meet the roof and to filter the light and air in mysterious patterns, and a delicate network of intricate carvings to support the roof.

## TRIVANDRUM
### Accommodation
*LUXURY:* **Hotel South Park**, opp. University College, Tel. (0471) 65666.
*MODERATE:* **Hotel Horizon**, Aristo Rd., Thampanoor, Tel: 66888. **Lucia Continental**, East Fort, Tel: 73443. **Mascot**, Palayam, Tel: 438990.
*BUDGET:* **Youth Hostel**, Veli, Tel: 71364. **YMCA Guest House** Palayam, Tel: 77690.
### Restaurants
The restaurants attached to Hotel Belair, Kovalam Beach Resort, Hotel Lucia Continental, Mascot and Jas Hotels are recommended.
### Museums / Art Galleries
**Napier Museum**, open 8 am-6 pm, closed Mon and Wed mornings. The **Sri Chitra Art Gallery** is in the same compound.
### Post / Telegraph / Telephone
**General Post Offic**e, Palayam, Tel: 73071. **Central Telegraph Office**, Statue, Tel: 61494.
### Tourist Information
**Kerala Tourism Development Corporation**, Trivandrum, Tel: 61897.

## COCHIN (Ernakulam)
### Accommodation
*LUXURY:* **Malabar Hotel**, Willingdon Island, Tel: (0484) 6811.
*MODERATE:* **Casino Hotel**, Willingdon Island, Tel: 340221. **Sea Lord Hotel**, Shanmugham Road, Ernakulam, Tel: 368040.
*BUDGET:* **YMCA**, Chittor Road, Tel: 355620. Fort Cochin has several inexpensive lodges: **PWD Bungalow**, Dutch Cemetery Rd. **Elite Hotel**, near the Church of St. Francis. **YWCA**, near GPO.
### Hospitals
**City Hospital**, M.G. Road, Tel: 38977. **Lissy Hospital**, Kariyil Road, Tel: 32102. **Susrusha Nursing Home**, Tel: 313799.
### Museums / Art Galleries
The **Pareekshith Thampuran Museum** on Darbar Hall Road, houses 19th-century paintings, ancient coins, sculpture, photographs, chandeliers, musical instruments, chinaware and mirrors. Open 9.30 am-12 noon and 3-5.30 pm. **Dutch Palace**, Mattancherry.
### Post / Telegraph / Telephone
**Head Post Office**, Fort, Tel: 24247. **Head Post Office**, Hospital Road, Tel: 31610.
Two post offices, Tel: 6270, 6065, are on Willingdon Island. **Central Telegraph Office**, Mattancherry, Tel: 25554.
### Restaurants
**R.K.Oberoi**, **Volga**, **Tandoori** and **Malaya**. **KTDC's** restaurant at the airport. Others are in hotels, Bharat Tourist Home, Casino, Malabar.

### Tourist Information
**Tourist Information and Guide Service**, Govt. of India Tourist Office (adjacent to Malabar Hotel), Willingdon Island, Tel: 6045.

### Accommodation
## KOVALAM
*LUXURY:* **Kovalam Ashok Beach Resort**, Kovalam, Vizhinham, Tel: 68010, 65323.
*MODERATE:* **Hotel Rock Holm**, Lighthouse Road, Vizhinjam, Tel: 306, 406, 407. **KTDC Hotel Samudra**, G.V. Raja Road.
## ALLEPPEY
Moderately priced rooms are available in lodges. The **Alleppey Prince Hotel**, Tel: 3752/58, is government approved.
## PONMUDI
**Tourist Bungalow**, **Guest House**, **Holiday Huts** offer accommodation at low tariffs.
## THEKKADY / PERIYAR
**Aranya Nivas**, Tel: Kumily 23. **Lake Palace**, Tel: Kumily 24. **Periyar House**, Tel: Kumily 26. **K.R.S.Rest House**, Tel: Kumily 71. **Spice Village**, Kumily Rd., Thekkady 685536, Tel: 04869-2134.
## KOTTAYAM
*MODERATE:* **Anjali Hotel**, K.K. Road, Tel: 3661. **Hotel Ambassador**, K.K. Road, Tel: 563293/94, 563755. **Hotel Aida**, M.C. Road, Tel: 61391-5.
*BUDGET:* **Homestead Guest House**, **Anurag Lodge.**

### Festivals
A ten-day *Utsavam* celebration takes place at the Padmanabhaswamy Temple, Trivandrum twice a year (March/April and October/November). Folk dance, music and an elephant procession are the highlights. This festival is also celebrated in other towns/ temples.

Between January and April there are colourful festivities at Suchindram (74 km from Trivandrum), Aranmula (128 km), Nagercoil (78 km, in neighboring Tamil Nadu), Tripunithura (8 km from Ernakulam), Ettumanoor Shiva Temple (11 km from Kottayam) and Guruvayoor (a major pilgrim center 29 km from Trichur). *Ararat* celebrations, at the same location (March/April) are marked by a display of fireworks.

*Onam* (August/September) is a harvest festival celebrated throughout Kerala; the exciting *snake boat races* held in Cochin, Kottayam (78 km), Aranmula and Alleppey (64 km) draw large crowds. Trichur (74 km) is the site of the *Pooram* festival. Devotees all over the state pray for prosperity on *Vishu* (April/May) the paddy rice sowing season.

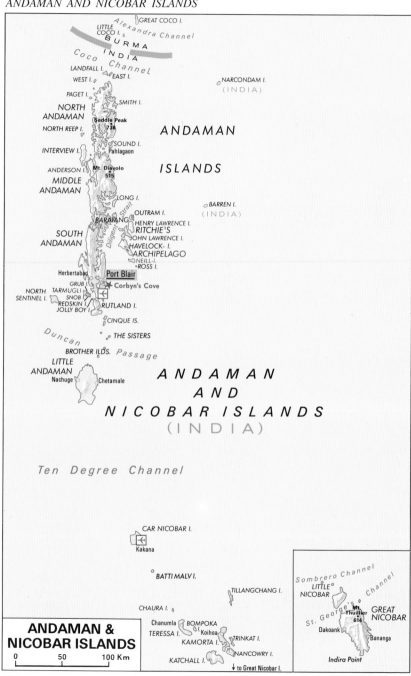

GREAT COCO I.

*Alexandra Channel*

LITTLE
COCO I.
**B U R M A**

**I N D I A**

*Coco Channel*

LANDFALL I.
WEST I.
EAST I.

NARCONDAM I.
(INDIA)

PAGET I.
SMITH I.

**NORTH
ANDAMAN**

Saddle Peak
738

**A N D A M A N**

NORTH REEP I.

INTERVIEW I.
SOUND I.
Pahlagaon

**I S L A N D S**

ANDERSON I.
Mt. Diavolo
515

**MIDDLE
ANDAMAN**

LONG I.

BARREN I.
(INDIA)

OUTRAM I.
BARATANG
HENRY LAWRENCE I.
**RITCHIE'S**

**SOUTH
ANDAMAN**

JOHN LAWRENCE I.
HAVELOCK- I.
**ARCHIPELAGO**

NEILL I.
ROSS I.

Herbertabad

**Port Blair**

GRUB I.
Corbyn's Cove

**NORTH
SENTINEL I.**
TARMUGLI
SNOB I.
REDSKIN I.
JOLLY BOY I.
RUTLAND I.

CINQUE IS.

*Duncan*
THE SISTERS

BROTHER ILDS.
*Passage*

**LITTLE
ANDAMAN**
Nachuge
Chetamale

**A N D A M A N**

**A N D**

**N I C O B A R   I S L A N D S**

(I N D I A)

*Ten   Degree   Channel*

CAR NICOBAR I.

Kakana

BATTI MALV I.

TILLANGCHANG I.

CHAURA I.

Chanumla
BOMPOKA
TERESSA I.
I. Koihoa
KAMORTA I.
TRINKAT I.
NANCOWRY I.
KATCHALL I.
↓ to Great Nicobar I.

*Sombrero Channel*
**LITTLE
NICOBAR**
*St. George's Channel*
Mt.
**Thuillier**
614
**GREAT
NICOBAR**
Dakoank
Bananga
*Indira Point*

**ANDAMAN &
NICOBAR ISLANDS**

0     50     100 Km

# EMERALD ISLANDS

**ANDAMAN**

**NICOBAR**

**LAKSHADWEEP**

## ANDAMAN AND NICOBAR

On a map they look like scattered emeralds. As you get closer, from the air, the Andaman Islands are like pearls rising out of the dark blue of the Indian Ocean. The water is so clear that you can see the outline of the islands in concentric rings of changing colour right down to the bottom of the seabed.

The **Andaman** and **Nicobar Islands** are a group of 293 islands that lie scattered halfway between Calcutta and the Equator stretching in a north-south direction over a span of 725 km (450 mi) and almost reaching the tip of Sumatra. Ethnically they are not part of India, and until recently were peopled by several tribes with different physiognomies and and languages. The capital of this Union Territory of India, **Port Blair**, is linked by air and sea to Calcutta (1,255 km/780 miles) and Madras (1,191 km/740 miles).

The existence of these islands was first reported in the 9th century by Arab merchants, who sailed past them on their way to the Straits of Sumatra. Marco Polo called it the land of the head hunters. The Andaman and Nicobar Islands were an-

nexed by the Marathas from the Indian mainland in the late 17th century. The first westerners to set foot on the islands were the Danes when establishing a settlement on the Nicobars which was left in 1768.

Thirty years later the British established a penal settlement on South Andaman which was abandoned in 1796 due to unhealthy living conditions. During the Anglo-Burmese wars, the Nicobars were used as a base for the East India Company. Finally, in 1872, both groups of islands were annexed by the British and remained untouched by time until World War II.

For many Indians, until the early part of this century the Andamans were a dreaded penal settlement known as *Kala Pani* or Black Water, where the most hardened criminals were sent, never to be seen again. This macabre fascination continues with the preservation of the **Cellular Jail** as a **Museum**.

During World War II the Japanese occupied the islands and created their own record of cruelty. They also built excellent concrete bunkers, noticeable from vantage points all over the main islands, and introduced fruit trees and edible crops that continue to thrive. The swallows who nest at **Chiriya Tapu**, a delightful picnic spot, were supposed to

*Preceding pages: Fisherman from Andaman Islands in his catamaran.*

have provided them with the delicacy known as Birds Nest Soup. After India had become an independent country in 1947, the Andaman and Nicobar islands became part of the Indian Union.

There are still a few tribes left on these islands: the Greater Andamanese who number around 26, and the Onges who live around **Dugong Creek** and **South Bay** on the Little Andaman Islands and are described as Negritos by race. They live by trapping and fishing, for which they make excellent drum-shaped pots.

The Onges number just a little under 100. The Jarawas comprise 250 persons, while the North Sentinelese are the most mysterious of all, Stone Age hunters who once attacked any intruders with their long poison-tipped arrows. The Nicobar Islands are peopled by tribes who show distinct traces of Mongoloid features and

consist of the Nicobarese and the Shompens. Since independence, groups of Indian immigrants have settled in the Andamans, which they like to call "Little India." There is a large naval base at Port Blair, which was named after Lt. Reginald Blair, the British naval surveyor who mapped out the area. There is also an excellent hotel, **The Bay Island**, built of hardwoods, including the rosy *paduk* that abound on the islands. Port Blair also has an **Anthropological Museum**, a **Cottage Industries Emporium** where one can shop and a Burmese temple at **Phoenix Bay.** A number of wood-based industries are also to be seen and a favorite tourist excursion is to watch the elephants engaged in logging operations in the jungle. **Corbyn's Cove**, just 10 km (6 mi) out of town, is a popular beach with an informal beach hotel resort.

Foreign nationals need a permit to visit the Andaman and Nicobar Islands, but this is available on arrival at Port Blair itself, whether by air or sea. The initial permit for 15 days can be extended for an-

*Above: A fisherman adrift on the blue seas of Lakshadweep. Right: A strange underwater encounter, off Lakshadweep Islands.*

other 15. Visitors can move freely in the area of the Great and Little Andamans, as well as to the islands within a radius of 70 km (44 mi) from Port Blair. The islands that may be visited include those known as **Grub**, **Snob**, **Jolly Boy**, **Redskin**, **Cinque** and **Brothers**.

It is possible to hire a boat and set off for one of these islands. Many are completely uninhabited but full of such natural splendor as to leave the mind in a state of perpetual enchantment. The islands are ringed with a fine white coral sand and one has only to wade in knee-deep to enter an underwater world filled with a dazzling variety of fish and corals. For snorkeling enthusiasts, the shallow waters provide an endless adventure.

If you have a reliable guide, a boat, and good company, you can camp on the islands during the day and sleep on board the boat at night. The best idea is to catch your own fish and leave it to the servants on board to clean it, cook it and salt it for drying while you slip into the water for a late evening swim. After dinner you can

lie back and watch the stars fall into the dark waters; every ripple glows with phosphorescence and soon even the restless birds are silent. You feel that you have entered paradise, yet even paradise can get lonely, so it is best to visit the Andamans in the company of friends.

## LAKSHADWEEP

Off the coast of Kerala, scattered in the Arabian Sea, are the Laccadive Islands, also known as Lakshadweep. Like the Andamans they form part of the Union Territories of India. Of the 36 islands covering a land area of 32 sq. km (12 sq. miles), only ten are inhabited. They are, in descending order of size, Minicoy, Androth, Kavaratti, Kadmat, Agathy, Ameni, Kalpeni, Kiltan, Chetlat and Bitral. The total population amounts to about 40,000. Most of the inhabitants are Muslims who speak Malayalam. Copra production from coconuts is the core of the economy on the inhabited islands. The archipelago offers good facilities for

cruising in the crystal-clear water of the lagoons, watching numerous varieties of fish from glass-bottom boats, and bathing on lonely beaches with white sand. During the monsoon, the islands tend to get cut off from the mainland. Four of the islands, **Kavaratti**, **Kalpeni**, **Kadmat** and **Minicoy**, are open to Indian visitors, while the island of **Bangaram** has recently been opened up for international tourists. The best way to reach it is by air from Cochin to **Agatti**, the island closest to Bangaram, which is accessible by boat. Two ships ply regularly from Cochin to Lakshadweep, but can take as long as 20 hours. Those who take the ship automatically get a permit to land along with their ticket. Others have to get a permit from the Lakshadweep Office on Willingdon Island at **Cochin**, **Kerala**.

The Ali Raja of Cannanore, of the only Muslim royal family of Kerala, annexed these islands for himself. This may ac-

count for the predominantly Muslim population on the islands. Since the 18th century, when a queen of Cannanore ceded the islands to the British, the populace has lived in almost com-plete isolation, depending on the cultivation of coconuts, some fishing, and also scattered efforts at boat building on Minicoy. The tourist is therefore left very much to his own resources both materially and mentally. The facilities at Bangaram are minimal and the island is so small that you can walk around it in no time and then settle down to the more serious business of underwater exploration of the coral reefs. There are "family huts" available on Kavaratti and Kadmat for about Rs 60. On Kalpeni, Minicoy and Kavaratti you can stay at inexpensive "beach resorts" for Rs 25. On Kadmat there is a youth hostel (Rs 10). All other luxuries and distractions are just not available, and the islanders, who were recently introduced to TV, returned their sets deciding they could do without it! The Lakshadweep Islands are the last frontiers of an enchanted world.

*Above: Two generations of working elephants on the Andamans.*

MANGALORE
Parambul
Bantval
Ullal
Manjeshwara
Puttur
Kasaragod
Kahangad
(Hosdrug)
Nileshwar
Payyannut
Taliparamba
Azhikode
CANNANORE

CHETTLATTI I.
BITRA I.
AMINDIVI ISLANDS
KILTTAN I.

KADAMATT I.
PERUMAL PAR I.
AMINI I.

BANGARAM I.
AGATTI I.
PITTI I.
ANDROTH I.

CANNANORE ISLANDS

Kavaratti
KAVARATTI I.

LAKSHADWEEP
(LACCADIVE ISLANDS)

L A K S H A D W E E P
(LACCADIVE ISLANDS)
(I N D I A)

CANNANORE
CHERIYAM I.
KALPENI I.
ISLANDS

LAKSHADWEEP

Nine    Degree    Channel

SEA

MINICOY I.
(INDIA)

Eight    Degree    Channel

INDIA
MALDIVES

MALDIVE            MALDIVES

IHAVANDIFFULU    KANDUFURI
ATOLL

ISLANDS
FILADU
TILADUMMATI ATOLL

## LAKSHADWEEP

0        50        100 Km

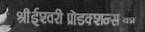

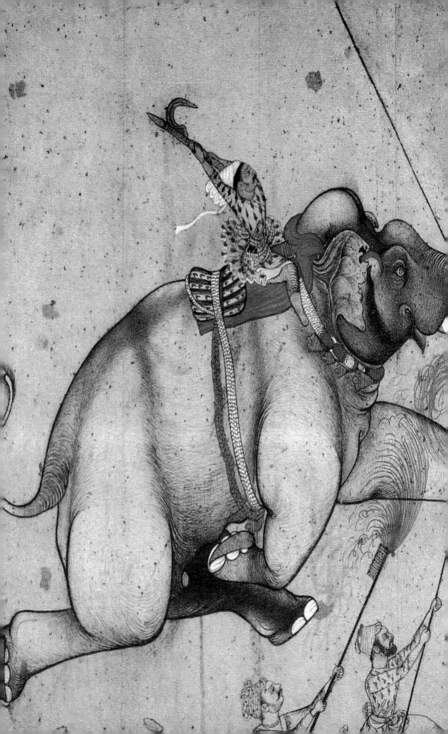

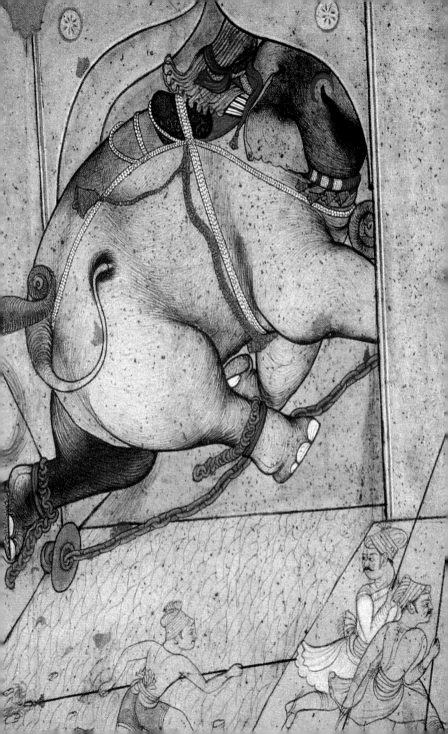

## THE GASTRONOMICAL TOUR

Indian recipes have been handed down orally from generation to generation, memorized and closely guarded. This is the reason why India's culinary art, despite centuries of refinement, is not as well known as that of France or China. There is also the fact that Indian cuisine varies from region to region. This confusion has perpetuated some misconceptions regarding Indian cuisine. It is reputed as being "rich" (some say "fatty") and "spicy" (some say "chilli hot"). Indian food is rich, but not fatty. It is true that food is sometimes cooked in excess fat, but the ingredientsthen expel all fat when fully cooked. The excess fat merely eases the cooking process and is supposed to be drained off before serving. (The drained fat or *rogan* can only be re-used once.) Similarly, Indian food is spicy, not chilli hot. Exotic spices are used for their special flavor and aroma. The use of red chillies is at one's own discretion.

### North Indian Cuisine

A culinary safari must begin with *Tandoori* cooking because it is the *tandoor* that has helped to popularize Indian cuisine the world over. North India's traditional clay oven, fired by charcoal, is probably the most versatile kitchen equipment in the world. One cannot make decent bread without it, nor can one savor the popular *kebabs* (though some *kebabs* are shallow or deep fried). Sauces and *dal* (lentils) made in the *tandoor* acquire a unique taste.

Punjab, home of the *tandoor*, has a robust cuisine influenced by invaders - Greek, Persian, Afghan and Mongol - who came from the northwest. The *tandoori* food which can be savored here, as

*Preceding pages: Film fantasies. Wall painting of elephants in combat. Right: A mango vendor waiting for customers.*

in other parts of the country, includes *Tandoori Jhinga* (prawns), *Tandoori Pomfret* or any other fish, whole or *tikka* (cubes), *Tandoori Murgh* (chicken), *Murgh Tikka* or its many variations (with mint, garlic or cheese), *Seekh Kebab* (minced lamb rolls, grilled in the *tandoor*), *Amritsari Machchi* (fish) and *Tawa ka Tikka*. Punjabi cuisine boasts equally good non- *tandoori* food. The remarkable aspect of this "other" cuisine is its simplicity. The earthy *Sarson-da-Saag* (mustard leaf spinach with knobs of white butter), *Makki-ki-Roti* or corn bread and *Lassi* or churned yoghurt is Punjab's eternal dish. The most popular - and commonly available - Punjabi dishes are *Murgh Makhani* (butter chicken), *Raarha Meat* (stir-roasted lamb), *Kadhai Chhole* (white gram or chicken cooked in the Indian wok), *Hara Chholia Te Paneer* (fresh Bengal gram and Indian cottage cheese), *Bhartha* (charcoal smoked au-bergine, cooked with onions and tomatoes) and *Dal Makhani* (the country's favorite lentil delicacy). Punjab's other grand contribution is the *dhaaba* - the roadside eatery that is an important feature of Indian highways.

Mughlai cuisine is actually the food of Hindustan, particularly the north. The Mughals provided patronage to, and became connoisseurs of, India's culinary art. In any event, the Indian kitchen flourished like never before and nowhere did it prosper more than in Awadh or what is today the **Lucknow** district of Uttar Pradesh.

The traditional Awadh cuisine found a champion in India's best known gourmet - Nawab Wajid Ali Shah. Awadhi delicacies include *Murgh Mussalam* (stuffed chicken), *Gosht Qorma* (an incomparable saffron, mace and cardamom flavored lamb curry), *Nahari* (essentially a breakfast lamb curry eaten with sour dough bread), *Subz Gosht* (a stew of lamb, turnips - or zucchini - and spinach, cooked in mustard oil), *Phaldari Kofta* (raw ba-

nana balls cooked in a rich tomato gravy) and *Dhingri Dulma* ( a combination of mushrooms and Indian cottage cheese tem-pered with black cumin). *Kakori* and *Galouti* are two *kebab* specialties.

## South Indian Cuisine

The small state of **Goa** offers an intriguing variety of cuisines - Christian and Hindu, Brahmin (both Hindu and Christian) and non-Brahmin (both Christian and Hindu), as well as Muslim and Portuguese and even Kashmiri since the Saraswat community originally came from Goa. There are subtle differences in the choice and use of ingredients, and in preferences, too. Hindus like lamb and chicken, Christians prefer pork. Both, however, prefer fish to meat. Goan food is chilli-hot. The fact that until a few years ago the men of Goa dominated the kitchens of the nation's finest hostelries is eloquent testimony to their culinary skills. The best Goan dishes are: *Goa Curry* (an exotic sauce that features *fruits*

*de mer*), *Prawn Balchao* (prawn pickle, usually eaten as an *entrée*), *Vindaloo* and *Sarpotel* (the two most popular pork dishes).

Hyderabad's dedication to gourmet eating has been unwavering over the last few centuries and the Hyderabadi Muslims will not brook any tampering with their cooking style. Despite a rich culinary heritage, it is difficult to find a distinctive meal in the city's restaurants. The food is authentic and tasty but there is little variety. The menu at most eateries is identical - *Kachchi Biryani*, plain and special, mutton, chicken and egg; *Nihari* served morning and evening and prepared with *zuban* (tongue) and *Paya* (trotters). *Haleem* replaces *Biryani* during *Ramzan* (Ramadan), and is enjoyed for the *tawanaee* (strength) and *rizaiyat* (nourishment) it provides during the month of fasting.

Tandoori Chicken has made an appearance on the menu, but the popular *kebabs* are *boti* and *seekh*, *Shikampur* and *Dum ke kebab*. The common desserts are *Dab-*

199

*Above: Tamil Nadu food, thali, served on palm leaves.*

*bal ka Meetha*, a Hyderabadi version of the ubiquitous bread pudding and *Qubani ka Meetha* a sweet prepared with dried apricots. It is a good idea to hunt for delicacies like *Pakki Biryani* (which takes nearly 40 ingredients to make), *Pasande ka Salan* ( a lamb piccatta curry), *Dum ka Murgh* (chicken simmered in its own juices with an assortment of spices), *Kairi ka do Piaza* (lamb and raw mangoes cooked with onions) and *Baghare Bengan* (aubergine cooked with peanuts and tamarind).

Andhra, Karnataka, Kerala and **Tamil Nadu** boast many superb culinary styles - Malabari, Tulu, Coorg, Syrian Christian, Cochin Jewish. Many of the recipes are common - with minor differences, of course - to every genre of southern cooking. There are some inexcusable - and unforgivable - misconceptions about the food of the south. While the West only knew of "curry," the ubiquitous *Madras*

*Soup* and *Mulligatawny*, what was even worse was that most Indians themselves were unaware that the region's cuisine was much more than *Dosai* (a rice pancake), *Idli* (steamed rice cake), *Bonda* (spicy potato balls), *Vadai* (doughnut-shaped lentil fritter, laced with pepper), *Sambhar* (the omnipresent lentil cooked with drumsticks) and *Rasam* (literally "juice" or "extract" of tomatoes) which are all breakfast foods, snacks and/or accompaniments. Without taking anything away from these delights, it must be said that each state has a varied cuisine. Just as inaccurate is the belief that southern food is "strictly" vegetarian. While the south has remained more or less vegetarian, the variety of non-vegetarian – especially seafood – delicacies is unmatched. The bewildering array of meat dishes notwithstanding, rice and *dal* (lentils) remain the heart and soul of a southern vegetarian meal and are supplemented by a plethora of vegetarian delights.

Other features of southern cooking are the liberal use of coconut, *kari* (curry) leaves, fenugreek seeds, tamarind and asafoetida. Contrary to popular belief, the food of the south is not chilli-hot.

The notable exceptions are the cuisines of Andhra (excluding Hyderabad, terribly hot) and Kerala (tolerably hot). Among the specialties are *Iggaru Royya* (prawns spiced with cumin, fenugreek and pepper), *Nandu Masala* (coconut-flavored crab curry), *Milagu Kozhi Chettinad* (a "devilled" chicken curry), *Vendakka Masala Pachchadi* (okra which has been simmered in a yoghurt-based sauce).

Incidentally, "curry" is an oversimplified form of the Tamil word *kari*, which means sauce. The word "curry" does not even exist in any Indian culinary dictionary. However, thanks to the Raj legacy – and much to the disgust of all Indians – the word became synonymous with Indian cuisine.

The insipid, colorless and tasteless stew a handful of *khansamah* (ill-trained cooks) prepared to pander to the sahibs' taste became India's culinary shame. The confusion was even more confounded when the sahibs themselves started cooking the stuff using "curry powder" which, again, is non-existent in any list of Indian condiments. Fortunately, the world is now learning to distinguish between the different styles of Indian cooking and between different sauces – not curries.

There are two schools of **Bengali** cooking – *Bangal* and *Ghoti*. The home of *Bangal* cooking was what is now Bangladesh, whereas the purveyors of the *Ghoti* style are the West Bengalis. *Ghoti* food is usually sweetened with sugar or jaggery. The use of mustard is limited to a handful of delicacies.

Like the Chinese, the West Bengalis hate to waste any trimmings. One of their best known accompaniments is *Chenchki*, which is gourd or pumpkin peelings, shredded, fried crisp and tempered with *panch phoron* (five spices) and red chillies. Both styles have a penchant for freshwater fish and tiger prawns. Also common is the use of mustard oil, which provides a unique flavor as a cooking medium. The dishes to look for: *Lau Chingri* (prawns and squash cooked with *randhooni* or *ajwain*), *Dohi Machch* (freshwater fish cooked with yoghurt), *Shukto* (coconut-flavored mixed vegetables), *Samukh Kumbra* (snails and red pumpkin cooked with mustard) and, inevitably, *cholar dal* (washed Bengal gram).

### Desserts

Another misconception is that Indian cuisine is considered notoriously weak in what westerners think of as desserts. *Phirni*, *Kulfi*, *Gajjar-ka-halwa*, *Gulab Jamun*, and *Rasmalai* are a few among the variety of Indian confections that are hard to match. The Rajasthanis actually make a dessert from garlic, which is delicious. And the chefs of Lucknow make a mutton and rice dessert where the meat is cooked as for any other curry dish and the rice is cooked sweet!

Mushq-e-Tanjan (*mushq* or aroma of the heavens and *tanjan* or treasure) is not only hard to imagine but also a delicacy by which the Awadhi Chef's skill is tested. The skill lies in getting the rice to absorb copious quantities of sugar without becoming caramelized and sticking to the bottom of the *handi*. A master chef can achieve a ratio of four parts of sugar to one part of rice. If you can achieve a ratio of 1:1 consider yourself a brilliant cook.

Indian food served at home has a perfect and subtle balance and Indians ate in courses before the French ever had a cuisine. Even the serving of sorbet between courses has been adapted from the Indian tradition of serving *sherbet* between the courses. Indian food should be a harmonious blending of different colors, aromas, flavors, shapes and textures, to be enjoyed by all the senses.

## THE TEMPLE TRAIL

The temples of south India are fascinating not only as artistic expressions from the past but also as living religious institutions where traditions, integral to the life of the people, are still preserved. This temple trail covers four groups of tem-ples, each absorbing in its own way.

The first group constitutes the Cha-lukyan temples at Badami, Mahakuta, Pattadakal and Aihole. Badami, the ancient capital of the Chalukyas, has the earliest Hindu temples of monumental dimensions in the south. Hindu sanctuaries from the 6th to the 9th centuries A.D. assumed different forms, among which cave temples were predominant. The origin of the cave temple is linked to the concept, articulated in the Upanishads, of the human heart being the abode of sanctity. The heart, in turn, is likened to a cave (*guha*). The four cave temples at Badami were excavated in the 6th century under the patronage of Chalukyan rulers. They are characterized by a boldness of conception, with an emphasis on adorning the ceiling, as well as the brackets above the pillars, with sculptures. Vigorous images of the gods were sculpted within the sides of the cave. There are also a few structural temples in Badami but these are interesting for their architecture rather than their sculpture. These ancient temples at Badami have now ceased to be centers of worship. In contrast, Mahakuta (10 km/6 miles) has one among many Chalukyan temples, where worship has been offered for nearly 1500 years. The main shrine is surrounded by several others, though these are not used for worship. Neither are the temples at Aihole and Pattadakal, which were thriving centers of worship at the time of the Chalukyas. One of the most striking features about the temples at these four sites is the

*Right: The temple priest at the holy well on Thirukalikundram hill.*

fact that they were built in clusters, yet in varied forms and always near a water source. While all the temples at Pattadakal are structural in form, Aihole has cave temples as well. The other striking feature is the co-existence of three styles of temples – the Dravidian, with the tower above the sanctum, the northern, exemplified by the vertical *sikhara*, or spire, and the Kadamba style with its stepped pyramidal superstructures.

Exuberant sculptures dominate the next group of temples, near Mysore, which are the creations of the Hoysala rulers. The temples at Halebid, Belur and Somnathpur appeared nearly 600 years after the Chalukyan group, and the intervening period witnessed a dramatic change in style. There are no cave temples, while structural forms had become more complex with the incorporation of twin or triple forms within a single plan. Simple, bold and realistic expression succumbs to a desire to over-embellish. Practically every inch of wall space has been carved with floral patterns and figures. The beauty of divine and human forms, highlighted by flowing lines and sensuous curves is seen beneath the elaborately worked details of jewelry and costumes. These Hoysala temples are perhaps unmatched in their profusion and intricacy of sculptural detail.

In contrast, the Gommatesvara at Sravanabelgola inspires an austere wonder. The naked figure here radiates a serenity in comparison to which everything around seems trivial. This Jain savior symbolizes one whose spirit has achieved absolute perfection, which is the ultimate aim of every Jain, and which is believed to be possible only through extreme non-violence and severe asceticism. The Gommatesvara stands in the attitude known as *kayotsarga*, or dismissing the body. It represents the absolutely perfected being, purged of all the idiosyncrasies that add variety to life. The Jain faith, which advocates a life of simplicity

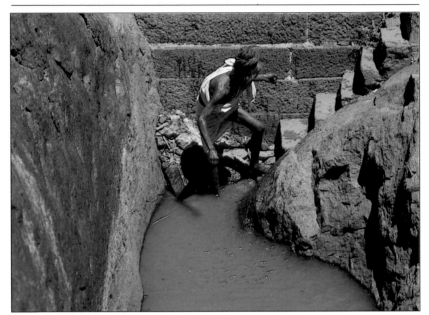

and asceticism, could not have created a more eloquent monument to its most cherished ideals.

Most South Indian temples follow a basic architectural pattern. Their orientation is eastwards. Two *gopura* (towers), one each in the east and south, rise from the rectangular boundary wall, although they may be built on the other sides too. Within the temple compound there are pavilions, tanks, courts and shrines. At the main entrance there is a *balipitha*, a "dispensing seat" which is a small stone altar on which Brahmins leave offerings of rice. Behind this stands the *dhvaja-stambha*, the "flagstaff", a tall mast with three horizontal perches that indicates the main sanctuary. Between the mast and the sanctuary, there is, in Siva temples, a recumbent Nandi (the bull, Siva's mount) facing the temple entrance; in Vishnu temples it is either the Garuda (a mythical being, half-man, half-eagle, and Vishnu's mount) or the monkey god Hanuman.

The main sanctum is quadrangular, and lit with oil lamps. Here is enshrined the anthropomorphic image of the god or goddess, or, in the case of Siva temples, the *linga*. Within the compound of the temple are shrines dedicated to the god's wife and children, the natural family unit. The walls and steps of these buildings are decorated with white and red vertical stripes, considered auspicious.

However, the most conspicuous part of the temple is the *gopura*, which is usually twice as high as it is broad. The monolithic doorposts are usually decorated with bas reliefs. The number of stories in the towering *gopura* is always uneven, and each is decorated with little pavilions, the central one being larger than the others and pierced with a single open window. Images of gods and goddesses and *dvarpalas* (door guardians) are carved on each story, the details being reduced in size, but not omitted, as the height increases.

Tamil Nadu is the land of great and beautiful temples that remain centers of devotion. At Madras itself is the Kapalisvara Temple in Mylapore, and the Partha-

203

sarathi (Vishnu) Temple in Triplicane, where daily worship and festivals are conducted exactly as prescribed in the ancient religious scriptures. Both are at least 1300 years old, and are mentioned in the hymns of saints of the devotional movement. The Kapalisvara Temple, which permits non-Hindus to enter, has all the components of a living Hindu temple. The temples at Mahabalipuram and Kanchipuram can be visited conveniently from Madras.

At Mahabalipuram, barely an hour's drive from Madras, the 8th-century Pallavas have left the best examples of their classical rock-cut art. Worship is not performed at these temples but their sculptural wealth is overwhelming. Even the monolithic *rathas* look like beautiful sculptures. There are several cave temples, 10 monolithic *rathas* and structural temples including the picturesque Shore Temple. There is a unifying order in these temples, yet each creation is different to the other in plan, elevation, sculptural form and arrangement.

Kanchipuram, the ancient capital of the Pallavas, offers the best scope for studying the evolution of South Indian temple architecture from the 7th century to the present day. There are over 100 temples. The well-known ones include the Kailasanath Temple and the Ekambesvara Temple, dedicated to Siva; the Varadaraja Temple dedicated to Vishnu; the Kamakshi Temple honoring the Goddess Parvati; the Subrahmanya Temple; and a Jain temple. Various structures, such as sanctum towers, entrance towers, enclosures, pillared pavilions and flag masts were added through the centuries, and they provide ample opportunity for the understanding of these features.

Chidambaram is the starting point for the last group of temples suggested here. Chidambaram is the abode of Lord Nataraja, the "cosmic dancer." The distinctive features of this temple are the bronze image of Nataraja, which is the main image of worship instead of the Siva *linga*, as in other temples, and the superstructure of the sanctum over Lord Nataraja, which is like a thatched hut, covered with gilded metal tiles. Nataraja was the family deity of the Chola emperors, who had the privilege of being crowned in the divine presence. Chidambaram is the "holy of holies" for Saivites; literature, religion, philosophy, music and dance evolved around this temple for nearly 2000 years.

Gangaikondacholapuram is about one hour's drive from here. The magnificent Siva temple of this Chola capital lies en route to Kumbakonam, which was an ancient township. There are several important temples at Kumbakonam, but two can especially be recommended – the Nagesvara Temple and the Ramaswamy Temple. The former, with a 9th-century structure, has the loveliest of all the early Chola sculptures. The Ramaswamy Temple, a 17th-century Nayak construction, is famous for its wonderful sculptures. On the outskirts of Kumbakonam is a beautiful later Chola temple (12th century) at Darasuram. The meandering road leads on to Tanjore, which rose to prominence in the 9th century as the capital of the Cholas.

The towering temple here was built entirely of granite by the illustrious Rajaraja I, around A.D. 1010. The sanctum tower is the loftiest in the south, encircled by a cloistered enclosure and two entrance towers. The temple is unique in all aspects – in its sculptures, bronzes, paintings, music, dance, inscriptions, rituals and also as an integrating center of the different regional languages.

Madurai is well known for its temple to the Goddess Meenakshi, who is one of the aspects of Parvati, Shiva's consort. Madurai city itself grew in concentric circles around the Meenakshi Temple. A unique feature of the city is that each street encircling the temple is named after a month of the year.

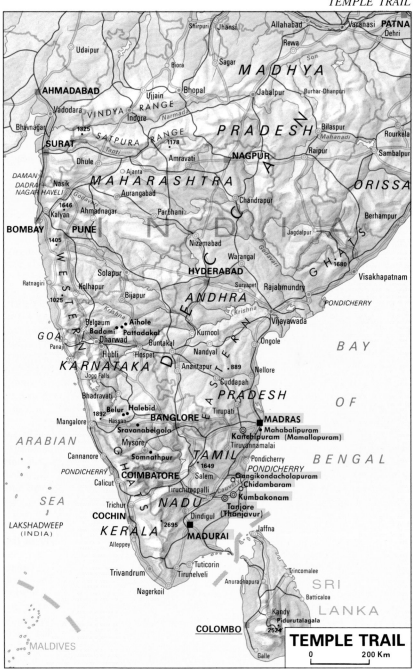

TEMPLE TRAIL

0    200 Km

205

## BEACH RESORTS

The beaches of India trace a shining garland of sand, rocks and pebbles around her pendant outline. The western shores are washed by the dark waters of the Arabian Sea. This is the aromatic Spice Coast that enticed the intrepid Arabs into a triangular trade between Africa and India. To the east are the warm waters of the Bay of Bengal and the Coromandel Coast, once known for its pearl fisheries and ancient seaports with their wood-fired lighthouses. The south yields to the sublime beauty of the Indian Ocean. At Kanniyakumari, Cape Comorin as the British called it, at Land's End there is a temple to the Virgin Goddess, forever young, forever free, where the traveler or the pilgrim may watch both sunrise and sunset. This 6,000 km (3728 mi) long coastline offers several beach resorts, best visited in the winter months.

### Gujarat

**Chorwad Beach** is on the Saurashtra coast of Gujarat. Its charm lies partly in its perfect isolation. It is 70 km (44 mi) away from the little visited but fascinating town of **Junagadh**. The airport at **Keshod** is 47 km (29 mi) away from Junagadh and linked by a daily flight from Bombay. The **Chorwad Beach Palace Resort** used to be the summer palace of the Nawabs of Junagadh. It has 75 rooms and all the usual facilities, including a swimming pool for those who may find the sea itself a little rough. Chorwad is also conveniently located for visits to **Palitana**, the fabulous hill-top Jain temples, the Hindu temple of **Somnath**, the birthplace of Mahatma Gandhi at **Porbandar**, and **Gir Forest**, the last home of the Asiatic lions. Just 20 km (13

*Right: Companions bathing after a hard day's work .*

mi) away from Chorwad is **Veraval**, a quaint fishing town where nimble-fingered girls from Kerala pack tonnes of lobsters, prawns, and shrimps in ice.

### Bombay

Further down the coast, at **Bombay**, local residents would consider both **Chowpatty Beach** and **Juhu Beach** as special places, but these are not recommended for swimming. More secluded, are the beaches of **Marve**, **Madh** and **Manori** (40 km north of Bombay) and accessible by rail or road most of the way. Of these, the first two are crowded on holidays and may be enjoyed only from the seclusion of a private cottage.

There are echos of the Portuguese at **Marve** which make for an interesting ramble. It is best to take the ferry from Marve (it also carries goats and pigs) to the curving tip of a piece of land known as **Manori Island** that is actually connected by a circuitous route to the mainland. From the leeward side to the beach it is possible to hire a bullock cart to take you to the private houses and cottage-style beach resorts that look out towards the sea. Here, too, the spirit of the Portuguese lingers in the style in which the local women dress and the small bakeries that produce a hard- crusted bread. The **Manoribel Hotel** is one of the more charming places to stay.

### Goa

The beaches of **Goa** will seduce you totally. **Calangute** must head the list, for it is not only a fine curving stretch of sand, backed by a hospitable grove of trees, but part of the legend of the colorful wave of flower children who washed over it. Nowadays they or their children are to be found further north in **Anjuna**, which has a well-known flea market, and on the beaches at **Mandram**, **Morjin** and **Vagator**. The up-market tourists make

for the **Aguada Fort Hotel**, just south of Calangute at the mouth of the Mandovi river, looking out towards the open sea from where the conquistadors came. The old **Fort** was so named because of the fresh water it provided to the ships, and it is closely linked with Alfonso de Albuquerque who, in 1510, extended a well-mailed fist, in the name of God and the Portuguese king, and seized the country that comprises Goa.

At Panjim, or Panaji, on the south bank of the Mandovi River, there are the small beaches of **Miramar** and **Dona Paulo**. It is worth while, however, to go further down and discover the white sandy beach at **Colva** that stretches on forever. In between there is the secluded bay of **Bogmalo** that creates an almost private beach for the guests staying at the five-star **Oberoi Beach Hotel** .

The fun of the Goan beaches, however, lies in the fact that the local folk enjoy them too and much serenading accompanied by guitars and drinking *feni* goes on. Goans are among the most hospitable people, and their cuisine is a memorable ingredient of any beach holiday.

### Kerala

**Kerala**, which has its own share of superb beaches and fiery sunset views, has been more pragmatic in the matter of encouraging tourists. It has gone out of its way to develop the **Kovalam Beach Resort** (only 11 km / 7 miles from Trivandrum) as a deluxe tourist resort.

There are now excellent hotels to cater to all levels of tourist and the local population has followed right on, providing refreshments in the best spirit of free enterprise. There are shacks on the way to the beach selling seafood, caught and fried right under your eyes, and friendly vendors of ripe papayas, pineapples, and mangosteen. You may drink the nectar from a freshly plucked coconut through a straw, or try toddy, the slightly fermented, mildly alcoholic drink that is made from the juice that drips from the trunk of the palm tree.

## Tamil Nadu

The beaches on the eastern coast are less well developed. At **Pichavaram** (15 km/9 miles east of **Chidambaram** in Tamil Nadu) there are the fascinating mangrove swamps that may well once have extended like a soft green sponge all the way down the coastline. Here the Tamil Nadu Tourism Department has provided a few cottages and a youth hostel. Boats are provided to row through the backwaters lined with mangrove trees that need the brackish water to grow. You can also row down to the beach for a swim. Though very much off the beaten track now, Pichavaram was once at the center of history. To the north is the former French territory of **Pondicherry** with **Karaikal**, another small enclave, south of Pichavaram. There is also the romantic old fort of **Tranquebar** that be-

*Above: Indian woman having a quiet moment on the beach. Right: Beachcombing can be a lot of fun for cows, too.*

longed to the Danes; and **Porto Nuovo** that once flew the Portuguese flag.

Further up the coast is **Mahabalipuram**, the once splendid port of the Pallava kings of south India, who sent their ships to southeast Asia. A stone carved lighthouse that used to be lit with wood fires may still be seen dominating the hill-top close to the new lighthouse.

Mahabalipuram is famous for its **Shore Temple**, the last of what tradition maintains were seven pagodas that were slowly eaten up by the sea; the world renowned bas-relief called **Arjuna's Penance**; and some of the finest sculptures to be seen in India. The beaches stretch all the way to Madras, and where people and nature have conspired to work together to create a place of relaxation, the results are very peaceful and satisfying. There are some excellent resorts and beach hotels, and delicious seafood is available. The sea is inclined to be rough. It is a pleasant experience to take a ride with the local fishermen in their rafts or *catamarans,* made by lashing together three, five or

seven logs, that have been carved slightly into the shape of a boat. Once you get beyond the surf the water is warm and buoyant. The ride back through the crashing surf under the expert guidance of the fishermen is the nearest thing to being on a surf board.

### Orissa and Bengal

The next best bet for beach lovers is high up on the coast of Orissa. There is a small but exquisite beach called **Gopalpur-on-Sea** by the British, and **Gopalpur** by everyone else. For Indian pilgrims, however, there is no other destination in this area than **Puri**, for they go there to the famous **Jagannath Temple**. The beach at Puri is the place for a ritual dip and devotees who may never have seen the sea before go into the water fully clad. They are assisted by *nolia*, the local fishermen in their conical hats, who are also supposed to act as informal lifeguards to those who might get dragged under by the current. The sea can be very rough. Towards the eastern end the beach is the special province of western tourists. Along this coast there are also the ghostly remnants of the once palatial houses of long dead wealthy landlords and princes that add to the strangeness of the place. A night spent on the beach is said to be a rare experience, for the darkness seems to be total while on the sands bands of phosphorescence appear.

Finally, there is **Digha** (185 km/115 mi southwest of Calcutta), a flat sandy beach that stretches for 6 km. From here onwards the fan-shaped channels of the River Ganga open and close over several islands. Of these **Ganga Sagar,** at the mouth of the main channel, attracts thousands of pilgrims. It is the end of a journey, or the starting point of a fresh one.

The biggest surprise to the beach lover is that so few of the beaches of India are known at all. They still are a carefully hidden secret, waiting to be discovered. Most Indians prefer holidays in the hills so most beach resorts are, therefore, blissfully uncrowded.

# INDIAN PAINTING

One of the unexpected surprises that awaits the traveler to India is its rich and distinctive modern art that is comparable to the best in the world. One is irresistibly caught by the vivid colors and the heady variety of forms that proclaim an international idiom as well as speak of a living connection to an ancient past. Some knowledge of this past will greatly help in understanding the nuances of contemporary art.

The recorded beginnings of painting date to the magnificent murals in the caves at Ajanta and Ellora (4th-century A.D.). Inspired by the Jatakas and other Buddhist themes, these somber paintings offer us evidence of a fully developed art, classical in the deepest sense. The figures have a flowing rhythm and their gentle curves and strong modeling suggest a volume that is almost sculptural. This classical form survived into the 11th century in south India, as can be seen in the lovely murals of the temple at Tanjore.

From about A. D. 800, we notice a marked change in the handling of the figure, as is evident in the Jain manuscripts of western India. The figures are treated spatially and show the artist's love for sharp angles and near-modern distortions of perspective. The calligraphy is chaste and a fine balance is invariably maintained between picture, text and empty space. The palm leaf manuscripts of eastern India have very small (as small as 13 sq. cm) but robust drawings, often on Buddhist themes. In these religious and secular texts, surfaces are alight with red, yellow, ultramarine, gold and silver - the first true expression of the Indian artist's inherent delight in color.

The imperial ateliers of the Mughals were set up around 1550. Akbar, during his reign (1556-1605), and Jehangir in

*Left: Three maidens under a willow tree, wall painting of 1810, Neogarh Fort.*

the 17th century, were the chief patrons of this genre which was defined by sumptuous coloring and austere elegance of form, the subject matter being court life, the Hindu epics, portraits (introduced for the first time), and studies of birds and other animals.

Flourishing around the same time were the so-called Rajput miniatures, centered in Rajasthan and the hill states. These utterly lyrical works show an almost startling ingenuity of composition and color orchestration, and generally focus on the theme of love, with Radha and Krishna as the divine lovers.

By the mid-17th century, Mughal painting had begun to decline, and in the 18th century there arose a hybrid Europeanized style far removed from the Mughal idiom, as painters were increasingly dependent for work on resident British officers and merchants. The subject matter of this "Company" painting was generally restricted to the picturesque surface of Indian life.

While the British admired our crafts, their attitude to Indian art was one of hopeless incomprehension, and as late as 1885, Sir Monier Williams could state with impunity: "... not a single fine large painting nor beautiful statue is to be seen throughout India."

The situation for the artist was made worse by the growth of an educated middle class Indian elite that subscribed uncritically to downgraded British taste and attitudes. This was partly because our own heritage remained undocumented. The first scholarly work on Indian architecture appeared in 1876, and on Ajanta in 1897. Miniature painting suffered an even more unfortunate fate, the first work on Mughal miniatures appearing only in 1908, and that on Rajput miniatures as late as 1912.

In 1905 the partition of Bengal took place and the country was afire with nationalism. Raja Ravi Verma (d. 1905) of the state of Travancore in south India had

already reintroduced Indian subjects in his large oil paintings. Bengal now became the center of a strong revivalist movement spurred on by a rediscovery of India's great cultural heritage, as more and more of it came to light.

Abanindranath Tagore led the artists in an outburst against British academicism but unfortunately they were swayed by nationalism rather than a serious involvement with artistic concerns. Not surprisingly, the result was mediocrity. Today, the small lackluster watercolors – the favored genre of that period – are mere curiosities, with the figures inspired by Ajanta, the themes taken from classical Indian literature, and all of it rather arbitrarily set in the format of the Mughal miniature.

In 1927, an event took place unique in the history of art. Rabindranath Tagore was already an internationally known poet and Bengal's leading writer when, at the age of 67, he took to painting. Indis-

putably he was India's first modern artist, and well aware of the folly of attempting to make an aged art young again. "When in the name of Indian art we cultivate with deliberate aggressiveness a certain bigotry born of the habit of a past generation, we smother our soul under idiosyncrasies unearthed from buried centuries. These are like masks with exaggerated grimaces that fail to respond to the ever changing play of life."

With no formal training except what he called "the training in rhythm – the rhythm in thought, the rhythm in sound", he turned instinctively to the right source, "the region of intuition, the unconscious, the superfluous." Haunting works in resonant colors poured from him "like lava" – 2000 watercolors between 1927 and 1941, that still speak eloquently to us today.

In the 1930s and 1940s, artists were well acquainted with the work of the Impressionist painters Van Gogh and Gauguin, whose paintings were reproduced in the English and American magazines

*Above: A drawing by Ram Kumar, 1966.*

that came to India. However, it is the art of China and Japan that had a decisive influence on pioneering artists such as Nandalal Bose, Ramkinkar Baij and Benode Behari Mukherjee. They used muted colors in the wash technique, and the expressive calligraphic stroke to record the luxuriant texture of Bengali landscape and the grace of its village folk. Jamini Roy, who turned to Bengali folk art for inspiration, pushed line and form towards bold simplification and gave up oils in favor of tempera and the colors of the village craftsman.

The first Indian artist to have a close familiarity with the best of European painting was Amrita Sher-Gil, who was an art student in Paris from 1929-34. Despite the short span of her life (1913-41) she left behind a small but impressive body of work, the Indian figure in repose being her favorite subject. The influence of Ajanta is marked in her colors, and generally in the gravity of her figures. Yet in the stylization and arrangement of forms, and in the handling of the pigment we see her declared intention of "approaching painting on the more abstract plane of the purely pictorial."

By the late 1940s, Delhi and Calcutta were centers of art, but the most significant activity was taking place in Bombay with the formation of the Progressive Artists Group (PAG) and the involvement of other painters who were informally associated with it. They were supported in their endeavors by the cosmopolitan ambience of the city and by the catalytic action of a handful of European émigrés who were the first collectors of modern Indian painting.

Just as in the past our culture had successfully assimilated and been enriched by its contact with foreign influences such as those of Persia and Greece, this time the eclectic imagination of our artists turned to the contemporary western masters such as Picasso, Braque, Klee, and the Expressionists.

F. N. Souza, who spearheaded the PAG, declared, "Today we paint with absolute freedom from contents and techniques, almost anarchic, save that we are governed by one or two sound elemental laws of esthetic order."

Our senior artists, who have put in four decades of work, have raised the stature of Indian art.

Most notable are the striking explorations of the human figure and bold graphic qualities in the work of M. F. Hussain and Tyeb Mehta. The figure in its more fecund and erotic aspect is seen in the work of K. G. Subramanyam and in the expressionistic canvases of F.N. Souza. Ram Kumar's abstractions, with their strong linearity and mature tones, evoke earth-sky-water, while the landscape as metaphor aptly describes the iridescent surfaces of Akbar Padamsee and the paintings of J. Swaminathan. In the realm of pure abstraction, V. S. Gaitonde and S. H. Raza stand unequaled.

Around the late 1960s a new generation of painters were attaining maturity, who were turning away from the west and leaning more heavily on their own tradition. Today's young painter is firmly rooted in India, and the sources of his inspiration are diverse - Tantra art, a wide range of folk and tribal art, the subtle geometry of our textiles, our rich calligraphic Indian epigraphy, and in a uniquely new way, our miniatures.

The subject matter of painting has widened to include women seen in a social context, the complexity and kitsch of our urban environment, the dreamscape, and a strikingly fresh interpretation of myth and legend.

Today, the Indian painter has a profound realization of the potentialities within his own tradition, as well as an easy acquaintance with trends in other parts of the world. His sensibilities are dynamic, and the repertoire of forms, images, and structures being created are a contribution to world art.

## ASHRAMS IN SOUTHERN INDIA

### Ramanashram

The Ramanashram at **Thiruvannama-lai** is a house of tranquillity at the foot of the great hill of Thiruvannamalai, also called Arunachalam. This ashram owes its origin to the sage, Ramana Maharshi, who lived here until a few decades ago. He was born of a Brahmin family at Thiruchuliyal village, about 70 km (44 mi) from Madurai, in 1879. Known as Venkatraman in his boyhood, he had an extraordinary mystical experience in 1896, when he felt that his body was different from his soul, a realization that prompted him to leave his studies and home, and come to Thiruvannamalai. The hill had been considered sacred since time immemorial. There is an important temple dedicated to Siva, and the hill and Siva are conceived as the glowing fire of knowledge celebrated in the legend of Siva's *linga* manifestation. Venkatraman entered an underground shrine in the temple complex and remained in meditation for over one year. It was with great difficulty that he was forced to re-accept consciousness of the world. His experience revealed that "one should realize one's own nature of infinite consciousness." He was not a preacher, but to those who approached him, he would say, "Know thy own self," or would urge them to enquire of themselves "Who am I?" Ramana, as he came to be called, had no use for rituals, sects, myths or miracles. Men were drawn to him by his radiant serenity. Several approached him with spiritual quests. His answers were not great philosophical exercises, but a simple and direct guidance to discover one's own potential nature. You are the Self, he says, nothing but the Self. Everything else is imagination. It is not necess-

ary to retreat into the forest. Carry on with your essential activities but free yourself from association with the doer of them. Always and at all times seek for the source of the ego, the apparent actor, and on the attainment of that goal, he tells us, the ego will drop away of its own accord and nothing will be left but the all-blissful Self.

Contemporaries record that the years 1935 to 1939 were the best at the ashram. The sage's health was good. Visitors flocked to the ashram from every corner of the world; there was hardly a country that was not represented at one time or another. The war interfered with the influx of foreigners but the number of Indian visitors steadily increased.

In his presence devotees experienced inexplicable quietude. He had infinite compassion for all living beings. Ramana Maharshi passed away in 1950. The ashram at the foot of the hill is open to all, and offers vegetarian food and accommodation. Thiruvannamalai is about 100 km from Madras, from where buses travel frequently.

### Aurobindo Ashram

Aurobindo Ghosh, the famous nationalist, humanist, thinker, and poet, combined in himself the briskness of the west with the illumination of the east. He was born in Bengal, and after a brilliant educational career, went to London to qualify for the Indian Civil Service. But his love for the freedom of the nation (which later matured into the freedom of the human soul), brought him back to India and made him an active participant in the struggle for independence. The British promptly imprisoned him, and charged him with conspiracy. When Aurobindo was in jail, he had a vision of Krishna, and at the end of one year, when he was released, he was a totally changed man. He gave up everything and came to **Pondicherry**. Aurobindo soon flowered into

*Right: Sadhus's retreat, with a lifesized image of his guru.*

one of India's foremost philosophers, who believed in directing the energies of the body, mind and spirit towards enlarging the boundaries of knowledge. He held that "it is not necessary to prove the existence of God. He is. In Him we live and move and have our being." He was no armchair philosopher: "Truth of philosophy", he said, "is of merely theoretical value unless it can be lived." His final word was that "we are, whether we like it or not, members of one another. Unless we realize this truth and act upon it, we shall never have peace and goodwill on earth."

Sri Aurobindo wrote several books; his essays on the *Gita*, and *The Life Divine*, are outstanding expositions. An illustrious French lady who came from Paris to Pondicherry was attracted by Aurobindo's philosophy. Later celebrated as the Mother, she joined Aurobindo as his disciple and took over the organization and administration of the ashram. Under her kind and efficient guidance, the Aurobindo Ashram at Pondicherry grew into an international center of community living. The ashram has acquired a number of buildings in Pondicherry. When Sri Aurobindo passed away in 1950, his Samadhi was built, wherein the body of the Mother was also interred in 1973 when she died. But before her passing away, she conceived the ideal of Auroville, a place of harmonious international coexistence, "where men and women could live in peace and progressive harmony with each other above all creeds, politics and nationalities." This was inaugurated at a ceremony on 28 February 1968. Situated at the outskirts of Pondicherry, in the midst of woods, Auroville affords a serene communication with nature. At its center is the Matri Mandir, a monumental structure, in which earth from all countries of the world is interred.

### Kanchi Sankaracharya Math

Quite in contrast to the ashrams described above, the Sankaracharya *math* at **Kanchipuram** gives the visitor an insight into the most traditional monastic institution and abode that has survived from the Upanishadic age.

The Sankaracharya *math* was established by Adi Sankara, the exponent of Advaita Vedanta, and is said to be nearly 2000 years old. According to tradition Sankara established five *maths* - four in the cardinal directions of India, where he nominated his disciples as heads, and the fifth called the Sarvanjna Pitha (the seat of transcendental knowledge) over which he himself presided. From the time of Sankara, an unbroken line of *sanyasins*, who are also called the Jagadguru Sankaracharyas, have served as the heads of this institution.

The present Acharya, His Holiness Sri Chandrasekharendra Sarasvati, is the most venerated sage of India. A man of extraordinary wisdom, simplicity and infinite love and grace, he personifies all that India has stood for for the past several thousand years. To the present-day Hindus, he symbolizes the Rishi of the Vedic Age. He has spearheaded a great movement to synthesize different sects, and approach godhood in the inner consciousness. He is seen by all, who, irrespective of caste, creed or sex, receive his blessings. He has already nominated two of his successors to carry on the mission. The *math* is very simple; visitors have to seek accommodation elsewhere in the city. Hundreds of visitors come each day to see the sage of Kanchi. His knowledge of world philosophy, and religious and current affairs is exceptional.

### Narayana Guru Ashram

Narayana Guru, whose birth centenary was celebrated in 1987, was born in Kerala of an Ezhava family, traditionally considered as outcastes. The oppression of the caste system urged him to rebel, and so he spearheaded a movement to emancipate the downtrodden. He encouraged his followers not to believe that they were low, but instead equal human beings. His main idea was to raise his kinsmen to the status of Brahmins. He appointed men from the lower castes to be temple priests. He also advised his men to discard the practise of sacrificing animals before gods and goddesses. He made his disciples learn Sanskrit and claim equality in all fields of knowledge. He built several centers in Kerala, including temples.

Soon he emerged as one of the beacons of social equality, was much respected for his wisdom and sagacity and came to be called the *Guru*, the enlightened one. His ashram is at **Varkala**, on a hill about 45 km from Trivandrum.

### Puttaparti Ashram

Puttaparti Sai Baba is a phenomenon in the spiritual life of the people of the south. Sai Baba is revered as a mystic and performs, according to his devotees, inexplicable miracles, which draw thousands of people around him. He encompasses the teaching of all religions - Hinduism, Christianity, Islam, Sikhism, and the like.

He speaks of the wisdom enshrined in the *Gita* and exhorts people to remember that God is constantly with them, watching all their activities. He encourages group devotional singing and philanthropic deeds. His devotees believe that he is God incarnate on earth and look to him for the removal of their sufferings.

Satya Sai Baba's main ashram – he has centers throughout the world – is in **Puttaparti** village (about 160 km from Bangalore), in Anantapur district of Andhra Pradesh. Called Prasanti Nilayam, the ashram is always bustling with activity. Accommodation is usually available, except on festival days, when there is an extra crowd. Situated on the banks of the River Chitravati, the ashram is near a hill called Vidyagiri, where there is also a university.

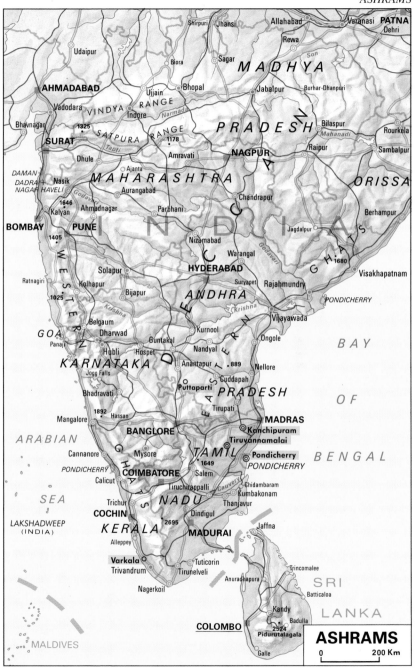

**ASHRAMS**

0          200 Km

217

## DANCE FORMS

"The heart and essence of the Indian experience is to be found in a constant intuition of the unity of all life and the instinctive and ineradicable conviction that the recognition of this unity is the highest good." (Ananda K. Coomaraswamy)

In a country that retains its philosophy through its ancient art forms of dance, music and drama, these words ring true when one is confronted with the diverse canvas that is Indian dance. For these sophisticated and stylized temple arts are not just skills to be learnt and perfected. Nor are they performances for the entertainment of a public. They are symbols of India's spirituality and a reflection of the socio-religious beliefs and development of a community over generations. There is a unity of thought, feeling, philosophy, myth and custom that binds all the dance forms of the country together. Yet, each of them takes on the fragrance, color, texture and appearance of that area from which it takes sustenance.

The south Indian dance forms are as varied and as similar as one can find. Basically, all dance in India has three broad visual streams – the solo performances where one artiste represents a classical style, the dance-drama traditions within these classical forms where a troupe of performers represent the style, and various folklore dance traditions in small or large numbers where the community is involved in celebration.

One cannot consider any of these from a merely technical viewpoint, nor in isolation from the literature, sculpture, musical surge and custom of the people of that state. For instance, the *Natya- Shastra*, an ancient Sanskrit treatise on dramaturgy written in the 2nd century A.D.,

that clearly lays down principles related to theater, music, poetry, literature and dance, is a text referred to and quoted by scholars of these disciplines from all parts of the country. Yet vernacular texts guide the spirit of each dance form imparting their special identity. This is true of the music, the poetry, the instruments used and the costume of these dance forms. The southern part of India, where varying traditions blend more gracefully with each other than their counterparts in the north, can boast of a style in every state: *Bharata-Natyam* from Tamil Nadu, *Kathakali* and *Mohini-Attam* from Kerala, *Kuchipudi* from Andhra Pradesh and *Odissi* from Orissa.

Bharata-Natyam, *Mohini-Attam* and *Odissi* were part of the tradition of *devadasis*, where maidens dedicated themselves in marriage to the temple-deity and were thus called "servants of God." This practice was referred to in early texts like the *Puranas* and evolved as a part of the temple ritual, within the temple precincts. There were *devadasis* in Karnataka as well, the most prestigious among them being those who danced in the temple. Others danced at marriages, or merely prepared temple offerings.

In Kerala, the daily rituals of preparing the flowers were also part of the duties of a *devadasi*. In Tamil Nadu, those who danced in the Siva temples were called *devadasis* and those who danced in the king's court were called *rajadasis*, or "servants of the King." Those who danced at festivals elsewhere were called *svadasis*. In spite of such rigid hierarchy, the dancers were a respected and envied community. In a society of harsh restrictions on women, a *devadasi* enjoyed freedom of expression, and, being the wife of God, she never became a widow. In fact, it was auspicious to look upon her when setting out on a journey. It is from this line of *devadasis* that the tradition of solo-rendering emerged to constitute a major strand of the art of dance in India.

*Right: An Odissi dance by Madhavi Mudgal. Far right: Bharatanatyam performed by Leela Samson.*

Siva – the god of dance – is the Creator, the Sustainer and, finally, the Destroyer. As Nataraja, a form seen in thousands of bronze and stone images in south India, he creates the universe through dance; sustains it with his rhythm and grants salvation: but he also destroys it. Every temple, and there were thousands, had to have an image of beauty for worship and to carry in procession during a festival. Thus the art of giving life to metal images of their God became a thing of unimaginable beauty.

It reflected the aesthetic and philosophical refinement of a people. Sanctified by daily worship, the images, now acclaimed worldwide, represent not merely an art, but the devotional fervor of the devotee. And although they were in the likeness of the human form, their contours and expressions were beatific, the point of perfection that the dancer in India today finds it difficult to better. Costumes worn by the dancers reflect the flowing garments in these statues, while the dance itself reflects their ornaments,

weapons, symbols and animals of carriage, and breathes life into the myths.

### Bharata-Natyam

Bharata-Natyam is a very dynamic and sophisticated dance form of **Tamil Nadu**. Its thematic content was regularized or given shape by the musicians of the Thanjavur court. It is accompanied by music sung in the classical style of the south, called the Carnatic school of music. Its instruments are also typical of this region - the cymbals, the *mridangam* (a single drum), the flute, the *veena* (a large stringed instrument with frets) and the violin. The style lends itself to both solo and dance-drama traditions. Visually it has a very linear quality, projecting a balanced measure of pure dance and expressional dance, of beauty and strength, of the slow and the fast. The dance-drama traditions of Tamil Nadu, on the other hand, are the *Bhagavata-Mela* of Thanjavur and *Therukootu* performed on street corners. The actors in

219

the *Bhagavata-Mela* were only men of a particular community and they presented stories from the *Puranas*. *Therukootu* was essentially an opera supplemented with impromptu dialogue between the *komali* (clown) and the *kattiakaran* (stage manager). Not surprisingly the most popular among these plays are episodes from the *Mahabharata*.

Bharata-Natyam is prevalent in **Karnataka** as well, and the dance-drama tradition of *Yakshagana*, a very forceful medium of storytelling, is one of its special arts. Like the *Kathakali* tradition of Kerala, it has elaborate costumes and make-up. Its crowns are similar to those used in *Otanthullal* of Kerala, but its drums are like the *Kathakali chenda*. A peculiarity of this drama is the ability of the actor not only to dance, but to sing as well, and to render dialogue on stage, a feat that conveys to the spectator the total

*Above: One of the dramatic moments in a Kathakali performance. Right: Radha and Raja Reddy performing a Kuchipudi dance.*

sense of drama represented in the ancient texts.

Kuchipudi comes from **Kuchelapuram** in **Andhra Pradesh**. It is based on the epics, and although it is a fusion of many aspects of drama, individual items from these are nowadays presented in solo presentations. Like *Kathakali*, *Yakshagana* and the *Bhagavata-Mela* dramas, *Kuchipudi*, too, was performed by men, many of whom were popular for their impersonation of female characters.

Kathakali is the grandiose story-play of **Kerala**. It has majestic form and high quality drama. With its billowy skirts and ornate make-up it is immediately recognizable as a vigorous male form of dance. It is a sophisticated and stylized art distinguishing between man and God, animal and bird, good and evil. Society in India recognizes these personages to be of the other world and once the mask-like make-up is completed the actor negates his smaller self to enter into the world of the superhuman. Primeval forces are made visual; the cries of evil are pitted

against the power of the gods. Swords and maces clash. There are leaps and dramatic movements and the drums sound loudly. Color distinctions range from green for mobility, green with red patterns and pith balls on the nose and forehead for noble characters in anger, black for demons and hunters, and orange for women and Brahmins. *Krishnattam*, *Teyyam* and *Kudiyattam* are similar forms. They are of a single tradition but vary in treatment. *Mohini-Attam* as its name suggests, is "the dance of the enchantress" and now a solo form in its own right.

### Odissi

Odissi brings to mind the waves of the ocean near **Konark**, Orissa, where the magnificent Sun Temple represents yet another lush stream of philosophical thought – the elaborate sculpture of dancing women and the *dharma* of Jagannath, the presiding deity of Puri. It is a very sculpturesque style of dance, sensuous and lyrical. Young Indian boys once performed a representation of it. Today, it has developed into the coming to life of sculpture.

To conclude, one should not fail to mention the martial-art traditions, the masked-dance traditions and the many folklore streams that nourish the more stylized forms. Happily, all these are receiving renewed attention and can still be viewed, if not on sophisticated platforms, at least,in their own environment where they belong. *Kalaripayattu*, the austere martial art of Kerala, requires the disciplining of body and mind to heighten reflexes. Visual concentration and controlled flow of energy allow for an alert culture of physical preparedness. The *Purulia* and *Seraikela Chhau* masked-dances of eastern India are attractive with masks of varied expression and beauty that speak of fine craftsmanship. "When the Actor beateth the drum, Everybody cometh to see the show; When the Actor collecteth the stage properties, He abideth alone in His happiness."

## TEMPLE RITUALS

In ancient India there was probably no other institution that could be compared to the temple for the variety of activities influencing the life of the people of the village around it. The deep effect of its cultural influence – it was a veritable treasure-house of art in all its aspects – was matched by its capacity to promote social intercourse, economic utility and moral action. An old Tamil proverb forbids residence in a village without a temple. The temple has lost this position in modern times, being confined now to the religious domain. A daily visit to the temple, however, is still a part of life, particularly in south India, and rituals are carefully observed.

Temple rituals are related to the location of the temple in the total layout of the village or township and its relationship with other temples and structures, the plan and elevation of the temple itself, symbolizing various metaphysical concepts, the daily rites and festivals. These rituals are codified in texts called *Agamas*, some of which date to the first century A.D. Two forms of rituals are recognized in these texts: temple worship, performed by initiated priests for the benefit of the community, and personal worship, at home. The different parts of the temple are conceived as manifestations of knowledge personified, and the whole temple structure symbolizes the totality of knowledge.

Worship is offered three times a day, in the early morning, midday and the evening. Depending upon economic circumstances, worship may be offered five or six times a day, although once a day is essential. The morning rituals begin with the invocation to the deity enshrined in the *sanctum*, and "the five purifications" of the precincts, the utensils, the priest's self, the image and the purification of the hymns by proper recitation. These are done by reciting hymns and sprinkling water. The Supreme Being is invoked in the symbolic image to receive the offerings and bestow blessings. The image is given a ceremonial bath and then decorated with clothing, jewels and fragrant garlands. The different names of the god (usually 108 in number) are recited in order and with each name a flower or *kumkum* (the auspicious red powder prepared with turmeric) is offered. The offering of incense is followed by that of food, which consists mainly of cooked rice and fresh sweets, by the offering of lighted lamps and finally of the great light with camphor (called *Deeparadhana*). This ritual consists of 16 parts. During each act of the ritual, Vedic hymns are recited, accompanied by specific gestures of the hand. At appropriate stages, instrumental music and vocal music are played. Earlier, dance also formed part of daily worship, which accounts for the institution of female temple dancers. The choicest of clothing, food, music and dance is offered to God and then partaken of as gifts of God. But even a simple leaf and a drop of pure water is sufficient if offered in the spirit of devotion.

In all the temples there are metal images, movable manifestations of the Immovable in the *sanctum*. During festivals, these metal images are taken out in processions. During the daily festival, the decorated metal image is taken around within the temple enclosure, to the accompaniment of music.

The annual festivals last for five, seven, nine or more days. On each day the metal image in one of its manifestations is mounted on a wooden, silver or gold-plated vehicle, like the bull, horse or elephant, and taken out along the main streets in procession. On the last day of the festival, the image is placed on a decorated chariot and taken through the main streets. This *ratha yatra*, as it is called, especially attracts crowds from distant places.

## WORSHIP OF THE LINGA

An important aspect of the cult of Siva, is the daily ritual worship of the *linga* which, as a phallic symbol, may be traced back to the pre-Vedic societies of the Indus Valley civilization (c. 2000 B.C.). Myths explaining the origin of *linga*-worship appear in the later layers of the epics, and are thereafter widespread. Foremost among these myths is the following, in which the *linga* symbolizes the illuminating pillar of light. Brahma the Creator and Vishnu the Protector once quarreled as to who was the superior one. When the quarrel reached a stage of frenzy there burst forth before them a glowing pillar of fire. Surprised at the sight of this, the two searched for its root and end. Brahma flew into the sky as a bird. Vishnu, as a boar, dived deep into the earth. But both failed in their attempts

*Preceding pages: At Thirukalikundram, feeding the holy birds. Above: A lingayat, wearing a silver linga. Right: Shiva linga.*

and returned humbled. From the middle of the shaft emerged Siva, bestowing knowledge on Brahma and Vishnu. Their quarrel, he said, arose from their egoism which shrouded their knowledge. This symbolic story summarizes the origin and essence of the Linga Cult. The *linga*, the cylindrical shaft, is the symbolic representation of Siva, the ever auspicious Lord. According to Saivite tradition, each individual soul is of the nature of limitless knowledge (likened to the illuminating light) and bliss. However, the ego veils knowledge and immerses it in darkness. When the self begins to realize its own true nature, the darkness of ignorance is dispelled and there emanates the illuminating consciousness that is Siva. This metaphysical concept is symbolized in visual representation as the *linga*. The *linga* enshrined in the *sanctum* is square at the bottom, octagonal in the middle and cylindrical at the top, which is visible to the spectator, the other two parts being hidden by the *pitha*. The square represents Brahma, the octagonal, Vishnu, and

*Above: Business and leisure at the cages in Bombays red light district Kamatipura.*

the cylindrical shaft above, Shiva. In effect the *linga* represents the Supreme Trinity of the Hindus.

There is another aspect that is sought to be conveyed by the *linga* - Siva as the potential cosmic energy, the Supreme Lord who is beyond form, color and actions. He acts through his kinetic form, the Sakti, poetically described as the female principle. Both represent one and the same principle, viewed from two different angles. This dual nature is symbolically expressed as the union of the male and female principles.

The *linga* represents the male and the altar on which it stands represents the female in their metaphysical and not physical sense. Thus the *linga* on the *pitha* is said to be the cosmic symbol.

There is yet another dimension to the *linga* given in some traditional legends, where it is said to represent the phallus, the reproductive organ of Siva. Interes-

tingly this legend stands for the total withdrawal from sexual indulgence. Siva is the ascetic par excellence, and the phallus is a symbol of the total rejection of sex. Siva is identical with Rudra, the Vedic god who is none other than the fire, Agni. Rudra, the pillar of fire, represents both the benevolent and malevolent aspects of fire. The *linga* is, in this sense, not only identical with the five basic elements; in some temples, it is said to be of the form of one of the elements.

When Hindus worship the *linga* they view it as the supreme symbol of knowledge and power and pray for the removal of ignorance and bestowal of grace. The *linga* in its ultimate aspect is the illuminating pillar of light and energy that arises in the mind of the spectator. Iconographically, the *linga* can also symbolize the synthesis of several elements of religious belief. With carvings on four sides representing different deities and the entire block shaped like a *linga* to represent Siva, it symbolizes the One and Absolute in its various manifestations.

## THE CASTE SYSTEM

Even though social anthropologists have identified caste-like social formations in many parts of the world, caste is widely known as a unique social institution in South Asia, and particularly in India. Not only has the caste system been an extremely resilient phenomenon among the Hindus, it has also retained its influence among converts to Islam and Christianity in India. What is distinguishing about the caste system is that it is a type of social stratification which is based on endogamous and hereditary subdivision of an ethnic unit occupying a position of superior or inferior rank, or social esteem, in comparison with other such subdivisions. Castes differ from social classes in that they have emerged into social consciousness to the point that custom and traditional law attempt their rigid and permanent separation from one another. The caste system is thus a fairly rigid hierarchical system in which higher castes are understood to be ritually pure whereas the lower castes are taken to be ritually polluted. However, according to Hindu theory, four castes (*varnas*) were instituted at the beginning and are eternal: *Brahmin* (the priest), *Kshatriya* (the warrior-ruler), *Vaishya* (the trader-cultivator) and *Shudra* (the untouchable who does scavenging, tanning, etc).

Despite caste being a very ancient institution among Hindus it is interesting to note that the *Vedas* of 1000 B.C. and beyond, did not have it in a substantially developed form. By Buddha's time, around the 5th century B.C., it was fairly prevalent; and the Greeks observed it a few centuries later. Any attempt to explain the caste system on the basis of a single factor is likely to be misleading. But religion has influenced it deeply, especially ideas regarding the immortality of the soul, its rebirth according to the law of moral causality (*karma*), and the earning of merit through abiding by the rules intended to safeguard the level of caste group purity. Members of the higher castes are also called "twice-born" because they are believed to have been born as human beings for the second time on account of good conduct in their previous lives.

In operative terms, however, it is the *jati* or sub-caste (sometimes simply referred to as caste) which is more concrete. The sub-castes are units of local populations within which the rules of caste behavior are effectively implemented. Easier means of communication now make it possible for *jatis* to stretch beyond narrow geographical confines, and this has become a significant basis of social and political mobilization by leaders of caste groups. Indian politics, though it is democratic and based on the principle of one-man-one-vote, has relied heavily on the phenomenon of caste for popular participation in the political process. Though the educated middle classes like to distance themselves from the caste system, caste remains an important social phenomenon and is a handy basis for professional networking.

It was mentioned above that the caste system has also influenced Muslims and Christians in India. The Christians of the Malabar Coast, who belong to the Syrian Church and who are divided into different groups may dine together but may not intermarry. Among the Roman Catholics, converts from the former untouchable castes sometimes also have their own churches. Among Muslims a basic distinction is made between the *ashraf* who are supposedly descendents of Arab immigrants and the non-*ashraf* who are Hindu converts. The *ashraf* group is further subdivided into Sayyids, Shaikhs, Pathans and Mughals. The non-*ashraf* are also divided into three groups on the basis of their status before conversion. But two of the principal ideas of Hindu castes, commensality and endogamy, do not appear as strongly in Islamic castes.

## UNTOUCHABLES

The phenomenon of "untouchability" is as unique as the Indian caste system. The very ideas of purity and pollution which informed the genesis of the caste system also constituted the ideological basis of untouchability. In the social division of labor those who traditionally pursued occupations such as scavenging, working with leather, removing dead cattle from the villages, etc., were considered to be untouchables in the sense that physical contact with them would defile the purity of the upper castes. In some parts of the country even the sight of an untouchable, or his presence within a circumscribed area, was polluting for a Brahmin. The untouchables, or *Shudras*, were therefore obliged to live in the outskirts of the main village. At different times in India's modern history these castes have been designated as "Backward Classes," "Depressed Castes," "Untouchables" and "Scheduled Castes". Mahatma Gandhi sought to remove the practise of untouchability through social reform in the course of the freedom movement. He named the untouchables "Harijan" or the People of God.

Untouchability in its traditional form is a complex phenomenon, with different caste groups maintaining different degrees of social distance from various untouchable castes. However, under the law of the Indian Republic the practise of untouchability is a punishable offence. Article 17 of the Indian Constitution says "Untouchability is abolished and its practice in any form is forbidden." Article 46 declares: "The State shall promote with special care the educational and economic interests of the weaker sections of the people, and, in particular, of the Scheduled Castes and the Scheduled Tribes, and shall protect them from social injustice and all forms of exploitation." The Untouchability (Offences) Act, 1955 and Untouchability (Offences) Amendment and Miscellaneous Provisions Act, 1976 reinforce the constitutional provisions and put them into effect. The Government of India also appoints a special officer called the Commissioner for Scheduled Castes and Scheduled Tribes who investigates all matters relating to the constitutional safeguards. Provincial, or state governments also have separate Welfare Departments to look after their welfare.

An important feature of the Indian political system is the policy of "reservations," a system of positive discrimination followed by the state to ensure that the former untouchables are provided with avenues of upward social mobility through education and employment. While these policies have made considerable changes in the social life of the scheduled castes, the struggle for equal dignity goes on. From the medieval period onwards untouchables have opted out of Hindu society into Islam, Buddhism and Christianity in order to escape from the rigors of untouchability. Within Hinduism reforms have been attempted from time to time.

Dr. B. R. Ambedkar, who was one of India's foremost constitutional experts and the moving spirit behind the making of the Indian Constitution, was a great champion of the rights of the untouchables. He converted to Buddhism and remained opposed to the policy of positive discrimination on the grounds that it would perpetuate the separateness of the scheduled castes from the rest of society. However, the state did implement positive discrimination, as a consequence of which a small elite has now emerged and finds a place in the civil service as well as in business. But going by the statistics of unfilled places in the "reserved" quota in institutions of higher learning it is apparent that the former untouchables are still not in a position to avail themselves of the limited facilities which the Indian state has to offer.

## LIVING STANDARDS

India is among the poorer countries in the world. But within the country the standards of living vary enormously and it is surprising that a nation which officially believes in socialism should allow such great inequalities of wealth. The really rich, who constitute a small but conspicuous percentage, possess the same amenities that their counterparts in other countries enjoy. They are mostly businessmen and industrial families and own extensive urban properties, and in some cases farms. This class is a reflection of the growing strength of the internal market in India. Though at most 2 percent of the population, it is large enough to sustain a fashion industry, five-star hotels and other luxury establishments. This class is followed closely by what might be called the upper middle class which is composed of smaller business people, but much more significantly of professionals and the upper echelons of officialdom. Without this class the consumer industry in India would be non-existent. They own their houses and cars, go on holidays and, in short, lead a comfortable existence without sharing in the affluence of the really rich. This group constitutes under 10 percent of the population.

What might be called the middle to lower middle class is mostly composed of salaried people in urban areas though it includes traders and shopkeepers as well as prosperous sections of the rural population. This section is, by and large, literate and articulate and attaches great importance to education and upward social mobility. It constitutes about 30 percent of the population and can be said to provide the ideological backbone of the public-sector oriented welfare model of the state. It is sometimes suggested that the better paid among the blue-collar workers are part of this section in terms of their standard of living.

*Above: The primitive Persian wheel, still much in use and a symbol of the cycle of life.*

The Sixth Five Year Plan (1980 to 1985) indicated that 50 percent of the rural population and about 40 percent of the urban population were living below the poverty line in 1979. The poverty line was drawn on the basis of a per-capita daily calorie intake of 2400 for rural and 2100 for urban areas. At 1979 prices the poverty line worked out to a per capita monthly expenditure of Rs. 76 for rural and Rs. 88 for urban areas. It was found that the absolute number of the poor was 317 million, of which 260 million were rural and 57 million were urban. Subsequently, because of the revision in population estimates based on the 1981 census, the figures for 1979-86 were revised and 339 million (51.1 percent) people were found to be living under the poverty line. It was claimed that in 1984-85 the population below the poverty line had come down to 36.9 per cent. The poverty line was based on the same calorie intake which was equivalent to a per capita income of Rs. 107 for rural areas and Rs. 122 for urban areas. Rural families with an annual income of Rs. 6,420 (39.9 per cent of rural population) and urban families with an annual income of Rs. 7,370 (27.7 per cent of the urban population) were said to be below the poverty line. The Seventh Plan expects to reduce the people living below the poverty line to 26 percent.

The theme of poverty alleviation has been central to Indian politics. It has shaped party policies and given rise to several specific government programs. The Congress Party declared that India would follow a "socialistic" path of development. Subsequently Mrs. Gandhi rose to great heights of political popularity on the basis of her slogan *Garibi Hatao* or "Remove Poverty." There are several government programs to assist the rural poor and provide employment for youth. In some states specially low-priced food and clothing is being made available to the poor.

*Above: A good harvest keeps the rural people busy.*

# THE POPULATION EXPLOSION

According to some estimates India's population is projected to touch the billion mark by the year A.D. 2000. Its rate of growth of population is about 2.3 percent per annum, which is high considering the fact that India adopted a family planning program soon after independence in 1947. But this rate of growth is not very different from other south and southeast Asian countries. Improvements in general hygienic and social health conditions have contributed to greater longevity and reduced the incidence of child mortality. However, these factors by themselves do not explain India's population explosion. A more appropriate explanation lies in the social and economic logic of a primarily poor peasant society where pauperization and bleak prospects for the future negate whatever real stakes there might be in reducing family size. On the other hand there is greater perceived security in having a larger number of children.

## Nutrition and Fertility

Under these conditions marginal improvements in nutritional levels result in greater fertility on account of the fact that the reproductive period becomes longer. Therefore many of the government's incentives for family planning have had limited impact.

Lack of adequate education has contributed to the slow erosion of traditional ideas about virility and fertility, especially in the rural areas. In the urban areas there is greater awareness about family planning partly because of wider exposure to modern methods of contraception and also because the resources of the urban family are seen as being clearly limited. More urban children go to school, and even though most of the schooling for the poorer sections is inexpensive, it makes parents aware of the investment they have to make in order to bring up their children. Not only do fewer rural children go to school but also rural parents tend to see children as assets who will help in the fields as they grow up.

## Family Planning

India's democratic system does not permit the use of coercive methods for family planning. An attempt at forcing the pace of sterilization was made during the constitutional Emergency of 1975-77 but it boomeranged badly on the government. On the other hand, economic incentives that the government can provide for family planning cannot be very large in a developing country like India.

It is increasingly being argued that while it is necessary to continue with the propagation of preventive methods, greater attention needs to be given to improving the living conditions of the poor peasantry. Greater economic security will gradually change the common man's attitude to the size of his family. The penetration of safe modern medicine deeper into the countryside will also diminish the risk of losing children in infancy. Consequently, anxieties on the part of parents about care in old age will also be taken care of.

It is well known that rapid population growth is a serious problem for countries such as India because the benefits of economic growth are eaten away by the roughly 15 million mouths that are added to the nation every year. Larger numbers also increase the already heavy pressure on the land, and in the ultimate analysis retard the process of capital growth that is vital for industrial take off. Therefore, in addition to the family planning program, attempts are being made to provide economic security for the poor through employment and development schemes. But more importance has to be given to the systematic education of women about the benefits of family planning in India.

## INDIAN WOMEN

In India, women are employed in almost every sphere of activity and the Constitution provides for equal pay for equal work for men and women. The prolonged struggle for freedom from colonial rule mobilized many women into political activity and social reform movements. Consequently, there are a large number of women in public life. Women hold some of the most senior positions in the Civil Services. They are well represented in higher education and in the fields of medicine, law and development. In the private, commercial and industrial sectors women work as executives, managers and technologists. Among the middle classes it is common for women to become graduates. And though many

traditional middle-class families have reservations about women working, there is a marked upward trend in women qualifying as teachers and office workers.

The largest segment of women are, of course, farm workers, usually paid a little less than men. This is also true of the unorganized sector in general. But millions of women also work in factories, mines and plantations. In the organized sector laws and regulations are sensitive to the woman employee's requirements. In fact, the stringency of the laws is such that employers find it cheaper and easier to employ men. Among some sections of the upwardly mobile working class and cultivating groups there is a tendency to withdraw women from the work force as the non-working housewife is seen as a sign of higher status. Upper-caste Hindu women usually do not engage in any manual work outside the house.

Increasingly, laws have given an equal place to women in matters of inheritance, marriage and divorce, especially among the Hindus. Muslims are regulated by a

*Above: For many Indian women, life affords little leisure. Right: Women play an important role in the workforce at construction sites.*

232

slightly different system of laws in civil matters, the Muslim Personal Law. On the whole the Indian social system is, nevertheless, weighted in favor of men. Working women have still to bear the burdens of housework and child rearing. Dowry, which is illegal, is still customary in most Hindu marriages.

In urban areas it has taken on increasingly menacing forms with the husband's family demanding large amounts of money and consumer goods from the bride's family at the time of marriage and thereafter. This leads to marital discord and, in extreme cases, to bride burning or suicide by women who are put under pressure. These factors show up the glaring contradictions in India's attitude to women.

In response to such trends as dowry deaths and harassment, and to women's problems in general, there is a growing feminist movement in India. Some feminist organizations pose the issue of women's rights as part of the overall democratic struggle against exploitation, while others focus specifically on wo-

men's issues. Major newspapers in India are sensitive to women's issues especially as many women journalists who specialize on these themes are active feminists. But independent women's journals, such as *Manushi* and *Equality*, are also published. Among the leading women's organizations are the All India Democratic Women's Association, the Janwadi Mahila Sangh and Saheli. There are also numerous centers exclusively devoted to women's studies.

The 1980s have seen an interesting development in the political system by way of its new sensitivity to the women's vote. This is partly on account of the fact that women are now believed to be voting differently from male family members. Some states have reserved a large number of seats in local councils for women not only for their adequate participation and representation but also in the hope that the induction of women into the councils would make the system more responsive and improve the quality of politics.

233

# THE MEDIA

In India, the radio and TV networks are entirely under the control of the central government while the press is almost entirely in private hands. Radio and TV are under government control because they are seen as agencies of mass education. However, there is substantial support in favor of autonomy for TV and a demand that provincial governments be given greater say in deciding programs for radio and TV.

A country like India, which has many languages and dialects, and a large illiterate to semi-literate population, requires an extensive radio and TV network with a wide range of programs. The All India Radio and Doordarshan (India's TV service) have been able to live up to such demands. In 1947, there were only six radio stations compared to 98 at present, covering 95 percent of the population and 86 percent of the area of the country. In another few years there will be 205 broadcasting stations to cover 97.5 percent of the population. It is estimated that there are roughly 20 million radio receiving sets in India. The All India Radio broadcasts news, light and classical music, plays, and programs specially designed for youth and for adult education. It also has a commercial service and various external services.

Doordarshan started in 1956 and is now one of the world's largest networks; its 238 transmitters reach about 72 percent of the population. Its rapid expansion in the last few years has been facilitated by India's own satellite system (INSAT) which enables Doordarshan to reach remote areas. In spite of the fact that Doordarshan tends to put out the official view, it has opened up the world to the widest section of India's population. Apart from the usual news and cultural programs, Doordarshan prepares programs on education, on agriculture, and on scientific and technological developments in the country. There is a general information service called INTEXT (on Channel II).

The press remains the most powerful and lively medium. It not only provides local, national and international information through well established news agencies, of which there are four major ones in the country, but is often severely critical of national and provincial governments. Though there is an autonomous Press Council which investigates complaints against editors and reporters, governments often berate the press for being "irresponsible."

There are at least 18 major English newspapers of which some, like *The Hindu*, *The Indian Express* and *The Times of India* are published from as many as 10 different centers. Languagewise, the largest number of newspapers are published in Hindi (6,370), followed by English (3,961), Bengali (1,662), Urdu (1,492) and Marathi (1,168). In terms of circulation, too, Hindi is the largest, followed by English. A whole range of glossies to serious news and pictorial magazines have appeared in the last few years in many languages, but especially in English. They are avidly read and have considerable influence in shaping middle-class opinion.

Films are possibly the most popular medium in India. It is well known that India leads the world in terms of the number of feature films made here. This is partly because they are made in all the 14 major Indian languages. The biggest film-making centers are Bombay and Madras. Most of the films are poor and revolve around fixed formulae, though they are often of high technical quality. Their appeal is due to star value.

However there is a good deal of serious cinema, too, by directors who not only make artistically good films but also address themselves to social themes. The largest number of films are made in Tamil, followed by Telugu and Hindi.

## THE COLONIAL EXPERIENCE

The Indian encounter with western ideas and economic practices during British rule led to many interesting changes in thought and ideas. Christian missionaries came to a land that already had deeply entrenched traditions of Hinduism, Buddhism and Islam.

Colonialism also brought in new ideas that led to rationalist interpretations of faith in India. This was to herald "the Indian renaissance," especially in Bengal and Maharashtra. Raja Rammohun Roy challenged many traditional Hindu practices, including *sati* – burning a widow on her husband's pyre. In the newly founded colleges of Calcutta and Pune students now learnt the natural sciences, geography and mathematics. Among the Muslims, Sir Syed and others sought to open up Islam to western scientific thought, and Hindu reformist groups such as the Brahmo Samaj and Arya Samaj were established.

The rural economy came under various new regulations and the general accent on commercialization led to important changes in traditional power structures in the village as well as in the relationship between town and country. Agricultural production now became linked to the international market and price fluctuations, especially in the cash crops, brought about severe distortions in the lives of the producers whose economic world had earlier been limited to the near locality. The international labor market also opened up as "indentured" labor was recruited to work in other British colonies. The penetration of machine-made goods from England into the Indian market saw the gradual decline of handicrafts and indigenous industry.

The introduction of English education had the desired effect of fostering a new Indian elite which was initially recruited to subordinate positions in the structure of British rule, but which could gradually aspire to higher positions as recruitment to the Indian Civil Service became open to qualified Indians. The Councils Act of 1862 introduced Indian participation in government through the Municipal Council. But this English educated Indian elite did not detach itself from its roots. The emergence of this group also nurtured an Indian political sensibility which led to the questioning of the benevolent nature of British rule. Indian nationalism soon came to be interpreted in terms of independence from colonial rule. The Indian National Congress, formed in 1885, did not reject imperial rule but held that Indians were equally if not more capable of governing India.

Mahatma Gandhi's entry into the nationalist scene led to a broadening of the social basis of nationalism. He used many of the ideas of the west to argue that the realization of nationalism required the democratization of society, the rejection of practices such as untouchability, the building of relations of trust between Hindus and Muslims, and a deeper understanding of the sources of Indian culture and the composite nature of Indian civilization. He rejected western ideas and practices which were identified as instruments of the west's dominance over India. Above all he distanced himself from the "modernism" of the west which included science, technology and industrialization.

Yet not all nationalist leaders shared Gandhi's faith in self-contained village-level democracy and a non-industrial society. Jawaharlal Nehru, who was among the nationalist leaders closest to Gandhi, believed in planning, industrialization, parliamentary democracy and a modern state. Such tensions in ideas have remained in Indian society even though it is the latter model which has prevailed. At a cultural level the crisis of modernization runs deeper as India makes its transition to an egalitarian, democratic and secular society.

NELLES MAPS / NELLES ROAD ATLASES

# Nelles Maps ...the maps that get you going.

NEPAL — NELLES VERLAG
KENYA — NELLES VERLAG
THAILAND — NELLES VERLAG
NORTHERN INDIA — NELLES VERLAG

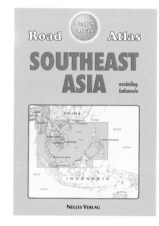

Road Atlas — INDONESIA — NELLES VERLAG
Road Atlas — SOUTHEAST ASIA excluding Indonesia — NELLES VERLAG

## Nelles Maps

- Afghanistan
- Australia
- Bangkok
- Burma
- Caribbean Islands 1 / Bermuda, Bahamas, Greater Antilles
- Caribbean Islands 2 / Lesser Antilles
- China 1 / North-Eastern China
- China 2 / Northern China
- China 3 / Central China
- China 4 / Southern China
- Crete
- Egypt
- Hawaiian Islands
- Hawaiian Islands 1 / Kauai
- Hawaiian Islands 2 / Honolulu, Oahu
- Hawaiian Islands 3 / Maui, Molokai, Lanai
- Hawaiian Islands 4 / Hawaii
- Himalaya
- Hong Kong
- Indian Subcontinent
- India 1 / Northern India
- India 2 / Western India
- India 3 / Eastern India
- India 4 / Southern India
- India 5 / North-Eastern India
- Indonesia
- Indonesia 1 / Sumatra
- Indonesia 2 / Java + Nusa Tenggara
- Indonesia 3 / Bali
- Indonesia 4 / Kalimantan
- Indonesia 5 / Java + Bali
- Indonesia 6 / Sulawesi
- Indonesia 7 / Irian Jaya + Maluku
- Jakarta
- Japan
- Kenya
- Korea
- Malaysia
- West Malaysia
- Manila
- Mexico
- Nepal
- New Zealand
- Pakistan
- Philippines
- Singapore
- South East Asia
- Sri Lanka
- Taiwan
- Thailand
- Vietnam, Laos Cambodia

236

## *TABLE OF CONTENTS*

## TRAVELING TO INDIA

This section provides general information on travel to India, as well as helpful tips for traveling within the country. For more detailed enquiries you should contact the Government of India Tourist Offices (GITOs).

### Arriving in India

**Air**: Nearly 50 international carriers operate over 150 flights a week to India's four major cities - Delhi, Bombay, Calcutta, Madras. Choose an entry point to suit your travel plans in India (Madras is only serviced by bi-weekly British Airways flights from London). Some chartered services fly directly to Goa.

**Sea**: Several ports dot India's sprawling coastline - Bombay, Cochin, Madras, Visakhapatanam and Calcutta. However, these ports are mainly used by cargo ships. The only passenger liner servicing India is the Queen Elizabeth II.

### Arrival Formalities

**Immigration/Visas**: A valid national passport and a visa (obtained from Indian missions abroad) are a must. If the visa is for 90 days or less registration on arrival is unnecessary. If otherwise, you must personally obtain a Registration Certificate and Residential Permit, within a week of arrival, from the nearest Foreigner's Registration Office. Four photographs are required and change of address and absence for more than 15 days has to be reported. Visas can be *collective* (issued to groups sponsored by a GOI recognized travel agency, it allows splitting up, visiting different places and reassembling before departure), *transit* (advance application to the Ministry of External Affairs, Delhi, required) or multiple-entry 90 day *tourist* visas.

Other types are issued if the purpose of visit is to conduct business, study, attend a conference, undertake media activity (e.g. make a film), participate in adventure sports (trekking, river-rafting, etc.) or study Indian culture (learn yoga or dance, for instance). Exit visas are unnecessary if you leave within the validity period of the visa (six months from the date of issue). Extension can be sought for a stay of up to six months.

### Climate

Temperatures in India can vary from sub-zero to over 50° C. Though October to March is the recommended travel season, visits timed otherwise can be as rewarding. In summer, when the plains are hot and dry, there are nearly 30 hill resorts to choose from.

A western bugbear is the Indian monsoon. This is a wandering phenomenon and follows a regular path around the country each year. Rain-bearing clouds arrive from June to September and since they do not expend themselves everywhere at once, they are just as easy to avoid as to seek!

In winter, some high altitude tourist destinations suffer inclement weather or are altogether inaccessible. The option is to head for the Indian coastline - studded with innumerable beaches. Except for humidity in the rainy season, these enjoy glowing weather round the year.

### Clothing

Your itinerary and its timing will determine this. Two pullovers, one light and the other heavy, are a must in winter. In some areas heavy woolens would also be required. For daywear light clothing will suffice; this will be suitable for the coastline destinations as well. Dispense with synthetics.

Ideal footwear would be open sandals in summer and walking shoes in winter. Except for the beaches, it would be wise for women to dress conservatively.

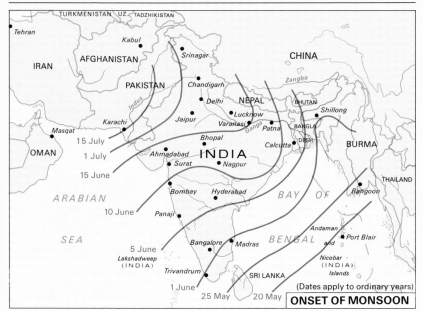

ONSET OF MONSOON

(Dates apply to ordinary years)

### Currency and Exchange

**Currency**: Coinage in India is decimal based with 100 paise to every rupee. Coins are available in denominations of 5, 10, 20, 25 and 50 paise and one and two rupees, while notes come in 1, 2, 5, 10, 20, 50 and 100 rupee denominations. It is illegal to export or import Indian currency. Rupee traveler's checks issued abroad are an exception.

**Banks**: Foreign and nationalized Indian banks conduct business from 10 am to 2 pm. Monday through Friday, and from 10 am to 12 noon on Saturdays. A few are open in the evening and on Sundays. Banks close on national holidays, June 30 and December 31.

**Exchange**: You can bring in any amount of foreign exchange in the shape of coins, bank notes and traveler's checks provided these are declared on arrival in the CD form (up to US$ 1000 or equivalent need not be declared, unless it is a currency draft). All encashments and exchange must be recorded and receipts maintained (including hotel bills and airline tickets) to facilitate reconversion of unspent money on departure. This is doubly useful for income tax exemption, in case your visit exceeds 90 days. Money should be exchanged only by authorized banks/money changers. Major credit cards are accepted by established hotels, shops and restaurants.

### Customs

Red and green channels exist for clearance. A random check of baggage may be conducted. Duty free imports include personal effects (jewelry too), a camera with five film rolls, binoculars, portable typewriter, radio, a tape-recorder, camping equipment, skis, etc; also up to 200 cigarettes and 95 ml alcohol. Vehicles can be brought in under a triptyque/carnet issued by any internationally recognized automobile association. Both professional equipment and high value articles must be declared. Import of the following articles is prohibited – dangerous drugs, live plants, gold and silver bullion, unlicensed weapons. These rules extend to unaccompanied baggage. Prohibited articles of export are antiques (over 100 years old), skins, gold jewelry exceeding Rs. 20,000 in value, other jewelry (including precious stones) valued at over Rs. 10,000.

## Departure

Reservations for departure must be reconfirmed well in advance. Also allow two hours for check-in as security checks can be intensive. All passengers (including infants) have to pay a **Foreign Travel Tax** (at the airport/seaport) of Rs. 300 prior to check in. Those headed for Afghanistan, Bangladesh, Bhutan, Burma, Nepal, Pakistan and Sri Lanka pay half the fee.

## Health (Regulations and Precautions)

A vaccination certificate is essential only if you have traveled through yellow fever endemic countries (mostly in Africa and South America), ten days prior to reaching India. Otherwise, you could face six days in quarantine.

No other certificate is required but it is advisable to get vaccinations for cholera, typhoid and tetanus. You will find a medical kit containing the following handy in India: anti-malaria, anti-emetic, anti-diarrhoeal pills, antibiotics, anti-allergens, an insect repellent, suntan lotion (for high altitudes), an antiseptic cream, band-aids and salt pills (necessary only in summer). These are available at medical stores in all towns and cities. Chemists attached to major hospitals are open 24 hours.

Boiled water, soda, mineral water or aerated drinks are recommended. Scrupulously avoid salads, peeled fruit and ice in smaller towns and establishments. Fresh food straight off the fire is comparatively safe.

## Statistics on India

Area: 3,287,263 sq. km; Population: (1986): 761070100; No. of States: 25; No. of Union Territories: 8; Religion: Hindus - 82.64%; Muslims - 11.35%; Christians - 2.43%; Sikhs - 1.96%; Buddhists -0.71%, Jains - 0.48%; Others - 0.42%.

# TRAVELING IN INDIA

## Accommodation

India offers accommodation to suit budgets and preferences ranging from luxury resorts and hotels to modestly priced travelers' lodges. If you want home comforts, stick to luxury hotels (a list can be obtained from your nearest GITO) which require prior booking specially during the tourist season (October-March). With the major hotel chains, reservations are centralized and options are offered. Accommodation is available at the four city airports as well as at most railway stations. The YWCA, YMCA, Youth Hostels and State Tourism outlets are cheap and comfortable. In smaller towns, the local district authorities can be contacted at least six weeks in advance for reservation of Inspection Houses and Dak-Bungalows, which are primarily meant for bureaucrats. Paying guest accommodation can be arranged by GITO. Camping sites exist in some areas.

## Bookstores / Libraries

English titles, whether published abroad or in India, are available at city bookstores which also stock international news magazines and newspapers. There are also public libraries countrywide.

## Cinemas

There are four shows a day. While cinemas in cities and larger towns screen

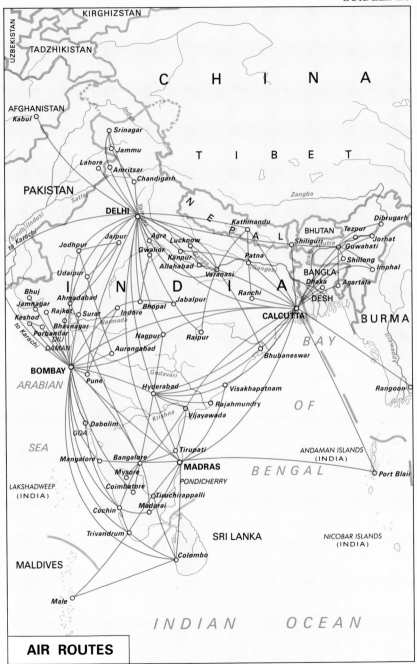

**AIR ROUTES**

English titles, smaller towns exhibit only Hindi and vernacular films.

## Domestic Airlines

The two domestic carriers are *Indian Airlines* (Air India handles outbound traffic) and *Vayudoot.* IA services over 61 domestic destinations and also operates to Afghanistan, Bangladesh, the Maldives, Nepal, Pakistan, Singapore, Sri Lanka and Thailand. Booking is computerized in Bangalore, Bombay, Calcutta, Delhi, Hyderabad and Madras. During the tourist season (October to March) please confirm reservations well in advance. Also, check in an hour before departure. A reliable coach service connects various hotels to the airport.

IA offers packages (available only against foreign currency) which can also be purchased outside of India: *Discover India* (US 400) permits unlimited travel within India for 21 days (with some routing restrictions) and the *India Wonderfare* (US\$ 200) allows unlimited travel for a week in a region (north/south/east/west) of your choice (US\$ 100 extra for those who opt to visit Port Blair from either Calcutta or Madras).

Further incentives are discount tickets for yougsters (25% discount for students/those under 30) and tourists heading south (30% off US dollar tariff on select sectors).

*Vayudoot*, a feeder airline, has a number of tourist packages. A big draw is the *Air-Trek* over the Himalayas. *Air-Trek* services are available from Delhi or from Dehra Dun.

## Electricity

A 220 volts (alternate current) 50 cycle system is in operation throughout the country. Good hotels provide step-down transformers to alter voltage to suit individual electric appliances. Confirm with the hotel information.

## Etiquette

It is essential to remove footwear (socks are acceptable) and to cover the head (this is insisted upon in *gurdwaras*) when visiting shrines (these include temples, mosques and memorials, and in Kerala, churches). Some religious places take exception to leather goods while others prohibit photography. So you should carefully read the rules displayed and act accordingly.

Indians are generally very warm and hospitable and will be pleased if you attempt to return their greeting, *namaste*, offered with folded hands. A handshake will be a nice gesture only with men. Indian women do not customarily shake hands even with their own men.

## Festivals and Holidays

Since most festivals are determined by the lunar calendar it is advisable to get a list of holidays for the current year from the GITO.

However, certain holidays have fixed dates: Republic Day - January 26; Independence Day - August 15; Gandhi Jayanti - October 2; Christmas - December 25. (See Guideposts for the important festivals of each state.) On Republic Day, Independence Day and Gandhi Jayanti even shopping centers remain closed.

## Guides

The services of English and other foreign language speaking tourist guides can be hired at all the major tourist centers. This can be arranged by a travel agent or GITO.

Guides should carry a certificate from the Indian Department of Tourism. Unapproved guides are not permitted to enter protected monuments.

At some monuments guide books from the Archeological Survey of India are available.

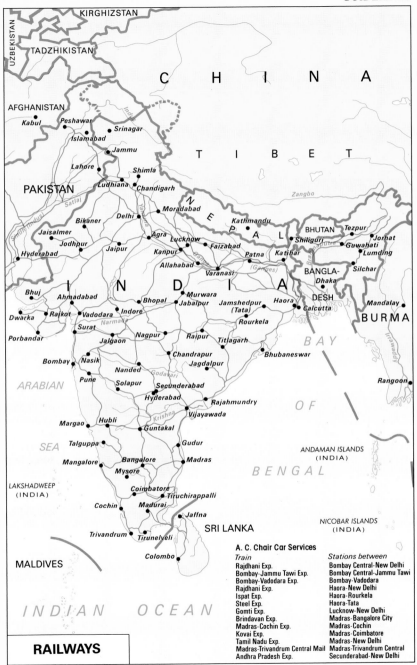

**A. C. Chair Car Services**

| Train | Stations between |
|---|---|
| Rajdhani Exp. | Bombay Central-New Delhi |
| Bombay-Jammu Tawi Exp. | Bombay Central-Jammu Tawi |
| Bombay-Vadodara Exp. | Bombay-Vadodara |
| Rajdhani Exp. | Haora-New Delhi |
| Ispat Exp. | Haora-Rourkela |
| Steel Exp. | Haora-Tata |
| Gomti Exp. | Lucknow-New Delhi |
| Brindavan Exp. | Madras-Bangalore City |
| Madras-Cochin Exp. | Madras-Cochin |
| Kovai Exp. | Madras-Coimbatore |
| Tamil Nadu Exp. | Madras-New Delhi |
| Madras-Trivandrum Central Mail | Madras-Trivandrum Central |
| Andhra Pradesh Exp. | Secunderabad-New Delhi |

**RAILWAYS**

## Liquor

Prohibition is in force in some states where permits are required; consult GITO to obtain one. Public holidays and certain days of the month are observed as dry days. While bars attached to starred hotels offer a wide array of drinks most city restaurants are not licensed to serve liquor. Liquor should be bought only from shops, displaying "English Wine" or "Indian Made Foreign Liquor" (IMFL) signs. Others sell country brews, best avoided.

## Local Transport

Next to rail, motor transport is widely used by locals as well as tourists to travel within and between cities.

**Taxis**: These are metered yellow and black, and non-metered tourist cars run by private tour operators. The latter can be air-conditioned or non-air-conditioned, of Indian or foreign make. Charges vary from state to state, nowhere exceeding Rs. 5 per km. The metered three wheel auto-rickshaw accommodates three passengers without extra charge. Due to frequent rises in fuel prices, meters often do not indicate the revised rates. Ask the driver to show the fare chart which indicates revised rates or pay 6 percent to 10 percent more than what the meter shows. Night charges are extra. From airports taxi numbers are noted as well as the name and destination of the passenger. International airports also have prepaid taxi services. For the convenience of passengers in transit, international airports have regular coach services to the domestic airport. It is in your own interest to make sure that the meter is zeroed to the minimum fare before your journey. Fare structure/rules vary from location to location.

**Buses**: These should be avoided during rush hours within the city. Inter-city connections are offered by several road transport companies who operate regular, deluxe and ordinary coaches. The deluxe occasionally have an additional feature - video films.

## Museums and Art Galleries

There is a select group of national museums which presents a comprehensive picture of the principal periods and styles of the 4000-year-old Indian civilization, and 21 on-site museums. Some are devoted exclusively to specialized areas like folk/tribal art or textiles.

Most museums remain open on Sundays and close on another day of the week as well as on public holidays. Entry fees to museums are incredibly low. Art galleries in larger cities periodically hold exhibitions-cum-sales of paintings, photographs, etchings, lithos, woodcuts, sculpture, ceramics and pottery (see Guideposts).

## Newspapers and Periodicals

The large number of English and vernacular publications reflect the great interest Indians have in current affairs. Leading English dailies include *The Times of India*, the *Hindustan Times*, *The Hindu*, *The Telegraph* and the *Indian Express*. Among magazines, *India Today* (a fortnightly) and *Sunday* ( a weekly) cover both national and international events. The *Illustrated Weekly* is a general features magazine, *The India Magazine*, *Imprint* and *Marg* cater to specialized interests. *Destination Traveller* is specific to travel and tourism.

## Photography

Photography is permitted in most places. Wherever there are restrictions such as at defense installations, bridges, certain monuments and areas, large notices inform you of this. Films are available and processing (barring Kodachrome) is possible. However, it is advisable to buy films from large stores.

## Postal Services

Mail services are generally reliable. So are poste restante facilities which are available at major post offices in the cities. Instead of posting (personally or through a bell boy) letters bearing high denomination stamps in a mail box, present them at any post office counter for immediate defacing (see Guideposts for each region).

## Railways

Covering 62,000 km (38,500 mi), the Indian Railway is the longest rail system in Asia and the fourth longest in the world, and recommended for a first-hand encounter with the diversity of India. Of the five categories of accommodation available, restrict yourself to air-conditioned first class, first class, two-tier air-conditioned sleeper and air-conditioned chair car. You can ask for bed rolls and extra blankets while purchasing the ticket. If possible, stay with the express trains. Food to suit western tastes is served in dining cars attached to all important trains. There are Tourist Information Centers at stations in Bombay, Delhi and Calcutta. Certain trains set apart a foreign tourist quota which gets you priority in reservations.

*Indrail Passes,* which cost between US$ 95 and US$ 690, for the categories advised, are now available from Asra-Orient, Kaiserstrasse 50, D-60329 Frankfurt, and Hari World Travel 13, Rockefeller Plaza, Shop No. 21, Mezzanine North, New York NY 10112. These are valid from a week to 90 days. However, these do not entitle reserved accommodation. Ask the agent instead for details on the *Indrail Rovers* scheme. Especially designed to cover tourist circuits, 32 itineraries ensure confirmed availability of train accommodation if booked 90 days in advance. For railway buffs there are still many delights like steam locomotives, narrow gauge lines and "toy trains" in the hill areas.

## Restaurants

Restaurants offering a choice of Continental, Chinese and Indian cuisine are many, and in the big cities those attached to luxury hotels further specialize in Italian, Cantonese/Szechwan, Japanese, Spanish and Thai food. There are any number of 24-hour coffee shops and fast food joints. Chilled beer and wine to go with the meal are, however, served only at select restaurants confined to the cities. Be cautious about eating at the ubiquitous wayside eateries called *dhabas*.

## Shopping

India has a long tradition of crafts, and even objects of everyday utility are fashioned with artistic skill. The range of handwoven textiles and ready to wear clothes is equally stupendous. If you fear you are being charged a "touristy price" for your acquisition, make purchases exclusively from government emporiums (and other approved establishments listed with the GITO and mentioned in the Guideposts).

## Tours

Conducted tours are run by nearly every state tourism department. They charge moderately for a day of sightseeing within a city and its immediate environs. There are also package tours, from a week to ten days, which link destinations within a state.

If you have a special interest, wildlife, museums, ethnic groups or adventure sports like hang gliding, trekking and river running, approach any of the following private agencies to chart a suitable itinerary: Shikkar Travels; Wildlife Adventure Tours; Alpine Travels & Tours; High Points Expedition & Tours; Thomas Cook; Sita World Travel; and Travel Corporation of India. Most of these are located in Delhi. Some of these agencies have branch offices in Bombay, Calcutta and Madras.

### Travel Restrictions

Some destinations or trekking routes can fall in the category of areas protected/restricted/closed to foreigners.

These include areas in Assam, Meghalaya, Tripura, Nagaland, Sikkim, Arunachal Pradesh, Manipur, Mizoram, West Bengal, Pubjab, Rajasthan, Jammu and Kashmir, the Andaman, Nicobar and Lakshadweep islands.

Ascertain details from your travel agent or GITO and accordingly apply (six weeks notice essential) to the Indian diplomatic mission or the Under Secretary, Ministry of Home Affairs, Foreigners Section, Lok Nayak Bhavan, Khan Market, New Delhi 110003, Tel: 619709, for a Restricted Area Permit. This can also be collected after arrival from any of the Foreigners Regional Registration offices at Delhi, Bombay, Calcutta and Madras. In some cases, immigration authorities grant permission on the spot. Seek details from the Mission GITO. The restriction can be on individual travel or the duration of stay (see Guideposts).

### Telecommunication

Facilities for making local, inland and international calls are available at certain Public Call Offices (PCOs) at airports, railway stations and post offices.

Other national and international calls can either be dialed direct or booked through the operator. Service is available on demand for 70 destinations in India and for the U.K. Collect calls (outgoing) can be made to 20 countries. International calls can take anything from 15 minutes to 24 hours. Telex and Fax facilities are available in select cities at a few post and telegraph offices. Some private operators offer Fax facilities (see Guideposts).

### Time

Despite the country's vastness, a single time zone exists. Indian Standard Time (IST) is 5 1/2 hours ahead of GMT and 9 1/2 hours vis-a-vis U.S., E.S.T. (Delhi: 12:00 hrs. corresponds to Bonn: 07:30 hrs).

### Tourist Offices

The Department of Tourism, Government of India, has 18 overseas and 21 inland information bureaus (see Guideposts). These are equipped to handle queries on all aspects of tourist activity - visa requirements, liquor permits, health and export regulations. They also dispense free tourist literature on each destination/region.

You may find directories (of services ) particularly useful as these list categories of accommodation and their tariff, taxi fares, distances between locations and facts under headings like local transport, shopping, banks and money-changers, "eateries" etc. Addresses (with telex numbers) are provided should you wish to book rooms in advance. GITOs as well as other state tourist information outlets in India do not make any travel arrangements. For this see a travel agent (listed with the GITO).

### Weights and Measures

India uses the metric system for both weights and measures. Gold jewelry and certain articles in silver are sold by weight, and weighed at many establishments in *tola*, a traditional measure equal to 11.5 gm. Gems are sold by the carat (0.2 gm). Indians frequently use *lakh* (one hundred thousand) and *crore* (one hundred *lakhs* or ten million) while quoting figures.

## Airlines

**Air France**. *Bombay*: Maker Chambers, V, Nariman Point, Tel: 2025021. **Air India**. *Bombay:* Air India Bldg, Nariman Point, Tel: 2023747, 2024142. *Madras:* 19 Marshalls Rd. Egmore, Tel: 847799, 848899. **Air Lanka**. *Bombay:* Mittal Towers 'C', Nariman Point, Tel: 223299. *Madras:* Connemara Hotel, Mount Road. Tel: 86315. **Alitalia**. *Bombay:* Dalamal House, 206 Nariman Point, Tel: 220795. *Madras:* 738 Anna Salai, Tel: 811306, 810936. **British Airways**. *Bombay:* Vulcan Insurance Bldg. 202 B Vir Nariman Rd., Tel: 221314, 220888. *Madras:* Fadun Mansions, 26 CMC Rd. Egmore, Tel: 474272/559/388. **Indian Airlines**. *Bombay*: Air India Bldg., Nariman Point, Tel: 2023031. *Madras:* Raja Annamalai Bldg. Meenambakkam, Tel: 477098/478333. **Japan Airlines**. *Bombay:* GSA Onkar Travels, 2 Raheja Chambers, Nariman Point, Tel: 233312/36. *Madras:* GSA Global Travels, 733 Mount Rd., Tel: 867957. **KLM Royal Dutch Airlines**. *Bombay:* 198 J. Tata Road, Churchgate, Tel: 221013/1185, 2965. **Lufthansa**. *Bombay:* Express Towers, Nariman Point, Tel: 2023430, 0887. *Madras:* 189 Anna Salai, Tel: 869095/ 9197/9296. **Pakistan Intl. Airlines**. *Bombay:* Oberoi Towers, Nariman Point, Tel: 2021455. *Madras:* GSA Bap Travels, Wellington Estate, 24 CMC Rd. Tel: 422611, 869985. **Royal Nepal Airlines**. *Bombay:* GSA Stic Travels & Tours, 6 Maker Arcade, Cuffe Parade, Tel: 2181431, 2181440. *Madras:* GSA Stic Travels & Tours, 142 Nungambakkam High Rd., Tel: 471195. **Swissair**. *Bombay:* Maker Chamber VI, 220 Nariman Point, Tel: 2870122/3461. **Vayudoot**. *Bombay:* Air India Bldg Nariman Pt., Tel: 2024142, 2028585.

## Embassies / High Commissions Consulates

**Australia**. *Bombay:* Maker Tower 'E', 16th Floor, Cuffe Parade, Colaba, Tel: 2181071. *Delhi:* 1/50 G Shantipath, Tel: 601112, 601238. **Austria**. *Bombay:* Taj Bldg. (3rd floor), 210D. Naoroji Rd., Tel: 2042044, 2044580. *Delhi:* EP-13 Chandra Gupta Mg. Chanakyapuri, Tel: 611512, 601238. *Madras:* Kothari Bldg. Nungambakkam High Rd., Tel: 476036. *Calcutta:* 96/1 Sarat Bose Rd., Tel: 472795. **Bangladesh**. *Calcutta:* 9 Circus Ave, Tel: 444458. *Delhi:* 56 Ring Rd. Lajpat Nagar III., Tel: 615668,699209. **Belgium**. *Bombay:* Morena, 11 M.L. Dahanukar Marg, Tel: 4939261, 4929202. *Delhi:* 50N Shantipath, Tel:608295. *Calcutta:* 5/1A Hungerford St., Tel: 443886. *Madras:* 23 Spurtank Rd. Chetpur, Tel: 665495. **Bhutan**. *Calcutta:* 48 Tivoli Court, Pramothesh Barua Sarani, Tel: 441301/2. *Delhi:* Chandragupta Marg, Tel: 609217, 609112; **Canada**. *Bombay*: 1 Walchand Hirachand Mg., Tel: 265219. *Delhi:*7/8 Shantipath, Chanakyapuri, Tel: 608161. **China**. *Delhi:* 50D Shantipath, Chanakyapuri, Tel: 690349. **Denmark**. *Bombay:* L&T House, Narottam Morarjee Mg. Ballard Estate, Tel: 2618181, 2614462. *Delhi:* 2 Golf Links, Tel: 616273. *Calcutta:* 'Mcleod House' 3 Netaji Subhas Road, Tel: 287476/78. *Madras:* 292 Mowbrays Road, Tel:83141. **Germany**. *Bombay:* Hoechst House, 10th Floor, Nariman Point, Tel: 232422, 232517. *Delhi:* 6 Shantipath, Chanakyapuri, Tel: 604861. *Calcutta:* 1 Hasting Park Road. Alipore, Tel:459141/43, 454866. *Madras:* 14 Bishop's Garden, Greenways Road, Adyar, Tel: 76013. **France**. *Bombay:* Datta Prasad, Pedder Rd., Bombay 26, Tel: 4949808. *Calcutta*: 23 Park Mansions, Tel: 298314. *Delhi:* 2 Aurangzeb Rd., Tel: 3014682. *Madras:* Kothari Building, Nungambakkam High Rd., Tel: 811469. **Ireland**. *Bombay:* Royal Bombay Yacht Club Chambers, Tel: 2872045. *Delhi:* 13 Jor Bagh, Tel: 617435. **Italy**. *Bombay:* Consulate General of Italy, Vaswani Mansions, 120 Dinsha Wachha Road, Churchgate, Reclamation, Tel: 2874773, 2874777. *Calcutta:* 3 Raja Santosh Road, Alipore, Tel: 451411/2. *Delhi:* 13 Golf Links, Tel 618311/2. *Madras:* 738 Mount Road., Tel: 83780. **Japan**: *Bombay*: 1 M.L. Dahanukar Marg, Cumballa Hill, Tel: 4933857/4934610. *Calcutta:* 12 Pretoria St., Tel: 442441/45. *Delhi:* 4-5 Block 50G Shantipath, Chanakyapuri, Tel: 604071. *Madras:* 60 Spur Tank Rd., Tel: 665594. **Nepal**. *Delhi:* Barakhamba Rd., Tel: 3329969. *Calcutta:* 19 Woodlands, Alipore, Tel: 452024. **Netherlands**. *Bombay:* 'The International' 16 Maharshi Karve Rd, P.O. Box 1135, Tel: 296840. *Calcutta:* 18A Brabourne Road, Tel: 262160/64. *Delhi:* 6/50F Shantipath, Chanakyapuri, Tel: 609571/4. *Madras:* Chordia Mansion, 739 Anna Salai, Tel: 86411/13. **Pakistan**. *Delhi:* 2/50 Shantipath, Chanakyapuri, Tel: 600603. **Spain**. *Bombay:* Ador House, 6 K. Dubash Marg, Tel: 244664. *Calcutta:* No.1 Taratolla Rd. Garden Reach, Tel: 235539. *Delhi:* 12 Prithviraj Rd., Tel: 3015892. *Madras:* Lawdale, 8 Nimmo Rd, San Thome, Tel: 72008. **Sri Lanka**. *Bombay:* 'Sri Lanka House', 34 Homi Modi St., Tel: 2045861/ 8503. *Delhi*: 27 Kautilya Marg, Chanakyapuri, Tel: 3010201/2/3. **Sweden**. *85,* Sayari Rd., Bhubesh Gupta Bhavan, Prabhadevi, Bombay 25, Tel: 4360493. *Calcutta:* 6 Poonam Building, 5/2 Russell Street, Tel: 213621. *Delhi:* Nyaya Marg, Chanakyapuri, Tel: 604011. *Madras:* 41 First Main Road, Raja Annamalaipuram. **Switzerland**. *Bombay:* Manek Mahal, 7th Floor, 90 Vir Nariman Road, Tel: 2043003, 2043550, 2042591. *Delhi:* Nyaya Marg, Chanakyapuri, Tel: 604225/6. **U.K.** *Bombay:* Maker Chamber IV, 2nd floor, Nariman Pt., Tel: 233682, 232330. *Calcutta*: 1 Ho Chi Minh Sarani, Tel: 445171. *Delhi:* Shantipath, Chanakyapuri, Tel: 601371. *Madras:* 24 Anderson Rd., Tel: 473136. **U.S.A.** *Bombay:* Lincoln House, 78 Bhulabhai Desai Rd., Tel: 3633611, 3633618. *Calcutta:* 5/1 Ho Chi Minh Sarani, Tel: 443611. *Delhi:* Shantipath, Chanakyapuri, Tel: 600651. *Madras:* 220 Mount Rd., Tel:83041.

## Govt. of India Tourist Offices Outside India

**Australia**: Levell, c/o H.C.I. 17, Castlereagh Street, Sydney NSW 2000, Tel: 0061-2-232-1600/17961. **Canada**: 60 Bloor Street, West Suite No. 1003, Toronto, Ontario M4W 338, Tel: 416-962-3787/88. **France**: 8 Boulevard de la Madeleine, 75009 Paris 9, Tel: 4265-83-86. **Germany**: Kaiserstrasse 77-111, D-60329 Frankfurt, Tel: (069) 235423/24. **Italy:** Via Albricci 9, 20122 Milan, Tel: 804952, 8053506. **Japan**: Pearl Building, 9-18 Ginza, 7 Chome Chuo ku, Tokyo 104, Tel: (03) 571-5062/63. **Malaysia**: Wisma HLS, 2nd Floor, Lot No. 203, Jalan Raja Chulan, 50200 Kuala Lumpur, Tel: 2425301. **Singapore**: 20, Kramat Lane, 01-01 A. United House, Tanglin Rd, Singapore 1024, Tel: 2353800. **Spain**: c/o Indian Embassy, Avenida 31-32 PIO XII., Madrid Tel: 28016, 3457339. **Sweden**: Sveavagen 9-11 Stockholm S-11157, Tel: 08-215-081. **Switzerland**: 1-3 Rue de Chantepoulet, 1201 Geneva, Tel: 022-21-813, 4677. **Thailand**: Singapore Airline Bldg., 3rd Floor, 62/5 Thaniya Road, Bangkok, Tel: 2352585. **U.A.E.**: P.O. Box, 12856, Nasa Building, Al Makhtoum Road, Deira, Dubai, Tel: 274848, 274199. **U.K.**: 7 Cork St, London WIX 2AB, Tel: 01-437-3677/78. **USA**: 230 North Michigan Avenue, Chicago IL 60601. Los Angeles: 3550 Wilshire Blvd, Suite 204, Los Angeles CA 90010, Tel: (213) 380-8855. New York: 30 Rockfeller Plaza, Suite 15, North Mezzanine, New York NY 10112, Tel: 212-586-4901/2/3.

## USEFUL TAMIL AND MALAYALAM PHRASES

There are 14 major languages and over 200 dialects. Tamil, Malayalam, Kannada and Telegu are the main south Indian languages. Tamil is understood in all the southern states, as is English rather than Hindi.

|  | **Tamil** | **Malayalam** |
|---|---|---|
| Greeting | *Vannakkam, namaskaram* | *Namaskaram* |
| Goodbye | *Poitt vaare* | *Vartae* |
| More | *Konjam koodi kodu* | *Aeneem* |
| Where is the ___? | *___ aenge irk apa?* | *___ evede?* |
| How far is ___? | *Aevlav dooram __?* | *___ettara dooram ana?* |
| How do I get to ___? | *Aeppadi poi varla ___?* | *___illekya enganiye ana ponade?* |
| How much does this cost? | *Inda villa?* | *Aenda vella?* |
| This is expensive. | *Raemba villa* | *Vella Kudutal ana* |
| May I see the menu?. | *Konjam menu kaat?* | *Menu kanikyamo* |
| Do not add ice. | *Ice poda venda* | *Ice venda* |
| Less sugar please. | *Shakara konjama podu* | *Panjasara korekyuga* |
| May I have the bill ?. | *Konjam bill tarunge?* | *Bill konduveru* |

| | **Tamil** | **Malayalam** | | **Tamil** | **Malayalam** |
|---|---|---|---|---|---|
| I | *aennake* | *njan* | water | *tanni* | *wellam* |
| you | *nningal* | *nningal* | coffee | *kapi* | *kapi* |
| yes | *amma* | *sheri* | rice | *saadam* | *chore* |
| no | *venda* | *venda* | tea | *chaya* | *chaya* |
| please | *daevayi* | *please* | milk | *paale* | *paale* |
| thank you | *nandri* | *thank you* | sugar | *shakara* | *panjasaara* |
| big | *perithu* | *velliyade* | yogurt | *taieere* | *taieere* |
| small | *chinna* | *cherriyade* | food | *sapad* | *bakshanam* |
| today | *indr* | *inne* | come | *inge va* | *varu* |
| tomorrow | *nallikye* | *naale* | go | *ange po* | *po* |
| yesterday | *naete* | *innelae* | salt | *uppe* | *uppe* |
| tonight | *inne raatike* | *innetae ratri* | chillies | *mellagu* | *aeru* |
| week | *vaaram* | *aariche* | less | *konjama* | *korekyge* |
| month | *maatham* | *maasam* | 1 | *onnru* | *onne* |
| year | *varudam* | *varsham* | 2 | *irandu* | *rande* |
| clean | *shuttam* | *virti* | 3 | *moonru* | *moone* |
| dirty | *ashinnam* | *virtikaettade* | 4 | *naale* | *naale* |
| hot | *choode* | *choode* | 5 | *ainthu* | *anja* |
| cold | *tannupe* | *taanittede* | 6 | *aaru* | *aare* |
| shop | *kadaa* | *kadaa* | 7 | *aeru* | *aere* |
| medicine | *marinnyu* | *marinnyu* | 8 | *aettu* | *itte* |
| how many | *aettana* | *aettariya* | 9 | *onpathe* | *umbude* |
| egg | *mutta* | *kozhimutta* | 10 | *paththu* | *pathe* |
| vegetable | *tarkali* | *pacchakaari* | | | |

## THE AUTHORS

**Shalini Saran** is a well-known travel writer and photographer whose profession has emerged from a desire to explore, understand and share the beauty of India. Widely traveled in India, her articles and photographs have appeared in *The India Magazine*, *Namaste*, *Swagat*, *Namaskaar*, *Udit*, *The Taj Magazine* and *Soma*, published from India, and *Orientations*, *Discovery* and *Sawasdee* published from Hong Kong. She has contributed to the *Rajasthan Insight Guide* and written the section on India for the *South Asia Insight Guide*. She has received two awards in the "Fotofest" organized by the Government of India for the Festival of India in Russia, and participated in "Pratibimba", an exhibition of Indian photography which has traveled to Russia and Britain. Based in New Delhi, Shalini has also worked as an editor with a publishing house.

After a distinguished career in archeology, **Dr. R. Nagaswamy** retired as Director, Department of Archaeology, Tamil Nadu. He is a leading scholar of Sanskrit, with a deep knowledge and understanding of South Indian art and culture. An internationally renowned expert on South Indian bronzes, he has been responsible for bringing to light many hitherto unnoticed images, and establishing their chronology. He has published over 20 books in Tamil and English, and more than 300 research papers. At present he is Director of a project on the Brihadesvara Temple, Tanjore, sponsored by the Indira Gandhi National Centre for Arts. He is also on several national committees related to art and culture. Dr. Nagaswamy is a poet, and composes dance-dramas in the classical tradition, as well.

**Shiraz Sidhva** is a well-known free lance journalist currently based in New Delhi. After completing her studies from Bombay University's St. Xavier's College she has held editorial posts in some of the country's leading publications - *Imprint*, *Business India* and most recently, *The Sunday Observer* of which she was the Assistant Editor. She has written on a diverse range of subjects, notably social issues, the media, culture and the arts. Her articles have appeared in *Sunday*, *Indian Express* and *The Times of India*, and in several travel journals.

**Varsha Des** works as an editor in charge of Adult Literacy publications, National Book Trust, New Delhi. She is a scholar of Sanskrit and Hindi and a regular contributor to several national dailies and periodicals in Gujarati, Hindi and English on subjects of artistic, cultural and literary interest. She has published books in Gujarati and Hindi, and being fluent in several Indian languages, has worked on translations as well. She belongs to Gujarat and travels widely in connection with her work.

**Geeta Doctor**, who has traveled extensively in India and abroad, worked as a free lance journalist in Bombay from 1970 to 1980. Since 1980 she has lived in Madras, and contributed regularly to leading newspapers and magazines, including *Swagat*, *Namaskaar*, *Silver Kris*, *The Sunday Observer* and *The Taj Magazine*. She is a correspondent for *Inside-Outside* and *Signature* and Contributing Editor for *Freedom First*. Her areas of interest are art, travel, drama and literature. She also has interviewed eminent personalities.

**J. Inder Singh Kalra**, who comes from a family of gourmets, is President (Asia) of the International Wine, Food and Travel Writers' Association. He runs a series of highly popular restaurant columns in leading dailies and is one of those writers in his genre who has given chefs their pride of place as true artistes. He has prepared the menu - and it is amongst the best in the country - for the Shiv Niwas Palace run by the Maharana of Udaipur. Kalra has also revived the authentic course-wise service of Indian food. He is now a Restaurant and Travel Consultant, specializing in gourmet - and other - tours.

**Mamta Saran** has been involved in book publishing for several years. Her other major interest is art, and she is herself an artist.

In today's classical dance world, **Leela Samson** has emerged as a gifted performer and sensitive teacher of the dance form *Bharata Natyam*, of which she is one of the leading exponents. Her formative years were spent at Kalakshetra College of Fine Arts, Madras, where she was deeply influenced by Rukmini Devi, the institute's founder. Well versed in the allied arts of music and literature, Leela appeared in major roles in Kalakshetra's celebrated dance dramas, which were staged in many parts of the world. As a soloist, she is esteemed throughout India as well as abroad. Amongst numerous recitals, she has danced for many visiting dignitaries, and in Europe she has appeared at Norway's Kuopio Dance Festival and at the Kulturfest in Vienna. In 1982, she was the recipient of the Sanskriti Award for Performing Arts. Apart from her concert schedule, Leela currently heads the Bharata Natyam Department at the Shriram Bharatiya Kala Kendra in New Delhi, where she teaches and writes on dance. Her publications include a book on the classical dances of India: *Rhythm in Joy*.

**Ashis Banerjee** took his M.A. in Political Science from Allahabad University where he has also taught for a number of years. He went on a Rhodes Scholarship to Balliol College, Oxford, where he took an M.Litt. He has been Visiting Fellow at the Centre for Policy Research, New Delhi, where he worked on problems related to the subject of national integration. He is presently a Fellow at the Nehru Memorial Museum and Library, New Delhi. All his publications are related to Indian politics and society.

**Poonam Kulsoom** has worked with the India Tourism Development Corporation in an editorial capacity for over six years. She has accomplished the painstaking task of gathering information for all the Guideposts with meticulous care.

## THE PHOTOGRAPHERS